A History of Auditing

The collapse in the US of Enron and Worldcom, together with their auditors, Arthur Andersen, has focused the public spotlight on the company audit and made it a highly controversial aspect of the accountant's work. In Britain, the recent legal action by Equitable Life against Ernst & Young is only the latest in a long line of scandals at BCCI, Maxwell and the Barings bank, among many others. *A History of Auditing* for the first time lifts the lid off the work of the auditors, and details how historically they have got themselves into the present situation.

The book draws on new evidence generated by a postal questionnaire and oral history among auditors both past and present, together with an analysis of company reports and exhaustive use of contemporary textbooks and articles, making frequent comparisons with American practice. The resulting history traces the evolution of the auditing process from its leisurely Victorian beginnings where armies of clerks checked and ticked everything in their client's books, to the transformation in the 1960s when, with the growing scale of clients, auditing became more a matter of checking a client's systems rather than the records themselves. The changes in the 1980s are also documented when because of the growing pressure on audit fees from clients meeting the threat of global competition, auditors began to put their faith in such nebulous techniques as risk assessment. Alongside all these changes auditors also had to cope with the advent of computerisation which robbed them of the audit trail.

This comprehensive history will be a useful reference tool for accounting, business and economic historians and will also be an enlightening read for all those with an interest in auditing procedures.

Derek Matthews is a Reader in Economic History at Cardiff University, UK.

Routledge New Works in Accounting History
Edited by

Garry Carnegie
Melbourne University Private, Australia

John Richard Edwards
Cardiff University, UK

Salvador Carmona
Instituto de Empresa, Spain

Dick Fleischman
John Carroll University, USA

A History of Auditing

The changing audit process in
Britain from the nineteenth century
to the present day

Derek Matthews

 Routledge
Taylor & Francis Group

LONDON AND NEW YORK

First published 2006
by Routledge
2 Park Square, Milton Park, Abingdon, Oxon OX14 4RN

Simultaneously published in the USA and Canada
by Routledge
270, Madison Ave, New York, NY 10016

Routledge is an imprint of the Taylor & Francis Group

© 2006 Derek Matthews

Typeset in Sabon by
Newgen Imaging Systems (P) Ltd, Chennai, India
Printed and bound in Great Britain by
Biddles Ltd, King's Lynn

British Library Cataloguing in Publication Data
A catalogue record for this book is available from the British Library

Library of Congress Cataloging in Publication Data
A catalog record for this book has been requested

ISBN 0–415–38169–X

Contents

Illustrations

Acknowledgements

I would like to thank the ICAEW Centre for Business Performance and the Leverhulme Trust who financed the primary research contained in this book. I am also grateful to Mr Jim Pirie, who carried out most of the interviews with accountants used here and additional background research, and to Profs Dick Edwards, Bob Parker, Roy Chandler and Salvador Carmona, who read drafts and gave useful comments at various stages of the book's development. As usual, of course, regarding any errors or weaknesses still contained in the book the buck stops with the author.

1 Introduction

Auditing today is clearly the most controversial aspect of the accountant's work. The collapse of Enron, and Worldcom, together with their auditors, Arthur Andersen, has put the spotlight in the past few years firmly on the company audit (*Economist* 30 November 2002). The scandals across the Atlantic were of course presaged by equally dramatic upheavals in the audit world in Britain in the late 1980s and early 1990s, with the performance of Price Waterhouse, the auditors of the Bank of Credit and Commerce International (BCCI), and Coopers & Lybrand, auditors of the Maxwell companies and Barings bank, among many other examples of audit failure (Mitchell *et al.* 1993).

Audit scandals of course have a long history in Britain going back through the performance of Andersens as auditors of the DeLorean company in the early 1980s, to the London and County affair in the 1970s, and the Royal Mail case in the interwar period. Yet apart from these negative aspects it is also the case that the rise of the British accountancy profession from the late nineteenth century down to the present day, and the world-wide success of its accountancy firms, were to a large extent based on the growth of the audit function (Matthews *et al.* 1997). In view of this background then it is remarkable how little attention auditing has received from accounting historians, and how relatively little published research there is on the subject. In the introduction to his collected edition of previous writing on the matter Lee (1988: xi) made the point that: 'As a subject, the history of auditing has received little attention.' Since then not much has changed.

The lack of interest in audit history can easily be demonstrated by surveying the accounting history literature. First, the various collected editions of essays on accounting history show the paucity of work on auditing. Out of 18 papers, Yamey's (1978) collection on *The Historical Development of Accounting* has none on auditing but, for example, five on cost accounting. Garner and Hughes' (1978), *Readings on Accounting Development*, contains two papers on auditing out of a total of 29; Lee and Parker's (1979), *The Evolution of Corporate Financial Reporting*, contains two papers discussing auditing out of a total of 17; while Parker's (1984), *Papers on*

Accounting History, has none out of 14 contributions. Parker and Yamey's (1994), *Accounting History: Some British Contributions*, has nothing on auditing, but again four contributions in their section on 'Cost and Management Accounting'. Finally, Lee *et al.* (1996) for their *Accounting History from the Renaissance to the Present: A Remembrance of Luca Pacioli*, commissioned seven chapters by leading accounting historians, ranging in subject matter from financial accounting and reporting, professionalisation and management accounting (two chapters), but again there was no mention of auditing.

The general histories of accounting, the few that there are – for example, Brown (1968), Woolf (1912), Littleton (1981) and Stacey (1954) – contain due reference to the auditing function but not in proportion to the extent to which the profession earned its living. Chatfield (1977), for example, in his *History of Accounting Thought*, has two chapters out of 20 on auditing. Edwards' (1989: 263–9) history of financial accounting has scattered references to the audit and a section of six and a half pages devoted to the process, but as with most accounting history the focus of the book is on accounting and financial reporting. The histories of accounting firms, for example those of Edgar Jones (1981) and (1995), usually give a fair treatment to the audit function but of necessity this is not the main focus of the story. Auditing also impinges on some events and issues which have been heavily researched, for example the Royal Mail case (Green and Moss 1982), but obviously this in no way adds up to a history of the process.

It is clear, therefore, that there has been very limited primary research into the history of the audit on either side of the Atlantic. There have been some notable articles on audit history, for example, Chandler *et al.* (1993), who set out to establish the changing purpose of the audit in the nineteenth and twentieth centuries, and Power (1992), who looked at the history of audit sampling. Yet these works are the exceptions that prove the proposition. Anderson's (2000: 385–93) list of the 154 accounting history publications for 1999, for example, contains only 15 on auditing topics and only 5 of those were British in focus. Moreover, this lack of work on auditing by historians is in sharp contrast to the huge amount of interest shown by writers on contemporary audit issues in recent decades. Despite both concluding that not enough was being done, Gwilliam's (1987) and Higson's (1987: chap. 3) surveys of auditing research give remarkable evidence of this: and since then there has been no let-up in the research and publications on present day audit themes. Equally significantly, of the little historical research there has been on auditing, almost none of it pays attention to what auditors actually did, again in contrast with, for example, the extensive treatment of the history of cost accounting techniques (e.g. Boyns and Edwards 1997).

One can only speculate on the reasons for this lack of interest in the audit process among historians but perhaps a major consideration is that, as one commentator has noted, 'there was very little information about how auditors actually conduct their work' (Higson 1997: 199). Power (1992: 39) writes of: 'The impoverishment of historical sources about audit practice', and as a result 'field studies of what auditors actually do, as opposed to studies of what auditors claim they do or would do, scarcely exist'. Myers (1985: 70) also concluded of the American scene that 'there remains very little evidence of what auditors do'. One reason given for this absence of information was that audit firms have not kept their old working papers and manuals, and moreover until the 1980s many accounting firms considered their audit methods to be strictly confidential (ibid.: 70; Higson 1987: 5, 1997: 199). Clearly, the audit is a relatively private activity, and from the historian's viewpoint it would seem that, apart from sporadic law reports and scattered information in the trade press (e.g. Chandler and Edwards 1994), there is a lack of solid data on the process of the audit as it was practised, rather than as the textbooks said it should be.

Another factor in the situation is that traditionally accounting historians have tended to use only documentary evidence, which, if this is as thin on the ground as seems to be the case with auditing, would itself account for the lack of published work. It is unfortunate that accounting historians have been somewhat reluctant to use oral history (although see: Loft 1990; Mumford 1991; Matthews and Pirie 2001) and accounting historians have been urged to use oral evidence more (Collins and Bloom 1991; Hammond and Sikka 1996). Also, accounting historians (or any other stripe of historian for that matter) have not exploited another technique widely used in the social sciences, namely the postal questionnaire. Academics researching present day trends and issues in accounting use questionnaires relatively frequently; there are, for example, the well known investigations of the shareholders' reading of the corporate report by Lee and Tweedie (1977) and Bartlett and Chandler (1997), Drury *et al.*'s (1993) work on cost accounting, and Beattie *et al.* (2001) on the auditor/client relationship. It is somewhat surprising then that accounting historians have not used the questionnaire technique.

In view, therefore, of the lack of published work and apparent shortage of documentary evidence it was decided to set up a project on the history of the audit which exploited both oral history and the questionnaire, made possible by the generous provision of funds by the Institute of Chartered Accountants in England and Wales (ICAEW). The oral history side of the research entailed a programme of interviews with retired and still active chartered accountants, and the evidence provided has been extensively drawn on here (and is discussed in detail in the Appendix at the back of the book). The other half of the ICAEW project was a postal questionnaire (again dealt with more fully in the Appendix) in which among other matters the respondents were questioned on the process of the audit which generated the crucial historical trends in responses reported in the tables here.

A third source of primary data used in this book is a survey of company reports, a project funded by the Leverhulme Trust, which involved the collection of a sample of quoted company reports. These yielded evidence on audit fees, while an analysis of the wording of the audit reports gives insights into the audit process itself (again the source is more fully discussed and the data used is given in the Appendix).

Finally, in addition to the new material generated by our programme of interviews, questionnaires and the survey of company reports, this book utilises the more traditional documentary sources, principally the trade press and the contemporary textbooks. In addition an analysis of the final audit examinations of the ICAEW revealed when questions on specific audit techniques were first asked, giving another indication of when they came into common use.

The aim of this book then is to give a reasonably comprehensive narrative history of the audit process in Britain. It should be emphasised that we focus relatively narrowly on the techniques used in the audit. The related and equally interesting matters of the purpose of the audit, its quality and cost and many other issues are only touched on where relevant to the audit process. Chapter 2 describes the traditional so-called bookkeeping audit as it was practised from the nineteenth century down to about the 1960s. New evidence is offered which emphasises that the characteristic feature of the audit in this period was the extent to which the auditors were also doing their client's accounting. The chapter also describes the labour intensive audit process known in the trade as 'ticking and bashing', but demonstrates that although mechanical this was usually not the cursory job that previous writers have assumed. The succeeding chapters describe the ways in which the bookkeeping audit has changed over time, although noting that the apparent innovations all had their precursors in early audit procedures.

Chapter 3 looks at the changes in the documentation involved in the audit, and traces the evolution of the early audit notebooks and brief sets of instructions into comprehensive audit programmes, working papers and voluminous manuals. The development of testing and sampling is discussed in Chapter 4, which finds that sampling was of necessity an aspect of the audit of large companies from the first, and, although it became increasingly used, probably did not increase in sophistication until the 1970s, when computers made statistical sampling a realistic possibility. Chapter 5 relates and quantifies the rise of the so called systems approach based on testing the client's controls rather than the underlying bookkeeping; and Chapter 6, after wrestling with the shifting meanings of the term 'balance sheet audit', gives evidence of the increased emphasis on procedures such as the attendance at stock-taking and the circularisation of debtors. Chapter 7 looks at the biggest single change in the audit in the period – the coming of computers – and how the auditors attempted to come to terms with the new technology, which took away their traditional source of evidence – the audit trail. Chapter 8 rounds off the narrative survey with a description of the most recent of the changes in audit technique – the coming to prominence of concepts such as risk, materiality and analytical review.

The book concludes with Chapter 9 which summarises the changes in audit procedures and offers explanations for these developments. The characteristic features of the history of the British audit are a diversity in practice based largely on the different types of clients the auditors served. Although all the changes in technique and their nomenclature seemed to emanate from America, the British adopted them in their own time. Leaving aside the upheaval caused by computers, the most important factor driving change, which distinctly accelerated in the 1960s, was the growth in the size of British companies. The most recent changes, coming into widespread use around 1980, were however driven by the commercial pressures bearing on the audit firms.

2   The bookkeeping audit

Nineteenth-century accounting and the rise of the professional audit

As is well known, the audit dates in Britain from at least medieval times, when the auditor on landed estates literally heard the accounts read out and checked on the lord's behalf that his steward had not been negligent or fraudulent (Edwards 1989: 37; for a summary of the early history of auditing see Higson 1987: 14–30). Then, as trading and manufacturing companies multiplied in the eighteenth century, accountants were commonly employed as auditors to check that all was in order with the investments of partners or shareholders. An audit certificate: 'Examined and found right, Bristol, December 20, 1797' forms part of the records of the accountancy firm of Josiah Wade (Howitt 1966: 245). But, as Lee (1988: xvii) has argued, the biggest fillip to the audit process was given by changes in the economic environment in the nineteenth century: 'developments in the economic structure of civilizations caused audit needs. Industrialization created the need for financing. This created, in turn, the need for incorporation. And this created the need for financial reporting of audited information'.

A major step forward for professional accountants in Britain was the coming of the railways, particularly resulting from the speculative mania of the 1840s (Kitchen 1988: 26). Railways were by a long way the largest companies spawned by industrialisation and they presented a major accounting challenge. The literature gives a mixed picture of railway accounting. Reed (1997: 5), for example, writes regarding the 1840s of 'the sophisticated accountancy required to integrate even a relatively small number of railways into a cohesive system ... and it was clearly essential to have a secure system to record takings and allow effective audit ... Most railways accordingly had well developed financial control mechanisms'. Even in the 1840s and 1850s railway companies usually had, as in the case of the Lancashire and Yorkshire, an accountant's office with teams of bookkeepers, and a treasurer or secretary capable of drawing up some form of accounts (Broadbridge 1970: 41). These, of course, were not the trained public accountants of the sort that were well established in the City of London and elsewhere by this time mainly involved in bankruptcy work, but they were often highly competent bookkeepers, a skill which helped them get to the top of the management ladder (Matthews *et al.* 1998: chap. 2). For example, Henry Tennant was, in the 1840s, the accountant of two smaller railways before moving to the giant North Eastern Railway in 1854, and in 1871 he became their general manager (Irving 1976: 15–16). Between 1846 and 1858, the general manager of the London & North Western Railway (LNWR) was the outstanding Mark Huish, whose knowledge of bookkeeping, learnt with the East India Company, had apparently helped gain him his first railway job (Gourvish 1972: 49).

But there was another side to early railway accounting. According to Gourvish (ibid.: 30) 'the early railways produced only the most rudimentary of accounts'. Often the speculative railway companies were fraudulently run and the payment of dividends and day to day expenditure out of the share-holders' capital was common (Jones 1995: 52). These rail companies' accounting systems were, perhaps as a result of the frauds, frequently in a mess, with no uniformity in a company's accounts from one year to the next, let alone comparability between companies. The *Times* in 1850 described the accounts of the Caledonian Railway Company as 'just such a tangle as one might dream of after supping on lobster salad and champagne' (Robb 1992: 43). Leading City public accountants, like William Quilter and William Deloitte, were frequently brought in to sort out railway company frauds and other financial problems, and were often largely responsible for putting their accounting systems on a sound footing (Jones 1984: 58; Bywater 1985: 792; Edwards 1985: 38). For example, professional accountants introduced a general balance sheet into the accounts of the Midland and the South Eastern railway companies for the first time in 1850 (Edwards 1989: 265).

The initial employment of public accountants to sort out a railway's accounting led on very often to an auditing role, while they also continued to take responsibility for the accounting. Although Quilter and Deloitte proba-bly did not originate the double account system, which separated out capital from revenue expenditure, they certainly refined and promoted its adoption by the railways (Jones 1984: 58; Bywater 1985: 792; Edwards 1985: 30; Kitchen 1988: 28). The double account system devised by Edwin Waterhouse, as auditor of the LNWR and other railways, probably acted as a model for the uniform accounts required of all rail companies by the 1868, Regulation of the Railways Act, which according to Pollins (1969: 138–9): 'after many years of chaos…marked a turning point in the history of railway accounting'.

After the 1868 Act, the published accounts of the railways were by far the most detailed, and probably the most accurate, of any public companies. The rail companies had for the most part settled down into stable bureaucracies with no need for outside public accountants to help them with their basic accounting, as had often been the case in the 1840s and 1850s. Gourvish has detailed the management changes wrought on the railways which 'led the way in developing relatively advanced techniques in business management, making progress in the fields of accounting, costing, pricing, marketing and statistics' (Gourvish 1972: 290). Huish, at the LNWR, for example, had introduced relatively sophisticated 'internal controls on costing and pricing' (ibid.: 267). By 1870, the Great Western also had a sizeable management team, indicated by the item in their accounts: 'Salaries of Secretary, General Manager, Accountant and Clerks, £20,170'; and by 1880 the company employed a chief accountant (Great Western Railway, Minutes of the Half-yearly General Meeting, 31 August 1870 and 9 February 1880).

Most of the other public utilities, like the gas companies, and also insurance companies, and the larger banks, had by the last quarter of the nineteenth century probably installed adequate accounting systems, and were also successfully handling their own accounting. According to Wilson (1991: 121–41, 158) gas engineers were responsible for drawing up their company's accounts, and they also had relatively large accounts departments producing their own balance sheets by the 1870s. In banking, Edward Holden, for example, joined the Midland as an accountant in 1881, and soon became secretary and later chairman, making his reputation on an ability to analyse the balance sheets of take-over targets (Holmes and Green 1986: 83).

In most of British business, however, where even in 1914 'introverted family groupings still dominated most British firms', it was a different story (Wilson 1995: 120, 132). Chandler has described in detail the amateurishness of management in Britain in this period: 'The small number of enterprises with administrative hierarchies and the smaller size of such hierarchies helped perpetuate a commitment to personal ways of management' (Chandler 1990: 242). Many British companies seemed reluctant to delegate responsibility to professionally trained managers (Wilson 1995: 120, 132). As a result the level of accounting in British companies was generally backward. Edwards (1989: 191) found that the company accounts filed for 1844–56, now in the National Archives, 'were often a jumbled collection of unrelated financial facts'. Even such a basic accounting practice as double entry bookkeeping (thought to have been developed in Italy in the fourteenth century) was slow to be utilised (Jones 1981: 23). The family-owned, Dowlais Iron company, for example, although the largest iron company in the world in the 1840s, and which kept a wide range of cost accounts on the performance of the works, still did not find it necessary to draw up a profit and loss account as late as 1860 (ibid.: 54). Again, when Waterhouse was called in to audit the accounts and prepare balance sheets for private banks in 1889 they were still using the single entry system (Jones 1995: 56); and, according to de Paula (1948: 22), in the 1890s it was 'by no means uncommon to find primitive records upon a single entry basis or alternatively most complicated double entry systems'. This backwardness is also confirmed by an article in *The Accountant* in 1892 which stated:

> It is extraordinary (although true) that in these days of advanced education, so many concerns (some of considerable importance) will

persist in adhering to the old system, if system it can be called, of single entry...The reason for such defective knowledge of the correct principles of bookkeeping among the majority of business men is not far to seek, and may be traced to the imperfect instruction on the subject given in schools.

(Quoted in Chandler and Edwards 1994: 144)

Again the accounting picture is patchy. Inevitably some companies were in advance of others, and this can be roughly identified by their employment of qualified accountants. We know, for example, that Ferranti, the electrical firm, had a chief accountant and an accounts department in 1889 (Wilson 1988: 73). Pilkingtons, the family owned glass makers, had an audit department before the First World War (Barker 1960: 196). Courtaulds, the rayon manufacturers, recruited chartered accountants as chief accountants by 1913 (Matthews *et al.* 1998: 175, 177). Lever Bros, had a chief accountant and (perhaps the first ever British) finance director before the First World War (Wilson 1954: 207–9). But Chandler suggests that these well run firms, like the Port Sunlight soap maker, were in a minority: 'Only in the case of Britain's largest, Lever Brothers, is there clear evidence that the owners [in the branded packaged goods sector of British industry] were assisted by an extensive hierarchy before World War I' (Chandler 1990: 266). Many, even large, British companies had non-existent or underdeveloped accounting departments. The Birmingham accountancy firm of Sharp Parsons, the auditors of Boots the chemists from the 1880s also handled their accounting, perhaps down to 1920 (Chapman 1974: 121, 136). Lucas, the engineers, did not have a professional accountant on their staff until 1922 (Nockolds 1986: 666). Again a sizeable quoted bus company like Crosvilles, which had undertaken many take-overs in the 1920s, did not employ its first full-time accountant until 1930 (Anderson 1981: 161); while Metal Box (63rd largest industrial company in the country in 1948) had no separate accounting department until 1940 (Reader 1976: 144; Chandler 1990: 685).

As with the railways it was the professional accountants who led the way in improving accounting practice among the backward companies. Accountants were frequently called in to prepare the accounts of even the largest companies and to put their bookkeeping on a sound basis. Appointment as auditor frequently involved sorting out the company's books, often converting them for the first time to the double entry system (Matthews *et al.* 1998: 105–6). Undoubtedly, however, it was the process of 'going public', seeking a stock exchange listing facilitated by the Companies Acts of 1856 and 1862, which was the main catalyst in imposing more rigorous accounting on the family firms. Under the terms of the 1856 Act in order to register, a joint stock company had to keep its books on the double entry basis, and unless it adopted its own regulations the balance sheet had to be drawn up in the fashion of the 'Table A' model provided (Freear 1977: 7). Although not a statutory requirement, a public accountant's name was usually considered essential on the prospectus of any putative company (Edwards 1989: 222). The reporting accountant gave a certificate as to the past and frequently the future performance of the company, and not infrequently drew up its first meaningful set of accounts (Chandler and Edwards 1994: 26, 85, 104). The accountant involved in the floatation then almost invariably went on to audit the new company.

Turning now to the growth of the audit function, it had been a long established practice in joint stock companies (like the old trading concerns such as the East India Company or the canals, gas and water works) for the shareholders, who took no part in the running of the companies, to elect at their annual or bi-annual meetings one or two of their number to audit the accounts, and so keep an eye on their investments (Littleton 1981: 290). The election of shareholder auditors at half-yearly meetings was made a stipulation in the Company Clauses Consolidation Act of 1845 (Robb 1992: 42). If not immediately they were formed then soon after, this practice was also adopted by the railways, where previously unprecedented amounts of capital, as we discussed earlier, came from a relatively large number of 'blind' investors who badly needed the assurance of the audit (Reed 1975: 197; Wilson 1995: 37).

But these amateur shareholder auditors frequently gave what accounts were presented to them no more than a cursory inspection on the day of the general meeting, which led them to be known as 'biscuit and sherry audits' (Robb 1992: 53; Jones 1995: 50). The auditors of the Eastern Counties railway, for example, 'visited the company twice in the half-year for a few hours at a time' (Robb 1992: 129). Understandably, in the face of the frauds perpetrated in the early years of the railways, the amateur audits were in the words of a contemporary critic – 'destitute of all efficiency' or 'a complete farce' (Broadbridge 1970: 40; Littleton 1981: 290). The amateurs, therefore, quickly began to employ the professionals to help them, often the same public accountants drafted in to sort out the frauds and the chaotic accounting (Jones 1981: 52; Littleton 1981: 292; Parker 1986: 7–8; Robb 1992: 129). Both the North Staffordshire and the Midland railways had public accountants assisting the shareholder auditors by 1850 (Williams 1876: 99); and Edwin Waterhouse built up his accountancy practice with this type of audit work for a number of railway companies in the 1860s (Jones 1995: 50–5).

Typical, with regard to the development of the audit function, was the Great Western railway (revealed by their annual reports held in the National Archives). There is no sign on the 1840 accounts that the then five-year-old company was audited at all. By 1850, the shareholders had elected two of their number as auditors, but already they must have felt inadequate to the task because for the first time that year they had called in Deloitte to assist them, indeed without informing the board they were doing so (Jones 1984: 57). The Great Western auditors recommended, and the board agreed, that henceforth the audit would be 'continuous' (Great

Western Railway, Minutes of the Half-yearly General Meeting, 14 February 1850). In 1867, an audit committee of shareholders was formed to oversee the auditors, composed by 1870 of three shareholders assisted by Deloitte. The item 'Auditors and Public Accountant, £600' appears in the accounts, indicating the cost of the professional help received (ibid. 31 August 1870). In 1889, Deloitte was elected auditor of the Great Western in his own right, which was typical of the other rail companies as gradually the amateur shareholder auditors abandoned the auditor's role to the professional accountant completely (Jones 1984: 58). In 1883, all the major railway companies had only amateur shareholder auditors; by 1900 they almost all had professional auditors, or a combination of one professional and one amateur auditor. Subsequently the amateurs were usually dropped altogether, although, in fact, the Great Western was the exception in keeping on its shareholder auditor until the railway was nationalised in the 1940s (data from *Stock Exchange Official Intelligence* and *Stock Exchange Official Yearbook*).

Regarding the auditing of the more numerous commercial concerns, as we have noted, it was the trend from the 1860s for companies to go public and to seek a stock exchange quotation, which gave a further boost to the professional audit (Jeremy 1998: 109). Edwards and Webb (1985: 188) found that, while not obliged to do so, between 1863 and 1900, 12 out of 13 steel companies going public chose a chartered accountant as their first auditor, usually the firm who had reported on the prospectus and drawn up the company's first accounts. In this way the chartered accountants won their one-sided battle with the amateur shareholder auditor among commercial concerns, probably by the time they had formed their professional body, the ICAEW, in 1880 (Matthews *et al.* 1998: 60). By 1886, over three-quarters of quoted companies were professionally audited, a figure which rapidly rose to over 90 per cent (Broadbridge 1970: 41; Parker 1986: 7–8; Edwards 1989: 265; Edwards *et al.* 1997: 8).

Auditing then, having taken over from insolvency, went on to become the largest single fee-earning occupation for the typical chartered accountancy practice. From less than 10 per cent prior to 1880, by that year auditing and accounting earned 22 per cent of the fee income of the firm of Whinney, Smith & Whinney; and by 1900 it was 70 per cent (Jones 1981: 47; Boys 1994: 38). In fact, the subsequent prosperity and the rapid growth of the accounting profession in Britain rested almost entirely on the back of the huge growth in audit business that followed from the expansion in the number and size of companies in the twentieth century (Matthews *et al.* 1997).

Accounting and the bookkeeping audit

There has always been (and still is today), in Britain at least, a spectrum of work undertaken by what are called auditors who are nominally conducting an audit. This work ranges from what accountants dubbed 'brown paper parcel jobs', so called because of the way the accounting records were often presented to them (Interviews with Muir, Hardcastle and Wilde). In other words, these were 'audits' using incomplete records of small (but some not so small) concerns, for which the accountant first had to put in order and make up the books, draw up the final accounts, then finally sign them off as the auditor. This type of 'audit' shaded into those for clients who kept good records but where nonetheless the auditor was still expected to close off the books, draw up a trial balance, produce a profit and loss account and balance sheet and then give an opinion on them in the audit report. Finally, at the other end of the spectrum to 'brown paper parcel jobs' came companies, invariably the larger concerns, that indeed presented the auditor with a full set of completed accounts on which he could perform what older auditors call a 'pure' audit (Interviews with Wilde, Beard, Carter, Sims, Niddrie and Boothman). In the early days, however, pure audits were a small minority of the average auditor's work. If today 'auditing can be viewed as the checking of the work of one set of skilled financial accountants by another' (Sherer and Kent 1983: 17) this has only relatively recently become the case.

The professional audit in Britain then was from the start closely bound up with bookkeeping and, as we noted above, this accountancy role often preceded that of auditor. From the 1860s, accountants seeing family and other firms through a stock exchange quotation frequently had to put the client's accounts in order, and when they subsequently assumed the role of auditor as a matter of course they continued responsibility for the accounts, indeed often doing their client's bookkeeping throughout the year. At least down to the 1960s, the majority of British 'audits' were therefore something of a polite fiction and not the pure audits which the articled clerks were taught in their textbooks. And although accounting historians like Jones (1981: 54) have been aware that, as Frederick Whinney said in 1891, accounting firms 'were frequently asked to finish the balance sheet and take out the balance, and write up the books', the extent of the practice and its longevity, not to say its full implications, have been largely overlooked by historians.

The reason for this oversight is probably due to the fact that there was something of a conspiracy of silence on the issue. This was possibly because the Companies Acts, although loosely worded and liberal with regard to how a company's accounts were to be presented and audited, were always unequivocal that there was a clear distinction between the directors' responsibility to produce a balance sheet and the auditors' job to give an opinion on it (Edwards and Webb 1985: 177). Therefore, from a legal standpoint, and from the point of view of the accountants' ethics, it was important for the young profession that the accounting and auditing functions were seen to be separate, and that the auditor apparently maintained his independence from the client's management, pursuing his role as the shareholders' watchdog.

This early conjunction of accounting and auditing had implications for the process of the British audit, and this is discussed more fully below. In passing we might note that the situation also, of course, had implications for the purpose and quality of the audit and, as we have said, for issues such as auditor independence. These are not the concerns of this book but clearly if the auditor is signing off accounts which he himself has drawn up he is likely to find them of an exemplary standard. There were also other dangers, as when, for example, the accountant/auditor was implicated in the fraud at Farrow's bank. As a witness at the resulting trial in 1921 the celebrated chartered accountant Gilbert Garnsey was asked: 'is there any real objection to the same firm of accountants keeping the books, and also auditing them at the end of the year?' Garnsey replied: 'Yes, there is really. I am perfectly open to admit there are a number of cases where it is done, but it is really objectionable because you cannot audit the same books that you keep yourself.' He was forced, however, to concede that this statement was somewhat disingenuous by the next question: 'But you will admit it is done in a very large number of cases?' 'I understand so', he replied (*Accountant* 9 July 1921: 53).

Evidence of the nature, extent and longevity of the conjunction of accounting and auditing in Britain comes from many directions. Several articles in *The Accountant* in the 1880s and 1890s indicated the accounting role of the auditor. A practising accountant, Trevor, in 1889 discussed 'the construction of the trading and profit and loss accounts – assuming that the preparation of these is entrusted to the auditor' (quoted in Chandler and Edwards 1994: 109, 111). Five years later, Carter, the senior partner in probably the largest practice in Birmingham, commented that the office of the typical client would have a cashier, a ledger clerk and an invoice clerk under the supervision of a manager, who in principle would hand the auditor balanced books, and 'a rough Balance Sheet and Trade Account'. However, Carter went on: 'In this district it is frequently left to the auditor to balance the books himself, and he is even required sometimes to write up the Private Ledger' (ibid.: 157, 159). Another accountant remembered his auditing experience prior to the First World War as follows:

> an audit consisted of 80 per cent checking everything possible, and 20 per cent preparing the final accounts. Every posting was checked; every conceivable addition was checked...Balanced books were the exception rather than the rule...Having at last balanced and checked everything, the senior gathered the necessary data on which the partner prepared the final accounts, which were signed, sent in, and there the matter ended.
>
> (*Accountant* 20 March 1937: 416)

'Doing the books' as well as the audit was even seen in the early days as positively desirable. An article in the *Accountant* in 1876 argued that it was a good thing that the auditor should take responsibility for setting up the client's bookkeeping system from the start, and then 'superintend the accountancy throughout' (quoted in Chandler and Edwards 1994: 11). In 1883, Pixley, the leading accountant and writer of the first textbook on auditing, stated in a lecture that he also preferred that the auditor draw up the accounts.

> It is far preferable for the auditor to prepare his own statements if his clients are willing he should do so, as he can then draft them in any form he pleases, whereas where accounts are submitted to him already prepared he may have to certify them, when perhaps he may not approve of the form, but cannot object as there may be nothing wrong with them.
>
> (*Accountant* 26 May 1883: 8)

The implications for the auditors' supposed independence if they also did the accounting perhaps gradually made them less open in public regarding the practice. In the first edition of his textbook Pixley (1881: 89–90) had been frank: 'In many Companies the duties of the Book-keeper terminate with the preparation of the "Trial Balance," the manipulation of this document, represented by the drawing up of the Revenue Account and the Balance Sheet, being frequently entrusted to the Auditor, when that official is a Chartered Accountant.' By the 1910, tenth edition, however, Pixley (1910: 345–6) had changed the tune somewhat:

> The duty of the preparation of the Accounts of a Company to be laid before the Shareholders devolves upon the Directors. When these Accounts are prepared they have to be formally approved by the Directors at a Board Meeting.... The Secretary should then intimate to the Auditors that the Accounts are ready for their examination. The preparation of these accounts therefore forms no part of the duties of the Auditors, but in many Companies it is the practice for the Directors to give them instructions to prepare the Accounts.
>
> In this case, however, the preparation of the Accounts is not performed by them as Auditors, but solely at [sic] professional Accountants; they are of course, paid a special fee for this duty, which is quite independent of their fee as Auditors.

The fiction of this separation of roles and remuneration was repeated in full by Pixley eight pages (ibid.: 355) later, and again in a later chapter (ibid.: 389), but the repetition does not make the assertion any more convincing.

By 1914, two of the other leading textbooks were following the same line as Pixley. De Paula (1914: 2–3) stated firmly:

> An audit is quite distinct and apart from accountancy – an audit does not entail the preparation of a Balance Sheet at all, but denotes something much wider, namely the examination of a Balance Sheet prepared by

others.... In practice, auditors often do prepare the Balance Sheet and Profit and Loss Account, which accounts they thereafter certify; but it must be observed that, when preparing the accounts, the accountant is acting *qua* accountant and not *qua* auditor, and that this work is additional to and quite outside his duties as auditor.

By 1957, the wording of the textbook had subtly changed to: 'In practice, *in the case of small businesses*, auditors often do prepare the balance sheet and profit and loss account, which accounts they thereafter audit' (de Paula 1957: 3, my italics). Spicer and Pegler (1914: 196) also asserted:

It is the duty of the Directors to prepare the Balance Sheet for presentation to the Auditor, and consequently the books ought to be presented to the Auditor balanced. It cannot be said to be the duty of the Auditor to balance the books, neither should he undertake to do so, unless specifically requested by the Directors, when he will be acting in the capacity of Accountant, and not as Auditor. Any additional work of this nature should be specially remunerated.

(Bigg 1951: 212)

This same wording was still used in Spicer and Pegler's tenth, 1951, edition.

Dicksee, who wrote another of the leading textbooks of the day, nowhere acknowledged that auditors also drew up the accounts, but his book included extensive reports from 89 court cases involving key accounting issues in the period between 1887 and 1936 (Waldron 1969: 769–1066). In 26 cases the audit process at work is made clear, and of these, 19, or almost three-quarters, indicated that it was the auditor who drew up the final accounts. Moreover, there seems to be no trend towards the pure audit. Of the 11 identifiable cases in the interwar period, in only 3 were the auditors not also doing the final accounting. Interestingly, on no occasion in these cases did the judge or anyone else allude to the fact that by law drawing up the balance sheet was the directors' responsibility, and that ideally the two activities, accounting and auditing, should be kept separate. Indeed, in the well known case of the London and General Bank in 1895 the judge (in error) was explicit on the matter: 'Mr Theobold's duty as auditor was confined to framing the balance sheets, which showed the position of the bank as disclosed by the books...' (ibid.: 780). In fact, Dicksee himself in editorial comments on the role of auditors in the court cases slipped naturally into referring to 'their balance sheets' (ibid.: 890).

The wording of the early audit reports often gives an indication of the work done by the auditors. From our sample of company reports in the early 1880s (of which those for the companies that also declared their audit fees are given in the Appendix) and 1900/1, 'Audited and found correct' or similar wording was the common, uninformative audit report. Often the reports were longer, though the wording, as can be seen, almost always preserved the public appearance that the auditors were examining a set of completed accounts presented to them. On only one occasion in our sample, in 1900/1, did the phrasing betray a different reality. Brewis & Rainie's audit report for the small company of stationers, Andrew Whyte and Son, read (my italics):

> We have examined the Books of Andrew Whyte & Son, Limited, for the Year ended 30th June, 1901, in connection with the Stock Sheets as certified by the Managing Directors, vouchers, and other instructions, and *have prepared* the foregoing Balance Sheet and Profit and Loss Account, which exhibit respectively a correct state of the Company's affairs as at 30th June 1901, and the result of the trading for the period mentioned, as shown by the Books.

Few companies in the early period declared their audit fees in their published profit and loss accounts. In the early 1880s, 23 such companies were found (see the Appendix), but in 1900/1 a larger and more representative collection of 121 company reports was garnered. The first point of interest, in view of the exhortation from the textbooks quoted above, is that no companies distinguished between accounting fees and auditing fees in their profit and loss accounts. The common titles of the relevant expenditure item were: 'Auditors' Fees', 'Audit Fees' or 'Auditors' Fees and Expenses'. Only 2 out of the 121 company accounts indicated that the auditors were performing two roles: 'Auditors and Accountant's fees – £143' at S. Blankensse and Son, and 'Registrar's Expenses, Audit Fees and Accountancy Charges – £1500' at the Welsbach Incandescent Gas Light company. Even there it must be noted the fee was not separately charged (or was not so distinguished on the face of the accounts) as the textbooks said they should. This practice of the auditors lumping the charges for all services into the audit fees continued until recently, if indeed it is still not practised. This can be judged by the fact that Chan *et al.* (1993: 772) found that the partners of the Big 6 firms interviewed in the early 1990s admitted that audit fees in the past had included payment for accounting and taxation services, but that 'for the larger clients at least the disclosed figures had become much "cleaner" in recent years'.

With a little subtle extrapolation, the level of audit fees can also be made to tell a story about the work done by the auditors. From Edwards *et al.* (1997: 17–21) and other sources (Pixley 1910: 38; Jones 1995: 59) it can be estimated that the average charge-out rate for an audit in this period was around two guineas a day, partners were more and articled clerks less. This implies a minimal amount of manpower expended on the smallest fee in our 1900 sample of company accounts – the one guinea J. W. Roach charged the tiny Exeter Coffee Tavern. However, the largest audit fee in our sample, the £1,500 that Deloitte, Dever, Griffiths earned from auditing the Welsbach Incandescent Gas Light company, would imply 714 man/days (or a team of 6 clerks for 6 months) and, as noted above, the wording of the audit fee item in the accounts indicates that additional accounting work was being done.

Sometimes the audit report also gave the game away. For example, the report of Turquand, Youngs on the accounts of the department store, William Whiteley, stated:

> Without devoting an amount of time which would involve a very great delay and inconvenience to the Company, we found it impracticable to examine in detail the very numerous papers making up the record of sales for the year. We have therefore adopted the daily totals of sales prepared by the permanent Audit staff of the Company after they had examined the original details.

Assuming that 'permanent Audit staff' refers to the shop's bookkeepers, Turquand, Youngs are effectively saying they had done all the accounts apart from add up the daily till rolls, thus justifying the huge 'audit' fee of £1000, or a notional four clerks for six months. There was no such tell tale wording in the accounts of several other of the largest companies in the country in our sample, but the clear implication of their audit fees is that a lot more than an audit was being undertaken. For example, Watney Coombe Reid, the brewers (audit fee, £750), Cunard, the shipping line (200 gns; NB a guinea was 21 shillings or £1.05 in today's currency), and the Salt Union (450 gns), all had fees greater or as great as the huge railway companies who, as we noted earlier, did their own accounting.

The reason the auditors did the accounting was of course that, as discussed in the first section, their client's did not have the personnel to do the work themselves. Another general indicator of the capacity of companies to do their own accounting is, therefore, the number of qualified accountants they employed. Obviously some unqualified accountants, bookkeepers, cashiers and company secretaries would have been capable of drawing up their company's accounts, but it would seem reasonable to suppose that most companies without a qualified accountant on the staff would be likely to require the auditors to draw up at least the final accounts. This is confirmed by our oral evidence. A typical response came from an accountant working in one of the largest practices in Reading in the 1950s: 'we mainly used to do the accounts... because they [the clients] had not got the qualified staff to do that. The records were good but they did not do the finishing work' (Interview with Partridge). On the other hand another interviewee talking of the early 1950s said: 'The three public companies we did had their own accountants and they would produce their set of accounts for the auditor to sign' (Interview with Colvin).

A crude measure of the number of qualified accountants working in industry in proportion to the work to be done can be gauged from Table 2.1. As can be seen, the number of accountants (composed of the English, Welsh and Scots chartered accountants, the certified, and the cost

Table 2.1 Qualified accountants working in business in Britain in comparison with
the number of public and private companies 1890–1991

	1890	*1911*	*1931*	*1951*	*1971*	*1991*
Accountants in business	128	642	6,253	17,491	39,960	94,917
Public companies	—	—	16,263	17,202	15,425	11,100
Private companies	—	—	95,598	241,063	503,232	998,700
All companies	13,323	51,787	111,861	258,265	518,657	1,009,800
Accountants per public company	—	—	0.38	1.02	2.59	8.55
Accountants per all companies	0.01	0.01	0.06	0.07	0.08	0.09

Source: Matthews *et al.* 1998: 90, 138.

and management accountants) working in 'business' (i.e. industry and commerce) increased rapidly during this period but barely kept pace with the increase in the number of limited companies; an increase almost entirely driven after 1931 by the growth in the number of private companies. If we focus on the number of accountants per public company (whose numbers have been declining from the 1950s to the present day, Matthews *et al.* 1998: 90) there was only approximately one qualified accountant (and only one in four of these was a chartered accountant) per company as late as 1951, and still only two and a half per company in 1971. Moreover, these estimates exaggerate the number of qualified accountants available to do the accounting in the public companies since some of them worked for private companies, while only between 65 and 70 per cent of ICAEW members employed in industry worked in the financial and secretarial roles, and were therefore in a position to be making up the accounts (ibid.: 223). Also it is worth noting, as a measure of the ability of audit clients to do their own accounts, that only 14 per cent of secretaries of publicly quoted companies were qualified accountants in 1931, still only 29 per cent in 1950, rising to about half by 1991 (ibid.: 125). Only one in five quoted companies had a qualified accountant on their board in 1931; two out of five in 1951, rising to four out of five in 1991. These figures, therefore, strongly indicate that even after the Second World War a sizable number of public quoted companies did not have the personnel capable of doing their final accounts, and therefore still left the job to their auditors.

A more precise measure of the extent to which British auditors also did their clients' accounting comes from our postal questionnaire. ICAEW members were asked if they drew up the accounts prior to conducting the audit at the start of their careers, and the results can be seen in Table 2.2. Almost two-thirds of respondents (with no particular trend) who qualified from the 1920s down to the 1950s said that they did their clients' accounts frequently during their training. Or put another way, up till the 1960s less than a

Table 2.2 My firm drew up the accounts prior to conducting the audit at the start of my career...

	Frequently[a] *(%)*	*Occasionally (%)*	*Rarely (%)*	*Never (%)*	*Total respondents*	
					(%)	*N*
Decade qualified						
1920/1930s	62.3 (25)	15.6	7.8	14.3	100	77
1940s	64.1 (32)	15.3	9.2	11.5	100	131
1950s	62.4 (33)	12.7	10.8	14.0	100	157
1960s	53.8 (38)	18.6	15.2	12.4	100	145
1970s	52.7 (20)	15.5	22.5	9.3	100	129
1980s	27.1 (9)	31.4	28.0	13.6	100	118
1990s	24.5 (1)	28.8	28.1	18.7	100	139
Respondent audited mainly...						
Quoted companies	20.6	28.5	31.5	19.4	100	165
SMEs	52.0	21.5	16.1	10.4	100	498
Sole traders and partnerships	67.8	5.6	13.3	13.3	100	90
Size of firm with which respondent qualified						
Top 20	33.4	26.4	25.4	14.7	100	299
Medium	57.1	17.7	11.7	13.5	100	282
Small	57.7	15.4	15.4	11.5	100	305

Source: Postal questionnaire, see Appendix.

Note
a Figures in brackets are the % of respondents who mainly audited quoted companies.

quarter of respondents said they rarely or never did their clients' accounts. As was expected, when the responses were layered on the basis of the type of companies audited, Table 2.2 confirms that drawing up the accounts was far more common on the audits of smaller companies. However, when those respondents who mainly audited quoted companies were analysed separately (the figures in brackets in Table 2.2), until the 1970s about a third indicated that they frequently drew up their client's accounts.

Of the total of 896 respondents to the question featured in Table 2.2, 12 made unsolicited write-in comments. Five, all training with small firms, one qualifying in 1981, noted that in their case by 'frequently' they meant they 'always' drew up the client's accounts. The rest queried the wording of the question, and were keen to make the point that drawing up the accounts came, not prior to, but in conjunction with or after the audit. Two respondents ticked the 'never' box for a reason unintended by the questionnaire, indicating that our figures in Table 2.2 may under-represent the extent of accounting done by the auditor. One of these, who qualified with the medium sized firm, W. M. Chadwick and Sons, Hyde, Cheshire, in 1939, stated: 'Except in the rare occasions when the clients' staff prepared the accounts my firm drew up the accounts at the *end* of the audit examination'. The other, who qualified with another medium sized firm, Mellor Snape in 1963, noted:

> if you had asked the question 'My firm drew up the accounts and regarded this as an audit', the answer would have been 'frequently'. I never heard of anyone preparing accounts and then auditing them. That is effectively doing the same thing twice.

Most accountants interviewed who worked in the earlier period also attested to the symbiosis of accounting and the audit. Some interviews indicated that occasionally one accounting firm would do the accounts and another the audit, although this was not common. An accountant recalling their clients in the 1930s said that for:

> the vast majority we would put the final accounts together. A few people who had their own accountant like the bigger building societies we would be doing proper audits. We had quite a number where, one firm of accountants would be their secretaries and keep all the records, and another firm would just come in and do a once a year check over and sign the audit certificate. We had a chain of cinemas that worked that way.
>
> (Interview with Goodwin)

Another interviewee remembered of the 1930s: 'One of our biggest clients was a chain of public houses with their head offices in the Strand. Another firm did their accounts but we used to audit them, and we'd always do a half-yearly audit (Joint interview with Fabes and Chapman).

However, the common practice was for one firm to do both jobs, although the interviews confirm that this was more common in the smaller clients. As one elderly accountant noted of his training with a small firm in Leicester in the 1930s: 'you were called an auditor, and indeed you gave an audit report, but 90 per cent of the job was getting the accounts out' (Interview with Aspell). Talking of the early 1950s in a small provincial practice, one auditor put it: 'With small or medium sized firms you did all the work for the accounts, and the tax work. Under those circumstances you were also doing the audit, you didn't divide the two' (Interview with Burlingham). But the practice was far from being the preserve of the small firms. A chartered accountant who trained with Peat Marwick in Swansea in the early 1950s remembered:

> in those days auditing and accountancy went together. The firm had few pure audits. Generally, the smaller the client the more likely it was we would be doing the total job. If the client was bigger then quite often it would have a trial balance, or possibly even full accounts for us to work on.
>
> (Interview with Davies)

Accountants writing publicly in the 1930s tended to portray the 'doing the books' audit as a thing of the past. W. J. Back, for example, recollected in the *Accountant* (22 September 1934: 403) that: 'In those old days...when the fathers of the profession built up their practices the professional accountant was a great deal more accountant than auditor...he would abstract his own list of balances and prepare the trial balance for himself.' This state of affairs, Back noted, had largely passed away, banished by: 'the greater capacity of the accountancy staff employed by the clients themselves'. But he conceded: 'There are, however, many small businesses, and some larger ones, in which the professional accountant [i.e. the auditor] acts as accountant to the business and has to complete the records, and balance the books'. It was, however, as we have said, in the accountants' professional interests to exaggerate the demise of the accounting audit, and it is clear from our oral evidence that it was still common even at large clients in the 1950s and 1960s. One accountant recalled: at 'the Carreras audit...I still prepared their accounts first, although they were a quoted public company in the early 1950s' (Interview with Keel). In fact, Carreras, the tobacco company, was ranked the 22nd largest industrial company in Britain in 1948 with a market value of £25.6 million (Hannah 1983: 191). Significantly, the audit report on the Carreras accounts, by J. H. Champness, Corderoy, Beesly, for 1950 still carried the familiar misleading wording: 'We have examined the accompanying Balance Sheet and annexed Profit and Loss Account which are in agreement with the books of account and returns...' (Carreras Limited: 11).

There are numerous other examples of the persistence of the accountancy audit among the larger British companies. A Manchester based accountant who qualified with Dearden and Farrow in 1953, and who audited quoted companies such as Chloride Electrical Storage, the battery makers, and Mather and Platt, the textile machinery manufacturers, was also asked how often his firm made up the accounts of audit clients:

> Well the answer is – always. I have never, I don't think, as a practitioner ever come across a pure audit in the sense that I was presented with a set of accounts which were complete. Usually the client probably didn't have a competent enough staff. The firm were known as the auditors but were actually always acting as accountants in the preparation of the accounts.... They [clients] might be able to balance the books but one always did do a certain amount of accountancy work, which makes it very interesting when you try to consider whether the auditors are in fact independent.
>
> (Interview with Gilliat)

Again, the experience of a future partner training with Peat Marwick in Leeds in the early 1960s and auditing wholesalers, textile companies and an iron company, was that: 'There were very few pure audits and it was quite a luxury if someone produced a trial balance for you. There would be very few instances where you were actually presented with a set of accounts' (Interview with Mordy). Moreover, this respondent dates the decline in the 'doing the books' audit as the early 1970s, consistent with our figures in Table 2.2. It is clear then that probably until the 1970s the bulk of what was called in Britain 'auditing' also involved accountants preparing a profit and loss account and balance sheet for all but their largest clients.

The decline in the British auditor's practice of also drawing up their client's accounts can be seen from Table 2.2. Only among the 1960s and 1970s qualifiers did the figure for those respondents who stated that their early auditing duties frequently included drawing up the accounts of their clients fall to just over half, and only among the 1980s and 1990s vintage did the proportion decline to a quarter. Of the respondents who mainly audited quoted companies even in the 1960s, over a third declared they frequently made up the accounts, although the decline thereafter is relatively steep, falling away to only a solitary respondent in the 1990s. The trend is less dramatic if, for all respondents, those frequently and occasionally drawing up their clients' accounts is combined. The proportion was 78 per cent of respondents training in the interwar period, while the figure was still 53 per cent in the 1990s. Another respondent who worked at Coopers & Lybrand in the early 1990s wrote on his questionnaire: 'for all but the biggest companies their auditors will prepare the full statutory accounts'.

The decline in the combination of accountancy with auditing, discussed more fully in the concluding chapter, was clearly due to the increased ability of the clients to do their own accounts, based on employing their own professional accountants. Some of our respondents, however, advanced the view that the decline was due to a change of attitude among some accountancy firms. An auditor who qualified with Peat Marwick Mitchell in the 1960s thought the reduction in accounting work came about due to: 'greater recognition of the potential conflict of auditing accounts which the firm had prepared'. Another put it as: 'I changed perception in that you can't audit what you've done yourself.'

Interestingly, the audit firms were not apparently sorry to lose this accounting work. One respondent to the postal questionnaire explained: 'The firm encouraged clients to develop their own accounting resources on the basis that a totally independent audit would be more valuable to them'. Another noted: 'the quality of clients' accounts staff improved, and we trained them up and assisted clients to recruit new staff'. A respondent at Ernst & Young in the 1990s also reported: 'larger clients who prepared their own accounts became favoured clients'. Finally, an accountant recently auditing at Coopers & Lybrand explained the still on-going trend downward in the amount of accounting done by auditors as due to: 'the changing size of the client base and the cost of performing the preparation work (this the client is encouraged to do themselves or is provided with names of good book-keepers)'.

The bookkeeping audit process

It was common in early British audits therefore for the auditor to do some of the client's bookkeeping and draw up their accounts. Nonetheless, an audit – simply stated as a check on the accuracy of the accounts and a guard against fraud – had by law from 1900 also to be conducted. The audit function was simply coincident to a greater or lesser extent with the accounting function.

How then was the bookkeeping audit conducted? We might first usefully introduce the personnel of the typical bookkeeping audit. The principal in charge of the audit would invariably be a partner in the accounting firm. He (almost never a she until the 1970s) would usually only be involved at the start and end of the process, but perhaps might (but frequently might not) keep a check on work done on his various jobs as they progressed (Interviews with Kemp, Aspell, Colvin and Mold). Depending on the size of the job, under the partner the personnel would commonly consist of a senior clerk (although later on and in larger firms there might be the intermediate posts of manager or supervisor). These seniors were usually trainees with several years' experience having passed their intermediate examinations, or were qualified accountants who had not yet been made partners. Seniors, however, would often be experienced but unqualified clerks who had been with the firm for years, probably never having taken articles, and had perhaps worked their way up into the position from office boy (Interview with Haddleton). The cannon fodder of the bookkeeping audit were the juniors – usually at least two in number on each job, who were articled clerks in the early years of their apprenticeship. Juniors were at the bottom of the audit hierarchy. As one auditor recalled, 'the people actually doing the audit weren't well treated and they weren't well respected. They were stuck in a nasty little room and they were regarded as a bloody nuisance [by the client]' (Interview with Grenside). On more propitious occasions the client's board room or some other room was used to conduct the audit, sometimes called 'the examination room' (*Accountant* 22 September 1934: 403). For the very smallest jobs the client brought their books into the auditor's office and the work was conducted there (Interviews with Partridge and Pearce).

Turning now to the techniques of the early audits, Littleton (1981: 307–8) notes that the essential skills of the bookkeeping audit, checking postings between books of account and ledgers and vouching transactions, dates from Pacioli and the Middle Ages. Certainly, the professional bookkeeping audit was a well-established process by the first half of the nineteenth century. Quilter was questioned on his role as an auditor by a House of Lords Select Committee on railway audits in 1849, and described a vouching and checking audit which would have been familiar to auditors a century later (Parker 1986: 29; Kitchen 1988: 26–9).

The typical nineteenth-century bookkeeping audit however is hazardous to describe. In a sense the variety of the work done was great since for one thing it depended on the size and nature of the client's business. For example, in 1900 audits by the same firm of accountants would range from those for a multinational company like Lever Brothers, to a local corner shop or solicitor's office. Spicer and Pegler (1914: xiv) discussed in some detail the various aspects of 37 different classes of audit which they considered needed special consideration; these ranged from insurance companies, clubs, bus companies to water works. The audit would also depend, of course, on how much of their own accounting the client did, and how reliable their accounting system was. Another major factor was the many varied auditing procedures between and even within accounting firms themselves.

On the other hand, fundamentally, the bookkeeping audit probably went through a process which was common to most audits, and was the standard procedure described in the textbooks such as Dicksee, de Paula and Spicer and Pegler. A first audit, of course, would start with a review of the book-keeping system used by the client and of their personnel (Littleton 1981: 311–12). Once this was established the work typically consisted of first closing off the books of account; reconciling the cash book and the bank statements; then checking the postings (the transfer) of figures from one account book or ledger to another, typically from day books or books of prime entry to the ledgers; vouching the transactions with documentary evidence such as invoices; casting or totalling the columns of figures in the cash book, various ledgers, wages books or the stock sheets; and finally arriving at or confirming a trial balance. In a pure audit the auditors' role would be to check that these procedures had been carried out correctly by the client's bookkeepers, but as we have said more usually the auditor would be performing these tasks himself for the first time.

This process of posting, vouching and casting was by far the most oner-ous in terms of manpower employed in the bookkeeping audit and by all accounts it was not pleasant work. As an auditor remembering the late 1950s put it: 'You were invariably working as a team and might be two, three, four, five people together. But invariably as a junior you are one of two people working together, which might be calling invoices and so on' (Interview with Patient). Another recalls: 'going out with a team usually in pairs, where one sat with the ledger, and calling out enormous numbers of entries over to each other, trying hard not to fall asleep' (Interview with Venning). Some had ways of not dropping off:

> come the afternoon one does tend to get a bit dozy. There was a test to find out if you were alert. He [a fellow auditor] would deliberately give you the wrong figure and if you accepted it then you paid a fine. But if the person being checked saw through it, the questioner had to pay a fine.
>
> (Interview with Thornton)

An auditor of the 1930s remembered another characteristic feature of the work: 'In those days, going out on an audit you had to tick everything'

(Interview with Palmer). All castings, postings and vouching once performed or checked had to be ticked, often with different coloured ink or pencils for different jobs. There were also different stamps, sometimes called a 'dabber', with distinctive heads to them, perhaps an initial, to distinguish who had performed the task (Spicer and Pegler 1914: 30; Interview with Thornton). Another articled clerk of 1950s vintage explained:

> You ticked off using different coloured inks or rubber stamps with your own tick mark. Mine was a pig's tail. Of course, as you ticked everything you tried very hard to get things beautifully lined up down the sides of the paper, because sometimes clients would say, 'What are all these awful ticks on my beautiful copperplate book?'
>
> (Interview with Beard)

Of the 1940s another remembered:

> In those days it was all hand-written stuff and the whole essence of the audit was the ticking of every single item you could find in the books. Everything was ticked at least once. It was ticked twice – in front for a posting and behind for a voucher. It was ticked three times for anything in the cash book. In front for a posting, behind for a voucher and underneath for a check to the bank pass book.
>
> (Interview with Livesey)

Thus the mind numbing work was known affectionately (or otherwise) variously as: 'tick and bash' or 'ticking and bashing' (Interview with Aspell, Sims, Atkinson and Whinney); 'ticking and blotting' (Interview with Boothman), or 'tick and touch' (Interview with Pearce).

A further aspect of the bookkeeping audit was that it 'was based on arithmetical accuracy which was the great key to it all' (Interview with Shaw). As another accountant put it: 'the theory in the small firms was – did the books balance? Were they arithmetically correct? And one searched for mistakes of a penny, believe it or not' (Interview with Middleton). Again: 'It all depended on absolutely balancing the books to a penny' (Interview with Aspell). This approach did not just apply to the small clients. It was still the rule when auditing relatively large companies, like Hays Wharf in east London in the 1960s, where they still: 'spent weeks adding up with comptometers' (Interview with Spens). And a trainee with PW in the 1960s remembers:

> There was a basic accounting machine for the rudimentary computerised punch card type stuff, but the accounting systems were forever producing wrong numbers and you spent a great deal of your time trying to establish that the numbers in the accounting systems were right.
>
> (Interview with Brindle)

Another retired auditor who qualified in the 1950s stated, 'I still have the ability to add a till roll in my head which not many people can do now. And I can still cast a column of figures off a page, virtually whilst discussing something else' (Interview with Patient).

> The most important thing was you had to cast quicker than any client. If you were in a client's office and there was a problem, it was considered a great disgrace if you couldn't add that up quicker than the chief clerk. It was a matter of pride.
>
> (Interview with Jones)

Although it is not possible to be specific, overwhelmingly the most man/hours of a typical audit were employed in checking the accuracy of the records of transactions. Although, Spicer and Pegler (1914: 159) stated in 1914: 'The most important duty of the Auditor, apart from his examination of the books of account, is the verification of the assets appearing in the Balance Sheet', this role was by far the less demanding in terms of manpower, indicated by the time devoted to the two aspects of the audit in the textbooks themselves. In the early editions of Dicksee (1904), for example, 'Auditing (up to the Trial Balance)', as he put it, took 205 pages, while 'From trial balance to balance sheet' was covered in 55 pages (in the 1969 edition the comparable figures were still 128 and 33 pages). The latter work consisted of the valuation and verification of assets such as stock or plant and machinery, and liabilities like bad debts; it also involved assessing the correct level for depreciation, the provision for reserves and verifying investments. But this was much less time-consuming than the work on transactions largely because, as we discuss in the following chapters, for one thing there was very little physical checking of the assets and liabilities. Littleton (1981: 312) surveying the verification of balance-sheet items in the 1880s concluded that: 'audit technique was weaker at this point than in the examination of bookkeeping details'.

Finally, if all had gone well in the bookkeeping audit then the final accounts were either drawn up or approved and then signed off by a partner, who may or may not have had much input into the process. The partner would, however, have been responsible for a final oversight of the completed accounts, reviewing the work done and seeing that the audit notebook had been correctly completed. The end product of the audit was the audit report (typical early examples of which are set out in the Appendix) and this too would probably be written by the principal. The accounts would then be handed to the client, and perhaps be discussed over a leisurely lunch with the board of directors. It might also be the practice for the partner to attend the client's annual general meeting.

A majority of our interviewees, however, were somewhat dismissive of the role of the partners. 'I often wondered what the partners did, they were shut in their rooms, or be out playing golf, they lived in a strange world' (Interview with Chapman); 'I didn't often see a partner on the job, no' (Interview with Haddleton); 'very much hands off' (Interview with Livesey); 'fairly remote' (Interview with Palmer), were typical reactions. Another recalled of a four partner City firm in the 1960s: 'I have no recollection of a partner ever going to see a client...We went out and did the work and brought the working papers back to the office, and the partner reviewed them, and that was that (Interview with Sharman). A minority said the partners did take an active role. And certainly matters changed in later years since another respondent who qualified with Touche Ross in the 1970s recalled: 'we were not the sort of practice where the partners never leave their office and only turn up to shake hands and eat lunch' (Interview with Scicluna). Also a trainee with Cooper Brothers in the late 1960s recalled that the partners worked extremely hard, imbued with the work ethic of Henry Benson at the head of the firm (I am grateful to Prof Dick Edwards for this comment).

Depth of the audit

Since there is some misapprehension on the matter in the literature it is worth taking some time to establish the depth and thoroughness of the early bookkeeping audits. As noted above, there were (and still are) differences in the work conducted by different firms and on different jobs, and there have been wide disparities in the thoroughness of the audit at all times during its history. Quilter in his Parliamentary evidence in 1849, alluded to above, asserted how thorough his audits were and that he would not just look at vouchers but at whether the item was charged at the proper price. He would take nothing for granted but 'require a justification for every entry, debtor and creditor' (Kitchen 1988: 28). To Quilter, an audit was not just a dry arithmetical duty but involved higher powers of judgement (ibid.: 27). Contemporary observers, however, were often vocal in the press as to the superficial and inadequate nature of the audits in the late nineteenth century, although it is important to distinguish between criticisms of the amateur shareholder auditors and those of the professionals (Chandler and Edwards 1994, xvi–xvii). Many of the criticisms, for example Sir George Jessel's evidence to the Lowe Committee in 1877, were probably directed at the amateur not the professional audit (Edwards 1989: 267). In court cases too, for example in the Leeds Estate Building and Investment company case of 1887, the erring auditor was often an amateur (Chandler *et al.* 1993: 449).

None the less there was a wide disparity in practice and thoroughness among the professionals. Carter, the leading Birmingham accountant, had no trouble, in an article in the *Accountant* in 1894, highlighting the conflicting auditing practice advocated by various early commentators.

For example, with regard to the heaviest part of the audit in terms of work-load,

> in checking postings to the personal accounts in the Ledgers from day books and Cash Books...while some think that all postings should be checked under all circumstances others think that they need not be checked at all if the books balance.
>
> (Quoted in Chandler and Edwards 1994: 157)

Also, Carter continued, the question was

> whether we should with Mr Pixley, look at vouching as a 'mechanical and most childish operation', or, with Mr Gourlay, as of 'paramount importance'; whether we should 'of course' agree the bank account in detail with the Bank Pass Book, or whether 'of course' it is unnecessary to do so.
>
> (Ibid.: 159)

Interest usually focused on the extent to which the auditor had to verify the underlying reality of the books of account, rather than just check that the resulting balance sheet showed a true and correct view 'as shown by the books' – a phrase enshrined in the Companies Act, 1879 (Chandler *et al.* 1993: 448). As Dicksee stated in 1892, there are some 'claiming that an auditor's duty is confined to a comparison of the Balance Sheet with the books, while others assert that it is an auditor's duty to trace every transaction back to its source. Between these two extreme views every shade of opinion may be found' (quoted in ibid.: 450). Although the words 'as shown by the books' continued to be used in subsequent Companies Acts, legal proceedings (principally that of the London and General Bank case in 1895) established (what Quilter had asserted almost 50 years earlier) that the auditor needed to take the 'trouble to see that the books of the company themselves show the company's true position' (ibid.: 449). Indeed, according to Chandler *et al.* (ibid.: 450) 'it was already established, in certain quarters, that auditors should go beyond the company's own records in search of audit evidence'. In a case in 1900, for example, the auditor was found liable for not using supplier's statements as a check on the creditors' ledger accounts (Chandler 1997: 70).

Recent historians, like Edwards and Chandler, have tended to side with the contemporary critics as to the superficiality of the early audits. Chandler (1997: 70) thought that Whinney, a leading accountant of the time, 'was an exception when he stated that an auditor must "see that the books themselves do correspond with the facts" '. Chandler concluded: 'It is clear that some "professional" auditors did little more than their amateur counterparts.' In turn, it is Edwards's (1989: 196) view that the 'mechanical' audit was widespread in this period and that: 'the fairly common certification "audited and found correct" further supports the idea that the nineteenth-century audit was often a fairly routine affair which ignored the difficult problems of valuation that are principal features of the auditors' duties today'. Edwards also argued that the small amount of time (seven days) allowed the auditor by the articles of association of some companies would have enabled them to undertake no more than a superficial examination of balance sheet figures.

Edwards's criticisms of the early audits turn to some extent on the definition of 'mechanical'. Edwards is correct that early auditors would spend little time on balance sheet valuations; they were usually prepared to take the word of management in this respect (as indeed they often are today). They took comfort from the well known and influential case of the Kingston Cotton Mill Company of 1895 where the judge laid down that the auditor was 'entitled to assume that they [the client's management] were honest' – unless there were suspicious circumstances (Chandler *et al.* 1993: 454). However, as we have discussed above, while with certain variations the senior audit clerks would run through a fairly mechanical set of procedures this did not equate with the audit being brief or cursory, as Edwards implies. The professional audit, properly carried out would often involve checking every transaction, and went beyond the books to the extent that ledger entries were typically vouched against the documentation of the transactions.

The bookkeeping audit then while mechanical in one sense was usually very detailed and certainly not brief. The amount and nature of the work being done in the early audits can be assessed to some extent from the evidence in our sample of 23 company reports for the early 1880s (set out in the Appendix). Since the companies ranged from the smallest, like the Redheugh Bridge company, a toll bridge, to the third largest company in the country – the Great Western Railway (Wardley 1991: 278) – and covered a range of industrial and financial sectors, the sample though small is probably fairly typical. An indication of the length of the audits can be gained from the time lapse between a company's accounting year-end and the date of the audit report. This, of course, is not an infallible measure of the time taken on the audit but it is certainly the maximum length (except for any interim work done), and for most companies is probably not far off the actual length. Using this measure, as can be seen from the Appendix, the mean audit period in our sample was two months, although that figure is inflated by the inordinately long year-end to audit date period of the telegraph companies (for which there is no obvious explanation). The mode and median periods of five and six weeks respectively are probably the more typical. Interviews with auditors involved also indicate that the typical bookkeeping audits lasted from less than a week for the smallest companies to three months for the largest (Interviews with Wilde, Atkins and Wilkes). An accountant who qualified in the 1940s 'can remember doing a departmental store, our largest client. I think it probably took me five weeks' (Interview with Mold). Moreover, this duration did not seem to change a great deal. A Manchester accountant estimated that in the 1950s: 'For the smallest client, you could be in there for only a week, but with our largest client, Combined English Mills, we took three months to do the job'

(Interview with Boothman). Vauxhall Motors audit took Deloittes about a month to six weeks in the 1950s (Interview with Milne).

These data on the length of the audit period, together with those on the audit fees discussed earlier, also allow some estimate of the manpower expended on the audit. If we take a typical audit like that of the Metropolitan Railway Carriage & Wagon company in 1881, the £105 (100 gns) fee for the five-week audit period would, using our rule-of-thumb of 2 gns a day charge-out fee, indicate a team of two auditors. But, since the mean number of clerks for the whole sample (estimated using our rule-of-thumb) was five, and both the mode and median was 4 clerks, this was probably a representative size for an audit team in the 1880s. This estimate is borne out using the data from the larger sample for 1900/1, for which the summary statistics are also reported in the Appendix. The average audit fee in our sample of 121 companies, £171, indicates 81 man/days worked (or around 4 auditors for a month). This seems in line with the length of an audit in those days, evidenced from other sources discussed below. As can be seen, the evidence for the 1880s and 1900/1 companies is similar, indicating little change in the period. Without stretching the evidence too far, therefore, it seems likely that a team of 4 clerks working for between 4 and 8 weeks might be taken as the typical audit of a quoted company in the late nineteenth century.

The audit reports given in the Appendix also offer hints at the work carried out by the auditors. For example the: 'We have examined the above Accounts with the Books and Vouchers of the Company and find them correct' wording of the audit report by Price Waterhouse on the accounts of the Artisan Labourers and General Dwellings company in 1882, may be taken as a reasonable description of what went on. There is also evidence that the auditors were actively attempting to improve the accounting practices of their clients. For example, Turquand, Youngs had, after some years, finally convinced the Marbella Iron Ore company to set aside funds for depreciation. There is an indication too that auditors were prepared to qualify their audit opinions, as with Robert A. Maclean & Co's 'subject to' qualification on the face of the National Safe Deposit accounts. Indeed in 1900, among our larger sample of 121 companies, 30, or a quarter of the total, contained some qualified audit opinion. The further important point is that the frequent brevity of the audit reports in the 1880s, such as the 'Examined and found correct' on the accounts of the City of London Brewery, or the 'Audited and approved' at the Crystal Palace company, give the wrong impression of an equally brief audit. In fact, the £200 audit fee would indicate a month's work for five auditors at the brewery, and 6 week's work for a team of 2 at the Crystal Palace.

Given this evidence then it follows that the typical professional Victorian bookkeeping audit was a labour intensive, time consuming and usually thorough, if mechanical, process, and not the brief, cursory, affair of which the auditors were often accused at the time (e.g. Chandler and Edwards 1994: 35) and by subsequent historians (Edwards 1989: 196).

Interim or continuous audits

Probably from the beginning of the professional audit, work was also performed outside of the year end period (which, of course, adds to the audit effort which was estimated by our calculations in the previous section). According to Spicer and Pegler (1914: 25):

> A Final or completed audit is commonly understood to be an Audit which is not commenced until after the books are closed at the end of the financial period, and is then carried forward continuously until completed. This is the most satisfactory form of Audit, and is usually adopted wherever possible.

However, Spicer and Pegler (1914: 22; see also de Paula 1914: 15) also described interim or continuous audits, which were:

> where the Auditor's staff is occupied continuously on the accounts the whole year round, or where the Auditor attends at intervals, fixed or otherwise, during the currency of the financial year, and performs an Interim audit; such Audits are adopted where the work involved is considerable.

Evidently the terms 'continuous' and 'interim' were often used interchangeably, although perhaps the former usually indicated a less intermittent process than the latter. Apparently a continuous audit could also have the connotation of the auditors doing something like an internal audit for management rather than it being part of the external audit for the consumption of the shareholders (I am grateful to Prof Dick Edwards for this opinion). As with many aspects of the audit therefore the meaning of terms is difficult to pin down.

The audit report of 1886 for the Birmingham Railway and Wagon company (given in the Appendix) is an example of a continuous audit, and many of our interviewees related how these interim audits were conducted in the 1920s and 1930s:

> We'd have up to seven or eight people and would be working on it virtually the whole year, doing a lot of interim audit work on a monthly basis. This was very regular for the bigger audits. We did the Trustees Savings Bank, that again was monthly.
>
> (Interview with Goodwin)

Of course, as we have argued above, what was often going on was not merely an audit but the client's bookkeeping, and Dicksee's early editions indicated that the continuous audit 'sometimes includes the preparation of the periodic accounts by the Auditor's staff' (Dicksee 1904: 12). By Dicksee's 1951 edition, this last comment had been dropped, however.

The motives behind the interim work were two-fold: first, to help get the year-end accounts out quicker and, second, since clients' year-ends bunched, to better employ the audit staff through the year (Cooper 1966: 33). As another respondent talking of the 1930s put it: 'all the sizeable firms would have an interim audit to save time at the end of the year, and of course to use the staff in slack periods' (Interview with Chapman). Another confirmed that the motive was:

> if you were slack in the office, and remember on those salaries we could afford to have spare articled clerks. So to fill up slack periods you would do interim audits. You could say – Joe Bloggs Ltd's ledgers are always a bit of a mess, go down and balance some of the quarters as opposed to leaving everything to the year-end.
>
> (Interview with Mold)

The auditor of Consett, the steel makers, in the 1950s also explained:

> You would audit it all during the year, trying to cut out the heavy weight of year-end work. Because, I think it's probably still true, for about seventy per cent of limited company audits, year-ends are December or March. So you get a disproportional weight of audits and you try to do a lot of work during the year.
>
> (Interview with Middleton)

The pressure to get the accounts out quickly in later years often came from American subsidiaries. A Price Waterhouse accountant recalled of the late 1950s: 'American clients like Bird's Eye wanted their accounts out remarkably quickly and therefore you had to do a tremendous amount of interim work' (Interview with Atkinson).

Since from the first, interim work was necessary for the larger clients, it followed that the practice would increase as companies grew. By 1951, Dicksee's textbook noted that 'all but the smallest audits must almost necessarily be, in some degree, continuous', and the wording remained the same in the 1969 edition (Magee 1951: 30–1; Waldron 1969: 30). For their largest clients, like Shell the oil company, Price Waterhouse were already employing the continuous audit in the 1950s, to the extent that they had personnel stationed with the client the whole year round (Interviews with Brindle and Stacy).

As the nature of audit work changed, the practice became established that certain aspects of the audit were conducted in the interim, leaving the year-end to complete the remainder. As one auditor described the process in the 1960s: 'the idea was to go in and comment on the internal control, and check certain work so that by the year-end you had done perhaps your work on the revenue account and the internal control, and at the year-end you audited the balance sheet' (Interview with Haddleton). The 1976 edition of de Paula confirmed that the interim audit was used for: 'generally covering the assessment and testing of internal control, together with detailed checking of transactions. In the case of a large client, such interim audit work may involve several visits during a year, or even a continuous audit' (de Paula and Attwood 1976: 17). In the first edition of Woolf's textbook in 1978 he indicated that the complete or final audit was now only for relatively small firms, whereas:

> In the case of larger clients the auditor will often find it necessary to proceed with the audit on an interim basis, in view of the volume of testing which is necessary ... [they] may be bi-annual, quarterly, or even monthly ... leaving the final stage of the audit relatively free for the verification of the year-end accounts, the assessment of the system and most detailed checking of the underlying records and documents having already been carried out.
>
> (Woolf 1978: 46)

Where, however, the internal controls of a client are fundamentally weak, Woolf noted, a continuous audit might be necessary. The same wording survived to Woolf's (1997: 46–7) sixth edition.

However, Higson's (1987: 323) interviews with practitioners in the mid-1980s indicated that there had been a reduction in interim work in recent years as a result of the general decline in the amount of testing being undertaken.

Summary

The characteristic feature of the British bookkeeping audit, which was the rule from the start of the professional audit in the early nineteenth century until the 1960s, was that it was closely bound up with also doing the client's accounting, since usually the amateurish family firms did not have the personnel able to produce a set of final accounts themselves. Until the 1960s about two-thirds of auditors also drew up the client's accounts. This fact ensured that the audit was heavily focused on the verification of transactions, arithmetical accuracy, and that the books balanced. Audit work entailed the checking of postings between books and ledgers, casting columns of figures and vouching transactions in a process known as 'ticking and bashing'. This was a mechanical though protracted affair taking, for the average quoted public company, 2 or 4 clerks 1 to 3 months. The balance sheet attracted much less attention on the bookkeeping audit and was far less time consuming than checking transactions; auditors were usually prepared to take the word of management as to, for example, the value of stock. Increasingly audit work was undertaken in the interim, leaving the year end for verification of balance sheet items.

3   Documentation

Audit programmes

Another aspect in which the early audit procedures differed between firms was in the extent to which the work was pre-planned and written down in an audit programme. From at least the late nineteenth century it was the practice of many firms to use audit note-books 'as a record of routine work performed and of queries raised in the course of an audit' (Dicksee 1892: 1–2). Trevor asserted in 1889 that:

> the practice of having an audit book for each audit is highly important, with columns for the initials of each person who has performed the work, and made himself responsible for its having been correctly and thoroughly done. By this means, much labour is saved on a second audit and thorough continuity secured.
>
> (Quoted in Chandler and Edwards 1994: 110)

Dicksee (1892: 1–2) reported G. P. Norton describing:

> certain printed instructions of a general character which are bound in small note-books, together with a number of spare blank leaves for memoranda. At the commencement of a new audit one of the note-books is appropriated to it, and the general instructions are carefully revised and special instructions supplemented. The clerk who has this book with him is thus shown precisely what are his duties with regard to the audit upon which he is engaged.

The term 'audit programme', which is effectively what the audit note-books were, would seem to be of later provenance, and was possibly American in origin. However, the British were not far behind, if at all. The term 'audit programme' appeared first in the ICAEW's Final Audit paper of 1929 (November, Question 10), but the term was used in the first editions of both Spicer and Pegler (1911: 29) and de Paula, (1914: 12–13); and as early as 1908, Spicer and Pegler (1908) published a book of model audit programmes, each especially tailored for a wide variety of audits – banks, railways, breweries and so on.

The chief motive behind the programmes in the audit note-books appeared to be the control of the audit clerks, since: 'In a large practice, unless some such method is adopted, the principals must of necessity lose a very large amount of control, and will be very much in the hands of their staff' (de Paula 1917: 12). To Dicksee, in his 1904 edition, the great advantage of the audit programme appeared to be because a 'definite system is undoubtedly preferable to leaving things too much in the hands of the audit clerk...the principal should always endeavour to keep the reins of every audit in his own hands' (Dicksee 1904: 5). Spicer and Pegler (1911: 28–9), in the first edition of their textbook, discuss the pros and cons of the audit note-book in the following terms:

> It is therefore desirable that some definite record should be kept of the work performed at each Audit, and in order to ensure uniformity, and to make certain that all the work is done which should be done, it is advisable to make out a programme of work, the clerk responsible for each portion of the work done initialling as it is performed.

The work done in a new audit was to form the basis 'for the preparation of an Audit Programme to be followed in the future'. This procedure, almost word for word, appeared in Spicer and Pegler down to the tenth, 1951, edition (Bigg 1951: 27–9).

Dicksee himself published a pro forma *Audit Note Book* in 1892, 'the demand for which', he stated in the 1904 edition of his textbook, 'is sufficient to prove that the use of such a book is very general among the profession... in point of fact, some sort of Audit Note-Book is almost invariably used by most accountants at the present time' (Dicksee 1904: 2). Dicksee described three versions of the audit note-book: first: 'a printed form of book containing an exhaustive series of headings, to comprise all those [duties] which might conceivably arise on any engagement'. It contained headings such as 'Cash balanced'; 'Day Book Postings and Additions'; 'Private Ledger written up'; 'Balance Sheet & Profit and Loss A/c completed' (Magee 1951: 32–3; note how this is further evidence of the auditor's accounting role). Some of these note-books were not taken out on the job but were kept in the accountant's office and written up from memoranda. Dicksee's second type of note-book had an audit programme drawn up by the principal at the start of each audit, and, third was the note-book which the audit clerk in charge wrote up, and 'is obviously suited only to those cases where the clerk is of a particularly responsible order' (ibid.: 34). These latter *ad hoc* programmes were apparently common down to at least the 1960s, since an auditor who qualified with a medium sized City firm in the 1960s recalled that the audit programmes in his firm were made up by the audit seniors and the junior clerks (Interview with Sharman). Another interviewee who qualified with a four partner firm in the 1960s, and who audited a subsidiary of Taylor Woodrow the quoted building concern, remembered: 'There were no systems of programmes commercially available that I was aware of. We used to create our own from job to job' (Interview with Kemp).

The audit note-book did service at least into the 1960s. Remarkably, the final – 1969 – edition of Dicksee continued, perhaps in the lazy way of text-books, the description of the audit note-book which, with only one or two alterations, was that given in the first edition of 1892 (Waldron 1969: 36). And the longevity of the audit note-book is confirmed by another interviewee who recalled:

> at the time I joined Peats [1958] and for a while afterwards, audit programmes were still tailor made year-by-year, invented by the senior in charge of the job, recorded in foolscap, bound books specially made with hard green covers. I remember the number of times I saw people running up and down the stairs on their way to see partners to clear an audit, filling in the audit programme on the stairs as they went, and it was very rare for the partner reviewing the job to spend much time on going through the audit programme. So even in the early sixties anyway, it was very much the old approach, but that was beginning to change.
>
> (Interview with Hardcastle)

The same audit note-book and programme could perform prolonged service in an audit firm. In the recollection of one auditor who trained in the early 1950s:

> The actual audit programme itself was in a long book, which you kept from year to year, using the same book. You'd tick off each item and if you did a month you'd put down which month you did and so on.
>
> (Interview with Beard)

One Price Waterhouse partner remembered: 'the audit programme went on from year to year. One I came across in 1957 was an audit programme dating twenty years back, with the senior partner's initials, NW, Sir Nicholas Waterhouse, down at the bottom of a column' (Interview with Stacy). An accountant who trained with Thornton and Thornton, the medium sized Oxford based firm, in the 1950s recalled: 'the jobs I worked on, I looked at the audit programme and it went back ten years, and the previous audit programme went back another ten years. They tended to stick a long, long time' (Interview with Haddleton). Another described how in the 1960s:

> It was structured from last year's audit programme, and the usual tech-nique was to take that and alter it up for changed circumstances. In those days coloured markers signified what you did in one year and

another colour the next year and so on. But it was probably 95 per cent unchanged from year to year.

(Interview with Patient)

Again at Peat Marwick the 'audit programme was probably the same for 15 or 20 years' (Interview with Mordy). Also, despite the textbook emphasis on flexibility, the audit programme was not always tailored to individual cases. Talking of the early 1960s another auditor noted: 'the same programme was used no matter what firm you dealt with. We'd turn up in many a different factory and carry out the same sort of procedure (Interview with Chapman).

However, the use of audit note-books or audit programmes was not universal, and Dicksee (1904: 2, his italics) also set out the rationale for not using programmes:

if a competent clerk is sent to undertake an audit (and none but competent clerks *should* be sent), it is much the better way to leave him unfettered with printed instructions but allow him to go thoroughly into the whole system in operation, and from the nature of the system, and from what he sees, let him outline his own methods of procedure. By this means there is not so much danger of his getting into a semi-careless groove of working, and moreover he feels that more responsibility is placed upon him, which acts as an incentive to do the work more thoroughly.

A tongue in cheek article by D. A. Bostock-Smith in 1949 stated:

Before commencing an audit it is necessary to have an audit programme. There are two kinds: (a) the programme firmly fixed in the head of the senior clerk, who left last week to rebuild the Empire somewhere East of Suez; and (b) the programme in the audit note-book. This article is concerned with programme (b), the rarer and more precious of the two.

(*Accountant* 12 March 1949: 198)

This view was probably too jaundiced, but another auditor reported that while training with a small firm in the 1940s there were: 'No strict systems at all. You just went out and did the job, and nobody told you what you'd got to do' (Interview with Brittain). Another confirmed the popularity of the mental audit programme, and that even in the 1960s:

The individual managers had their own styles and were left very much to themselves. I remember one who in fact kept very few records, being on the job for 10 years, 15 years, 25 years and was a law unto himself. So often it was in the guy's head rather than on paper.

(Interview with Niddrie)

Even later at Stoy Hayward: 'our first proper audit approach came in about 1972. I would like to say that when I started there was an audit programme but it was still in its infancy' (Interview with Martin).

The wide divergence in the use of audit programmes can be seen from Table 3.1, where our questionnaire evidence reveals that from the interwar period through to the 1960s only around 50–60 per cent of audit firms were always or often using them. Put another way, even in the 1960s around 45 per cent of trainees never or only sometimes used audit programmes. Not until the 1970s was there a significant increase in their usage, when the figure for those always or often using audit programmes increased to around 70 per cent; by the 1980s it was over 90 per cent, and in the 1990s – 96 per cent. Table 3.1 also reveals that use of programmes was not so much a function of the size of the audit firm with which the respondent trained, as was implied by some of the evidence above, but more due to the size of the company being audited. Taking all those respondents with auditing experience from the interwar period down to the 1990s, 90 per cent of those who mainly audited quoted companies, and two-thirds of those auditing small and medium sized companies, often or always used audit programmes, compared to only a third auditing sole traders and partnerships. One of our interviewees confirmed that programmes were used by

Table 3.1 While I was undertaking my articles/training, my firm used audit programmes...

	Always (%)	Often (%)	Sometimes (%)	Never (%)	Total respondents (%)	N
Decade qualified						
1920s/1930s	39.3	20.2	28.1	12.4	100	89
1940s	38.9	17.6	25.2	18.3	100	131
1950s	35.4	16.5	30.4	17.7	100	158
1960s	46.3	9.5	31.3	12.9	100	147
1970s	58.5	12.3	19.2	10.0	100	130
1980s	78.3	12.5	5.8	3.3	100	120
1990s	92.8	3.6	2.2	1.4	100	138
Respondent audited mainly...						
Quoted companies	84.4	5.4	6.0	4.2	100	167
SMEs	56.9	14.3	20.1	8.7	100	411
Sole traders and partnerships	20.4	15.1	38.7	25.8	100	93
Size of firm with which respondent qualified						
Top 20	69.4	8.3	13.1	9.2	100	314
Medium	50.2	12.2	25.8	11.8	100	287
Small	49.7	16.8	21.9	11.6	100	310

Source: Postal questionnaire, see Appendix.

the same firm on the larger jobs but not the smaller (Interview with Norris). It would seem reasonable to argue therefore that the growing use of programmes was due to the increasing scale of the audits, which accelerated in the 1970s and 1980s.

Working papers

The audit programme in Britain then was usually contained, if there was one, in a bound audit note-book, and they continued in common use until at least the 1960s. The note-books were also in widespread use at an early date in America, where they 'typically contained printed instructions of a general nature, blank pages for instructions applicable to the particular audit and specially ruled pages for the work done on the various accounts...the clerk who assumes responsibility should initial his work' (Myers 1985: 54). American auditors, however, had abandoned audit note-books in favour of working papers at least by the time of the first edition of Montgomery (1912: 242–6), the leading US audit textbook. The reason for dropping the note-book was given by Montgomery as due to the decline in America of the bookkeeping audit for which it was best suited. The Americans came to rely more on what they called 'working papers'. These however did a similar job to the note-book, and Montgomery (ibid.: 73–7) said they should contain the audit programme, files of among other things – work done and errors found. The files were indexed and placed in folders in a binder and carried over from year to year on the same audit (Montgomery 1934: 47–53). An article by Waldron H. Rand, published in 1915 in the *Journal of Accountancy* (the official journal of the American Association of Certified Public Accountants), discussed the importance of working papers; and a book, *Audit Working Papers – Their Preparation and Content* by J. Hugh Jackson, was published by the American Institute of Accountants in 1923 (Waldron 1969: 373–2).

The Americans, therefore, placed emphasis on the importance of working papers before the British. A British accountant who qualified with Thornton and Thornton in the 1950s testified to this:

> The only time I came across the working paper or schedule which was specifically required by an audit programme, was when I worked in Canada for a big firm for a couple of years and the American attitude seemed to be that you audit the balance sheet and therefore you write lots of things down about the assets on the balance sheet. Make notes on it.
> (Interview with Haddleton)

However, to some extent the loose documentation which inevitably accumulated in the conduct of an audit, and which was sometimes carried forward from year to year, was also a feature of the British audit from the start. The first edition of de Paula (1914: 12–13) suggested that: 'all working papers should be filed and kept, as also should drafts of accounts, and the schedules appertaining thereto'. The working papers' serious litigious purpose was also made clear since: 'should anything go wrong...if proper records are not kept, the auditor might find himself in a position of considerable difficulty'. But Dicksee, on the other hand, was slow to discuss the issue. The 1951 edition describes but does not use the term, working papers:

> We have spoken throughout of a 'book', but a plan which has been growing in popularity of recent years is to place all the papers relating to an audit upon an audit 'file', one for each periodical engagement, so that ready reference may instantly be made to all the papers relating to any particular year's audit...also a 'permanent' file containing such matters as articles of association.
>
> (Magee 1951: 34)

The collection of working papers in Britain then was a haphazard process that varied from firm to firm. When they were accumulated working papers originated on British audits more in the natural course of events, and this was also influenced by the fact that the auditors were frequently doing the client's accounting. As the Thornton and Thornton trainee quoted earlier explained:

> Accountants generate working papers with that sort of job because they need to. You start off by balancing the bank, then you balance the cash...then you post it up to the nominal ledger...and then you prepare draft accounts. And all along the way you are generating working papers. I don't recall ever specifically setting out to generate a certain working paper....
>
> (Interview with Haddleton)

An accountant who qualified with Mellors, Basden & Mellors, the medium sized Nottingham firm, also testified that in the 1950s the firm 'still prepared the accounts from the books. We did the audit as we went along, but the emphasis was very much on accountancy, and the working papers were very possibly initial calculations and arithmetic as opposed to verifications' (Interview with Hewitt).

Early British working papers were therefore unsystematic and less voluminous than they were to become. Another accountant recalled that they:

> were merely there to explain and show what you had done. So anyone with a query could see what had been done. You kept them year after year. I've got working papers now going back to 1939...In those days the working papers were not so prescribed, so the working papers in the Cardiff office would be different to those in Newport. Today there is more standardization.
>
> (Interview with Jones)

Another accountant from the same era recalled: 'a typical file of working papers would be a quarter of the size that it is today, or even less than that per-haps' (Interview with Whinney). An articled clerk of the 1950s remembered:

> When I think of our modern files and then what they were like in those days. They were pretty primitive. There wasn't even a standard order of the working papers, and everything was more geared to the prepa-ration of the accounts than it was to the audit.
>
> (Interview with Shaw)

Another trainee with a small City firm in the 1940s said they didn't keep working papers at all (Interview with Ainger), and one interviewee offered a practical reason for this: 'there wasn't encouragement to build up too much, a) because of the shortage of paper, and b) simply because there weren't photocopiers like there are today' (Interview with Atkinson).

There was then a wide diversity of practice based on: the individual firm's procedures, the size of the client, and the extent to which the accounts were being made up during the audit. By the 1940s, however, some major firms at least had given thought to the working papers and the form they should take. One landmark on the issue was a paper given to the Oxford summer school of the ICAEW in the late 1940s by a Price Waterhouse partner, Stanley Duncan. He recalled: 'What I did was display the way that PW pre-pared their working papers, so that they showed what had been done and to substantiate the various figures' (Interview with Duncan). Henceforth, the working papers at Price Waterhouse, and possibly other firms were modelled on that paper. Another PW partner remembered that in the 1950s their papers:

> went through each of the balance sheet headings and gave you a specimen lead schedule with movements from last year to this year of fixed assets, breakdowns between sundry debtors and trade debtors, and bad debts and provisions. Possibly it had an indication of sample audit procedures to test those balance sheet items and we all tended to follow that pattern. So one would produce a set of working papers which would have enabled the partner and the manager on reviewing the audit to look at the accounts and say, 'Oh, the fixed assets or the debtors are up a lot, I wonder why?' and find the answer in the working papers. It was an analysis of the accounts that we were pre-senting. I think the Price Waterhouse working papers were very logical, and did actually give you a fair insight and quite a profound analytical review.
>
> (Interview with Stacy)

Some firms had no audit programmes but good working papers and vice versa. An accountant who qualified with a small firm in the 1950s stated: 'Audit programmes were effectively non-existent, but by contrast, we were expected to keep up a most meticulous set of working papers on every client' (Interview with Boothman). Likewise, and interestingly in view of the fact that the founders of the firm wrote a standard textbook, Spicer and Pegler had no strict system of audit programmes in the 1950s. A trainee with the firm at that time explained:

> Common sense was always paramount. You were expected to produce a good set of working papers. It showed up when they went to the tax department [at Spicer and Pegler] if you didn't. If... the information they needed wasn't there, they made a complaint pretty vigorously. But the dominant consideration was professional judgement.
>
> (Interview with Denza)

Almost certainly, as with audit programmes, the universality of systematic working papers dates from the 1970s. Again remarkably little had changed in the wording of the treatment of working papers from de Paula's first edition in 1914 to the thirteenth edition in 1966 (de Paula 1966: 15–16); but by the fifteenth edition in 1976 the content of audit files and working papers was more fully set out and reference was also made to the ICAEW's statement U12, issued in 1969, entitled: 'Auditor's working papers', which advocated their use (de Paula and Attwood 1976: 18–21, 268). The 1969 edition of Dicksee added a completely new chapter on: 'The Auditor's working papers', detailing all the papers to be kept and listing the advantages of the procedure. Top of this list was: 'The papers constitute the auditor's main defence from criticism (or even prosecution) if he should prima facie appear culpable in his work or his findings' (Waldron 1969: 373). Spicer and Pegler's sixteenth, 1978, edition says curiously little about audit programmes, but gives full details of the working papers to be kept, distinguishing between the 'current audit file and the permanent audit file' a distinction which had been made, as noted above, in Dicksee's 1951 edition, and was also laid down in Cooper's *Manual of Auditing* in 1966 (Cooper 1966: 7; Waldron 1978: 60–2).

Audit manuals

The audit programme and working papers were methods of making the audit a more systematic procedure, and this was also true of the audit manual, or the set of instructions of a general nature usually kept in the firm's office which auditors could refer to and apply perhaps with modifications to all audits. The first edition of Dicksee's (1892: 2–4) textbook reproduced a list of 22 such instructions, which it was stated had been drawn up and followed in the office of the well-known accountant of the period, David Chadwick, 'many years ago', and which had been published in the *Accountant* (29 September 1883: 8–9). This list of instructions started, for example, with: '1. In commencing a new audit you should obtain a list of all the books kept and all the persons authorised to receive or pay money and order goods'. Dicksee explained the list as follows:

> In some offices it is customary to maintain as a kind of preface to all these stereotypical forms of audit note-book a set of general instructions common to all audits, presumably in order to remind all clerks of the general scope which it is expected their work will cover.
>
> (Magee 1951: 32)

These instructions were clearly an embryo audit manual, dating from perhaps the 1860s, and a number of firms had expanded on this format by the 1950s. At Thornton and Thornton in the fifties an accountant noted how the manual acted as a sort of corporate memory to avoid repeating mistakes:

> there was also some sort of office manual which I think was typed.... I can remember reading examples in it which showed why a piece of work got into the programme. It might be because somebody had been caught out in 1920 or 1932, and we weren't going to get caught again. So we were going to check the insurance cards and count the stubs or whatever.
>
> (Interview with Haddleton)

But none of these early manuals matched the innovation at Cooper Brothers after the Second World War. The Coopers' *Manual of Auditing* was apparently written by Henry Benson, who had recently become the leader of the firm with John Pears, and was first issued to staff in 1946 (Benson, 1989). According to one source the main motive behind writing the manual had been labour control:

> I remember talking to Henry Benson and their big worry was keeping control of the staff. There were huge numbers of people, they didn't know what they were getting up to; they were scared out of their wits and this was the origin of the audit manuals.
>
> (Interview with Goodwin)

The preface to the manual, however, states that it was found to be: '...of value to those returning from service in the forces and other spheres of war-time activity, as many of them were out of touch with current thinking in the profession' (Cooper 1966: vii).

Designed to grow with the firm, the Cooper's manual was held together with extendible brass screws so that sections could be added. The original accounting areas covered included: liquidations, investigations, taxation, company accounts, and executors and trustees, as well as auditing, but it was the latter aspect that was eventually published in 1966 as, it was said within the firm, Henry Benson's gift to accountancy (*C&L Journal* No. 31, June 1979: 15; Cooper 1966: vii). According to a senior Coopers man:

> It was published because Henry Benson felt that we should help the profession by showing what we'd done. We were in the vanguard of getting the Institute to produce technical [guidance] in the members' handbook. A large part of that was based on our work. They were taking parts of our manual and effectively putting them in to tell people how to audit the inventory or debtors or something of that kind.
>
> (Interview with Hobson)

The manual was published in the name of a partner, Vivian Cooper, as a way of attaching the firm's name to the publication without breaching the no advertising rule of the Institute (Interview with Middleton), and it was praised in the *Accountant* (9 July 1966) as follows: '...lucidity throughout is an outstanding characteristic of this sophisticated survey and its public appearance will be welcomed by those practitioners who are conscious that their own systems stand in need of a comprehensive reappraisal'.

The 620 page manual was based on a foundation of five audit procedures (Cooper 1966: vii): first, the classification of clients from A to E (and their treatment accordingly), where A was a large client with good internal controls and an internal audit and E was a small company with no internal controls and with the accounts in the hands of one person (ibid.: 26); second, the use of internal control questionnaires (an example of which took up 135 pages of the manual); third, detailed audit programmes (specimens of which took 99 pages); fourth, the writing of letters of weakness to clients; and finally, the use of a clearly defined system of working papers.

The Coopers manual was highly influential on auditing practice both before and after its publication, and a number of interviewees argued that on the basis of the manual Coopers were ahead of the other big firms in terms of audit practice and quality in the 1950s and 1960s. 'Cooper Brothers had been the byword for regimental audit efficiency...and led the way' said one interviewee (Interview with Hewitt). An accountant who eventually became the senior partner at Coopers in the 1970s remembers:

> We were working with a manual all my time as a partner from 1953. I can recall working on a prospectus in 1950 and we had a manual of what to do in that area at that time, which our joint auditors, Price Waterhouse, did not have. They had nothing. They just sent their people into bat without any instructions at all.
>
> (Interview with Hobson)

Coopers' influence spread through the profession prior to the manual's publication. One interviewee from Thornton and Thornton remembered working on the BMC, the motor company, audit in the 1960s where his firm were joint auditors with Coopers:

> we followed their audit manual and so they were very influential on my auditing. My father had been with Coopers for four or five years in the 1950s before he joined Thorntons, so he was well ahead of his time in the way auditing was done.
>
> (Interview with Atkins)

Firms that were taken over by Coopers were forced to adopt the manual, or experienced 'Cooperising' as one accountant involved put it (Interview with Middleton). When another's firm was taken over in 1967 he was impressed that: 'Coopers' audit systems...were and probably still are very advanced' (Interview with Livesey). But the process was not always viewed with favour. One interviewee reported that when his firm was taken over in 1965:

> The audit system changed completely as soon as we joined Coopers. Coopers brought in their own manual, which was quite different to the way we conducted an audit and we had to conform...and it wasn't nec- essarily what the client wanted. We'd begun to work out methods of sampling that were tailored to the individual client and we used to explain to the client why we were doing what we were doing. And then the Coopers manual came in and the old system went out of the window.
>
> (Interview with Palmer)

The Coopers' manual was, of course, probably even more influential after publication. Writing in 1970, Waldron stated that:

> There can now be no practising accountant who is unaware of the Coopers Manual and few who do not have copies in their offices for constant reference by themselves and their staff. It is not every office which can spare the time or effort to produce its own manual, yet every office needs a working reference book of this sort.
>
> (*Accountant* 19 February 1970)

Other firms felt obligated to follow Cooper's lead. A retired auditor recalled of his medium sized City firm:

> I can vividly remember when the first audit manual was written in the firm because I was involved in it. It coincided with, or it followed, the publication of Coopers *Manual of Auditing*, which was a great step forward in the profession, and almost drove every firm to either adopt the Coopers manual or to produce a manual which set out its firm's procedures, even if it just contained model audit programmes which you then took out and applied to the jobs.
>
> (Interview with Patient)

A former partner recalls that at Price Waterhouse:

> Our first audit manual was produced by Charles Bailey...while he was waiting to become a partner...That was in 1969 and that did get much more into talking about...testing controls. That was when we really started moving more towards trying to understand the systems of control.
>
> (Interview with Stacy)

By the 1980s every audit firm of any size had its own manual and some like Thornton Baker (1981) and Thomson McLintock (1983) published them (Turley and Cooper 1991: 7). Humphrey and Moizer (1990: 225) found from their interviews with 18 audit managers that the audit manual was still used for its original purpose of establishing control over the labour process or: 'to narrow differences in the approaches and judgements of audit teams within the firm'. They found that the manuals had a significant influence on the determination of levels of audit work carried out within firms. However, by some managers interviewed: 'the audit manual was consistently portrayed as merely establishing a loose framework in which expert audit judgement could be exercised' (ibid.: 225–6, 228).

Summary

The documentation involved in the early audits varied from firm to firm. Between 50–60 per cent of firms in the period down to the 1960s used audit programmes always or often, with the main factor determining use being the size of the audit clients since the main role of the programmes was labour control. The usual form of programme was the bound audit notebook, which recorded what was to be and what had been done in the audit, and who had performed the task. The notebook assigned to each audit would do service over many years. Many firms however followed no formal programmes apart from that carried in the head of the senior clerk. Other firms relied on the practice more common in America of carrying loose working papers from one year to the next. From the 1960s on, however, the use of audit programmes and working papers grew until, now much more standardised and formal, they became all but universal, except on the smallest audits. The use of audit manuals or more generalised audit instructions also date from the start of the professional audit, but the manual introduced in 1946 at Cooper Brothers represented a major advance and was influential on British audit practice before and after it was published in 1966. Subsequently all sizable firms had their own manuals the aim of which was again the control of audit labour.

4 Testing and sampling

Testing

Accounting historians have tended to underestimate the amount of testing in the early audits. Littleton (1981: 312), in his survey of lectures published in the *Accountant* in the 1880s, found that 'so little is said regarding the way to test-check that the conclusion is inescapable that very little of it was done'. Lee (1988: xviii) also concluded that there is 'little evidence of test checking prior to 1900'; while Brown (1968: 698) dated its implementation to the 1890s. Indeed, the first edition of Pixley's (1881: 164) textbook laid down: 'A thorough and efficient audit should embrace an examination of all the transactions of a Company', and the book still contained this wording in the tenth edition (Pixley 1910: 541). Victorian accountants like Quilter, as we noted above, would be reluctant (as with the fact that they were also doing their clients' accounting) to admit that they did not check everything since they were conscious of the criticism their work was receiving, in part as a result of the well publicised court cases involving audit failures in the 1880s and 1890s, such as those involving the Leeds Estate, Building and Investment company, the Liberator Permanent Benefit Building Society or the Millwall Dock company (*Accountant* 15 May 1909: 687–96). Indeed, in a legal judgement in 1885 it was declared to be the duty 'of an auditor to check and verify by vouchers or otherwise *every item* before he passed it' (quoted in Chandler 1997: 64, his italics).

Yet self-evidently an examination of all transactions for all clients was impossible from the very beginning of the professional audit. The railway companies, for example, were so large as soon as they were being formed from the 1820s on that for an auditor to vouch every transaction was already impractical and meant test checking was a feature of many professional audits from the start. Indeed, a number of speakers and lecturers in the 1880s did admit the fact. J. C. Bolton at an ICAEW meeting in 1888 stated:

> I cannot see in many businesses how it is possible for the whole of the work to be audited; when one bears in mind . . . a bank like Coutts' at the West end of London . . . How would it be possible for any of us, who

are fortunate as to be appointed auditors for such an institution, to audit every item? We must accept certain results, and only audit a part of the work.

(Quoted in Chandler and Edwards 1994: 85)

This stance was reiterated by a number of speakers. Monkhouse said: 'It is practically impossible to talk about carrying out the checking of details of large companies. The larger the company, the less proportionate work in detail the auditor does, or could possibly do' (ibid.: 87).

As we have already noted, in 1894 Carter attacked previous writers on auditing for inconsistency, and he also criticised them for maintaining the need to check everything whereas in practice this was clearly impossible. Carter admitted, though, that in his attack on 'the comparatively useless mechanical checking recommended by writers I have quoted...the grounds which justify an auditor in using tests instead of checking everything is a difficult one' (ibid.: 159). Indeed, even where, like Carter, auditors admitted in public to the practice of testing they were usually not specific about the methods used. However, in the ICAEW meeting in 1888 quoted earlier, Murray discussed testing different parts of a business each year, or what became known as rotational testing: 'we must not follow the same course on each occasion; but if desirable make a change so that we may in time, extend the audit to the whole work in connection with the Company' (ibid.: 87).

Gradually, testing was admitted to be a legitimate part of the audit. In the judgement in the London and General Bank case in 1895 there was evidence of the use of sampling by the auditor. The judge stated that 'in practice, I believe business men select a few cases haphazard, see that they are right and assume that others like them are correct' (Brown 1968: 698). And Dicksee (1892: 8–9) in his first edition stated: 'it cannot be denied that (except in concerns of comparative insignificance) a minute scrutiny of every item would be quite impossible to the Auditor'. He quoted Joseph Slocombe F.C.A.: 'There are some cases wherein an audit, to be efficient should comprehend an examination of every entry in the books; there are others – more numerous – wherein the accuracy of the accounts may be verified by tests which render the checking of every posting unnecessary' (ibid.: 9). The first edition of Spicer and Pegler in 1911 made the distinction between the 'complete' audit where everything was checked, and the 'partial' audit, necessitated because:

in most businesses of any size...the amount of detail is so voluminous, and the time involved in checking the whole of it would be so excessive, that reliance for the accuracy of the detail is, to a large extent, placed upon the system of Internal Check in operation in the office itself, and the Auditor, after making such tests of the detail work as commend themselves to his judgment, is then able to devote his attention to questions of principle.

(Spicer and Pegler 1911: 22)

They continued:

> if discrepancies are found he should carry his examination further. If, on the other hand, the transactions he has examined are in order, he is entitled to assume that the remainder can be safely passed...The vouchers should be tested exhaustively, either by taking a certain consecutive period, or by examining all vouchers over a certain amount

descriptions of what became known respectively as 'block' and 'stratified' testing (Spicer and Pegler 1914: 56, 72). Again:

> Where the Sales Ledgers are numerous, and there is a good system of Internal Check in operation, it will be sufficient for the Auditor to test the postings. This can be done either by taking an individual ledger and clearing that, or by taking individual accounts in different ledgers...Note should be taken of the ledgers selected for test, so that in the course of a period of years, the whole of the ledgers may come under notice in this manner.
>
> (1914: 99)

Remarkably, this procedure was still described almost word for word in the sixteenth edition of Spicer and Pegler in 1978 (Waldron 1978: 113).

Power (1993: 37–62) has argued that audit 'tests' should be distinguished from 'sampling' (a word first used in the 1933 edition of Dicksee) since the former did not incorporate the concept of 'representativeness', which had to await developments, unconnected with auditing, in the discipline of statistics in the 1920s. In practice, however, the distinction between testing and sampling is merely semantic since, as we noted above, although they did not explicitly use the terms the early professional auditors were undertaking random tests on the understanding that they were to be taken as representative of the whole. If mistakes were found during a block test of any one month, for example, then that was indicative of a general weakness and therefore necessitated further investigation. As an auditor who worked in the 1930s put it: 'We'd probably select a month or two, and having worked through, if too many difficulties, errors or weaknesses did not occur we would accept that evidence. On the contrary if the outcome was unsatisfactory, checking would then be extended' (Interview with Keel).

As is suggested by the unvarying treatment of the subject in successive editions of Spicer and Pegler, testing procedures probably changed little from the start of the professional audit down to the 1960s. Our oral and questionnaire evidence confirms the type of testing carried out in practice. In the postal questionnaire respondents were asked to write in the sampling techniques used when they were training. There was considerable variety but generally the methods seemed to boil down to: first, block testing based on time periods. Typical responses were: 'two months in 12 months'; '1 or 2 months' entries and the year-end month'; 'either a week or a month depending on number of transactions involved'; 'one week in every month, one day in every week'; 'full audit of selected periods'; '100 per cent audit of a short period'; 'alphabetical/specified periods throughout'. Block testing continued to be popular into the 1960s: 'We took a month and checked everything' was how one auditor of quoted companies put it (Interview with Spens). Certainly, selecting one month and a different month each year, duly noted in the audit programme, was still the rule at PW and Peats in the 1960s (Interviews with Stacy and Grenside).

A second type of testing that might be distinguished was a variety of block testing where, as a respondent to the postal questionnaire described: 'samples were chosen almost at random such as, for example, by taking every tenth item in selected blocks'. This was of course closely related to a third popular testing method – taking a certain proportion of records at random. Sometimes the selection of samples was haphazard with no particular rationale to it as in: 'every 10th document'; '1 in a 100, or 5 items per month' or 'Random numbers, typically a sample of say 132 out of a total of 10,000 transactions'. Respondents wrote of taking a 'random percentage of entries'; 'random numbers for 3–4 per cent of population'. Turquand, Youngs were using 'rudimentary percentages' in the 1950s. Sometimes there was a logic to the choice of percentage as in: 'Random selection expressed as percentage. Percentage dependent upon standard of records/management'. At Peats in the 1950s the auditors, as well as block testing, would also sometimes take 'for example, 20 per cent of purchase invoices, 10 per cent of sales invoices, etc.' (Interview with Evans).

Fourth, there was from the beginning of the professional audit an element of stratified sampling, or applying a different procedure depending on the size of the transaction. In the 1930s this could involve: 'Every tenth small account (every large account) plus two large and one small entry at random on every page of prime entry.' Or samples were taken: 'Generally at random at discretion of audit manager and targeted large items', or 'the largest, plus as random as possible'. Fifth, there was early evidence of testing what were perceived as the weakest elements in the accounts, as in this response from an accountant qualifying in the 1940s: 'random testing with special emphasis on vulnerable aspects'. Finally, testing was often tailored according to the client, which could lead to one-off and often complicated arrangements. One respondent remembered that in the 1960s: 'in one large quoted company, we had a procedure for "proving" the financial figures by a fairly complex system of reconciling them with statistics taken from the production records'.

A major characteristic of testing in the bookkeeping audit was the diversity of practice, even within the same firm and sometimes on the same job. One respondent who trained in the 1930s wrote in the questionnaire: 'sampling varied from visit to visit and depended on the size of company and other factors'. Another put it as: 'Sometimes on a time basis, sometimes on percentage, sometimes haphazard according to assessment by the partner or senior, and completely unscientific.' At Peats in the late 1950s testing included: 'a) detailed vouching and postings checks – 2 or 3 months of the year, b) review of remaining months for large or exceptional/unusual items c) proof of various ledgers etc. and control accounts'.

This diversity of practice was further increased by the innovation of what became known as 'testing in depth', 'depth testing', 'walk-through testing' or 'cradle to the grave' testing. This involved taking a relatively small number of individual transactions and verifying them through all their bookkeeping stages. For example, one item would be traced from the raising of the original order, receipt of invoice, entry in a journal, posting to purchase ledger, and entry in the cash book. It is not clear where or when this technique was first introduced but it was used almost exclusively in testing a client's system of controls and therefore grew in popularity with the systems approach (discussed below) in the 1960s. The technique was, however, known and perhaps used long before then. As quoted above, the first edition of Spicer and Pegler (1914: 99) which described 'taking individual accounts in different ledgers' seems to indicate early testing in depth. Then in 1951, William Lawson, a partner in the accountancy firm, Binder Hamlyn, and President of the ICAEW in 1957–8, set out in a paper to the Oxford summer school the elements of a 'state of the art' audit. He described (without using the phrase) the practice of depth testing used by the auditor to 'satisfy himself that the [client's] system is operating effectively' (*Accountant* 6 October 1951: 306–7). Rather than testing 5 per cent or 2.5 per cent of entries, an alternative approach, he stated, 'is to select a certain number of accounts for complete checking through all stages of the accounts'. The ICAEW's, 1961, statement on the general principles of auditing – U1 – stressed the need for an assessment of the client's system of internal control where: 'It is important to include examinations "in depth"...tracing a transaction through its various stages from origin to conclusion' (*Accountant* 18 May 1963: 645). It recommended

> auditors to select one hundred payments to creditors for goods supplied and verify them by examination of the paid cheques...only a proportion...would also be verified with the suppliers' invoices and statements; a still smaller proportion would be verified in addition by evidence that goods had been recorded in the stock records; and so on until a comparatively small proportion had been verified completely in depth.
>
> (Waldron 1969: 356)

However articles published in the early 1960s advocating depth testing indicated that the practice was still not that well known at that time (*Accountant* 2 December 1961: 718–19; 2 November 1963: 573).

Depth testing then was closely linked to the growth of so-called 'compliance' testing of the client's systems in contrast to the 'substantive' testing of actual transactions. A point needs to be made here, however, that in practice the distinction between the substantive testing of transactions and the compliance testing of systems was often blurred since of course to test a system usually required testing a transaction through the system, so in many firms both tests were being carried out at the same time. Indeed, when the terms compliance and substantive tests were first used in an Auditing Standards discussion draft in 1978 many in the British profession had not come across the American terms before and clearly did not make the distinction in practice (Hatherly 1978: 378–80). And although Higson (1987: 242) found that most firms by the 1980s maintained a conceptual distinction between the two tests at least one major firm did not bother.

Finally, mention should be made of a form of testing which seems to have been introduced in recent decades with the aim of cutting audit costs known as directional tests (Higson 1987: 244–5). This is based on the principle that, if in the double entry system the books balance, checking for an overstatement in assets and expenses and understatements in income and liabilities should show up all errors with effectively half the amount of testing. However, there is no evidence as to how common this practice was or is.

Statistical sampling

The difference between testing/sampling and so-called statistical sampling is only one of technical sophistication, which indeed should not necessarily imply a superior audit. Statistical sampling is testing by taking strictly random samples and applying the laws of probability to the number of errors found in order to extrapolate to the level of error in the whole population. Without going into detail the most common techniques borrowed from the world of statistics were: 'estimation sampling', the estimation of the total population from a sample, for example of total sales or debts, and then accepting or rejecting the client's stated figures on the basis of the estimates; this could be used for substantive or compliance testing (Sherer and Kent 1983: 64–9). Alternatively, 'acceptance sampling' was a plan for compliance testing where the auditor would set predetermined rates of unacceptable error and accept or reject the client's procedures on this basis. 'Discovery sampling' took smaller sample sizes but accepted no errors and was most suitable in testing for fraud (Gray and Manson 1989: 174). 'Monetary unit sampling', or MUS, suitable for substantive testing, sampled, for example individual $s or £s, as opposed to discrete transactions or physical units as in the previous systems. It was an attempt to overcome the problem of the heterogeneity of accounting items in that larger more significant transactions stood a proportionately greater chance of being caught by MUS. Finally, 'Bayesian sampling' allowed a combination of judgemental (or utilising the auditor's experience or 'feel' in any given situation) and statistical sampling for compliance testing.

Statistical sampling was apparently an American innovation (the use of the word 'sampling' in the audit context was also of US origin). Although Montgomery (1934: 36) in his early editions noted that 'the use of tests is a part of the normal procedure in nearly all audits' for some reason he chose not to be specific as to how the tests were to be carried out. However, by the 1940s Montgomery *et al.* (1949: 46) were arguing that:

> The auditing technique known as test-checking is based on the mathematically founded assumption that an analysis of representative samples of a group of items indicates the quality of the whole ... By thoroughly checking all the items in a representative sample, the auditor may assume under the mathematical laws of probability, that the number of errors found in the sample appears in the group as a whole in about the same proportion as in the sample. The auditor, therefore has justifiably reduced the extent of his detail examination by the use of the test check or sampling method.

Yet in practice sampling in America still used the same tried and trusted methods as carried out in Britain and detailed earlier.

> The auditor may check all items included in a specific period; he may check all the items over a certain minimum amount for the entire period; he may select a percentage of larger items and another percentage of smaller items; he may check a percentage of a total, either in dollars or number of items; or, in examining accounts filed alphabetically, he may select those under certain letters.
>
> (Montgomery *et al.* 1949: 46)

In theory at least statistical sampling had been well understood from an early date. A letter in the *Accountant* (15 November 1958: 605) claimed that the first suggestion of a statistical approach was an article in the *American Accountant* in 1933 by Lewis Carman. The leading early populariser, however, was an academic, L. L. Vance, who published an influential paper on statistical sampling in 1947 advocating the use of acceptance sampling. A sympathetic review of Vance's key textbook, *Scientific Method for Auditing*, appeared in the *Accountant* (31 March 1951: 316); and McRae (1982: 143), a Scotch accountant turned academic, in his book advocating the technique thought Vance's paper could be regarded as 'the birth of statistical auditing'. McRae (ibid.: 139) claimed, not that convincingly, that there were four waves of development in statistical sampling between 1948 and 1980, each initiated by co-operation between academic statisticians and practising accountants. Certainly there was fertile collaboration between theoreticians and practitioners; for example PW in America collaborated with Professor Herbert Arkin to work out practical methods of statistical sampling in the 1950s (ibid.: 147). In 1963, Arkin, whom Sherer and Kent (1983: 66) deemed almost entirely responsible for the development of acceptance and discovery sampling in auditing, published a *Handbook on Sampling for Auditors and Accountants*, which contained sets of sampling tables for use by auditors (*Accountant* 2 May 1964: 554).

The American accounting firm of Haskins & Sells seem to have taken the lead in working out practical applications of statistical sampling, and in the early 1960s one of their partners together with a professor of statistics at

Princeton University developed a precursor to MUS known as 'cumulative monetary amount' sampling, or CMA, which was said to be in 'widespread use in the firm by 1966' (McRae 1982: 152). A little later the same firm was involved in developing the MUS system, and the first public presentation of MUS was made by Meikle in 1972 (ibid.: 54).

The precocity in the practical application of statistics by American auditors must, however, not be exaggerated. Of the Securities and Exchange Commission registered auditors surveyed in 1979, 45 per cent said they used statistical sampling, but only 13 per cent stated they had started doing so before 1970 (ibid.: 181). Even in 1979 only 20 per cent of the American audit firms sampled said they often used the technique, while of course there were 55 per cent who said they never used it.

The British were not apparently behind in the early theory of sampling. That the laws of probability could be applied to audit testing was first explored in a brief article, which acknowledged no American influence, in the *Accountant* (8 October 1932: 444) in 1932, and a more lengthy exposition appeared in 1935 (ibid. 16 November 1935: 679). Rowlands' 1933 rewriting of Dicksee's textbook had argued that: 'The "test" ought to be more scientific', and the auditor should take, 'in the statistical sense, fair samples' (Power 1993: 51). Yet the three standard British auditing textbooks in their post-Second World War editions: de Paula (1948), Spicer and Pegler (Bigg, 1951) and Dicksee (Magee, 1951), still made no mention of statistical sampling as such. Dicksee's 1951 edition continued to talk of the need for tests to be more 'scientific', and the taking of 'fair samples' but still gave no detail as to how to carry out procedures to bring this about (Magee 1951: 38–9).

By the early 1950s, however, the use of statistical sampling techniques was being frequently discussed in accounting circles in Britain. The first article in the *Accountant* (22 August 1953: 218–21) to analyse in detail the mathematics required for statistical sampling, and acknowledging American leadership in the techniques, appeared in 1953. Interestingly, in view of the venerable nature of the procedure, the author referred to test checking 'as the modern technique in auditing the accounts of large businesses today' (ibid.: 218). Academic-led seminars on the mathematics of statistical audit sampling were first organised in this country by the Society of Incorporated Accountants and Auditors in 1954 (*Accountant* 6 February 1954: 158–9). A series of two articles in the *Accountant* (25 October 1958: 491; 1 November 1958: 527) by H. C. Mackenzie, a non-accountant lecturer in Economic Statistics at Bristol University, discussed the issue on the grounds 'that at present accountants do not have any generally accepted and soundly based procedures for determining the amount of inspection to undertake'. There were many articles in the *Accountant* in the 1960s (see 15 April 1961: 430–4; 2 December 1961: 718–19; 20 October 1962: 492–5; 22 June 1963: 805–9; 2 May 1964: 554–8; 28 November 1964: 665–7; 7 September 1968: 312–17) advocating statistical methods but their practical use was slow in arriving.

The first mention of statistical sampling in a British textbook came in the thirteenth edition of de Paula (1966: 26–7), but it did not give the technique a ringing endorsement:

> Considerable attention has been directed to the use of statistical sampling techniques to determine the extent of test checks. However, they have not been adopted to any great extent either here or in America, and in the writer's view it would be in most cases either unwise or unnecessary to do so... because statistical sampling is unsatisfactory in determining the quality of errors, he [the auditor] must rely on his own judgement... Statistical sampling may be useful in certain limited applications, such as when selecting debtor accounts for direct verification with the debtor; but... It is not a substitute for sound judgement.

The 1970 edition of de Paula (1968: 32) continued merely to note that statistical sampling is 'still only used by the larger firms' but 'seems to be spreading'. Other textbooks gave more credence to the technique and if anything were a little ahead of its application in practice. Considerable detail was given in the 1969 edition of Dicksee's *Auditing*, which stated that statistical sampling came from America, and referred the reader to Arkin's handbook (Waldron 1969: 357–8). Spicer and Pegler also had a significant section on the issue by its 1969 edition (Bigg 1969: 63–71).

Yet despite being well publicised since the early 1950s, statistical sampling made little headway as a practical audit technique in Britain, as in America, until the 1970s. Power (1992: 58) has argued that when statistical sampling was adopted it was as: 'less an explicit technology and more as playing a role for members of the profession by positioning them as credible monitoring agents on behalf of capital'. Again Power's view cannot be accepted. The audit is a private affair and firms that adopted statistical sampling made no particular attempt to broadcast the fact. Indeed, it is clear that those firms that did adopt statistical sampling did so because they believed it improved their work, or at least cut down the work they had to do. But most damning for Power's thesis is that if statistical sampling was merely a public relations exercise it would be difficult to explain why so many in the audit profession were resistant to its introduction on the stated grounds that it was a flawed technology.

This practitioner resistance, which has continued to some extent down to the present time, was based on a number of considerations. Perhaps the most fundamental of these is that the science appeared to detract from the application of the auditor's cherished tool – judgement. An accountant who was at Price Waterhouse in the late 1960s articulated this as follows:

> There wasn't a great deal of it [statistical sampling]. Mathematical approaches to selection weren't really worthwhile and I don't think they are today really. Samples were usually selected by judgement... and even as an articled clerk you would select them yourself.

(Interview with Carty)

A major firm told Higson (1987: 313) in the mid-1980s that even with statistical sampling a 'vast amount of judgement' was still required (on materiality, confidence levels etc.), and that 'auditors were attempting to put precision on things that are not precise'. Based on his interviews with auditors in the early 1980s McRae (1982: 297) also noted that: 'Traditional audit procedures are highly subjective and intuitive... [and] there is little sympathy for a more scientific approach to auditing among many accounting firms.' These firms might have included Arthur Andersen. Surprisingly, given the fact that in America they apparently pioneered MUS in the 1980s (Higson 1997: 200), a former senior partner of the British branch of the firm noted:

> Arthur Andersen never went in for statistical sampling to any extent, largely on the basis that we are not trying to come up with a statistically valid conclusion. The end result of an audit is a judgement on the view given by the financial statements. That's the key thing rather than going through a mechanical process, which some of the other firms have gone through but have tended to abandon since.
>
> (Interview with Plaistowe)

Another sceptical firm, at least in the earlier years, was Cooper Brothers. Despite their reputation as a progressive firm they were also not convinced by the technique. The Coopers manual of 1966 discussed sampling methods but no reference was made to statistical sampling (Cooper 1966: 297–300). The 1981 edition declared:

> Whilst the possibility of using statistical sampling techniques should always be borne in mind, the authors consider that generally it is preferable to determine initially whether judgmental sampling will provide the auditor with the assurance that he is seeking. They recognise that some auditors and many statisticians would not agree with this view, but draw attention to the consideration that in their view, auditing is fundamentally a judgmental process.
>
> (Coopers & Lybrand 1981: 96)

A Coopers partner who retired in 1982 stated:

> Coopers didn't ever like statistical sampling. When I was there we never used it. We went for the internal control... rather than just shooting in the dark as we used to say. You know where the problems lie and you concentrate on the bits where the monetary affect of the problem would affect the balance sheet.
>
> (Interview with Middleton)

Another Coopers man, who qualified in 1989, when asked in the postal questionnaire what statistical techniques they used, stated that they were: 'invalid justifications for sample sizes. Hence none'.

A further objection to statistical sampling by practitioners was that accepting a margin of error was part of the process. Amusingly, one respondent related how as a young enthusiast he met a frosty response when he brought the good news back to Mellors, Basden & Mellors in the early 1950s:

I went to an Institute summer school in 1952 and met a member of the Whinney family. He'd heard of sampling and lent me a book, and I came back to Nottingham and presented to the partners some ideas on sampling, and it was quite an occasion. But I made the mistake of starting off by saying: 'The first thing you have to do is to decide what margin of error you will allow'. And that was fatal because the senior partner immediately said, 'I allow no errors'. So we didn't do any statistical sampling for very many years, and I think that even 20 years on in Price Waterhouse in the seventies it was still more talked about than acted upon.

(Interview with Hewitt)

Another interviewee remembers:

as a manager [with Price Waterhouse] in 1960, I was sent to the USA, and one of the tasks I was given was to study the American techniques and come back and write a paper on statistical sampling. But we never really used them to any great extent for a long time, the firm was not convinced of their validity. We were somewhat discouraged by the probability that things could go wrong.

(Interview with Ainger)

A further problem was a perceived need for large sample sizes and therefore an increase in costs (Sherer and Kent 1983: 68). Another Arthur Andersen man remarked:

my observation quite early on was that if you were going to apply statistical sampling to audit work, your samples had to be so big to attain the sort of probability and error margin that you needed that it was going to be uneconomic. By and large, it seemed much better and much more likely to be practicable to assess and attack risk. Subsequently, the business was all about risk assessment.

(Interview with Currie)

Although McRae (1982: 297) did not think the criticism was justified, his interviewees in the early 1980s also said they did not use statistics because they thought it would need an increase in sample size. He found, particularly where the audit fee was under pressure, that the 'auditor may plead that he cannot afford to draw audit samples large enough to satisfy proper statistical evaluation procedures'. Clearly this was particularly a problem in firms who relied on internal control evaluation, and where: 'Substantive testing may either be zero, or very small "walk through" samples'.

But at the heart of the problem with the use of statistics in auditing was the undeniable fact that the laws of probability rested on items in a population being identical, whereas financial transactions came in all shapes and sizes with a distinctly unequal possibility that the accounting of them could be wrong. A letter in *Accountancy* (June 1977: 121) in the late 1970s argued that statistical sampling fell down because 'so much of what is being audited is not homogeneous', therefore the technique 'must occupy a subsidiary position to the auditor's judgement'. McRae (1982: 297) also put the lack of enthusiasm in Britain for statistics as down to the fact that the skewed nature of accounting populations could make statistical methods inaccurate. Finally, McRae found that British auditors were also impressed by the fact that statistical sampling carried no greater weight than traditional methods in a court of law (ibid.: 28–9).

The practitioners were therefore well capable of arguing their corner that statistical sampling was technically flawed in the practical audit context, and opposition was often on the grounds that it was being foisted on the profession by academics. A letter to the *Accountant* in 1964 (16 May 1964: 631–2) pointed out that the serious practitioners (such as the unnamed international firm cited) were dismissive of the academic origins of statistical sampling, and that, moreover, the academics themselves admitted that: 'the correct method of applying statistical sampling to auditing had not yet been discovered'. On its own 'audit in depth', the writer argued, was as capable of replacing mass vouching as statistical sampling.

All this professional criticism of statistics received support from a new audit textbook written by Woolf (1978b: 152–3) in the late 1970s:

> the experience of most firms which have at one time or another sought to use such techniques is that their usefulness has turned out to be more limited than was at first anticipated. Many firms have indeed come full circle, and now require their audit technicians to obtain the prior sanction of a manager or partner before spending time on statistical sampling....

And the same wording remained in the 1997 edition (Woolf 1997: 149). In their interviews among the leading practitioners, Turley and Cooper (1991: 112) still found in the 1990s: 'a notable reluctance to make full use of statistical sampling' due to 'a lack of understanding, and more basic doubts about the applicability of statistical methods to audit problems'.

Yet despite this scepticism in the profession, statistical sampling undoubtedly gained in usage in the 1970s. Here, however, it is clear that the figures in Table 4.1, reporting the questionnaire results on the use of statistical sampling, must be treated with caution since there is a problem of definition in the use of the term 'statistical sampling' used in the question.

The intention was to identify the use of techniques such as CMA and MUS, where the laws of probability are used to precisely estimate errors in the whole population of data from a small sample. However, since our narrative makes clear that these techniques were not being employed at all in the 1920s and 1930s, the third of our respondents who stated that they used statistical sampling at least sometimes in the interwar period obviously had something else in mind. This is confirmed by the fact that as respondents were also asked to give the techniques used, they often described, for example, block sampling. Nonetheless, despite the ambiguity in the replies for earlier decades, Table 4.1 does show a clear upward trend in the use of statistical sampling from the 1960s to the 1970s. Whereas only about 15 per cent of respondents who trained in the 1960s said they used statistical sampling techniques always or often, by the 1970s this had doubled to about a third of trainees.

Moreover, corroborative evidence for the timing of this upswing in the use of statistics in auditing comes from a number of directions. The first respondent to our postal questionnaire who reported a premeditated system of sampling qualified in 1966, and wrote that at the time his firm used: 'Random sampling by pre-arranged numbers.' And a 1968 qualifier wrote

Table 4.1 While I was undertaking my articles/training, as the auditors we used statistical sampling techniques...

	Always (%)	*Often (%)*	*Sometimes (%)*	*Never (%)*	*Total respondents*	
					(%)	*N*
Decade qualified						
1920s/1930s	2.5	8.6	21.0	67.9	100	71
1940s	3.1	7.1	19.7	70.1	100	127
1950s	0.6	4.4	15.2	79.7	100	154
1960s	4.1	10.3	22.6	63.0	100	146
1970s	13.1	18.5	29.2	39.2	100	130
1980s	25.2	35.3	26.9	12.6	100	119
1990s	29.0	37.0	21.7	12.3	100	138
Respondent audited mainly...						
Quoted companies	24.7	26.1	12.9	36.3	100	163
SMEs	9.3	15.8	26.4	48.6	100	601
Sole traders and partnerships	2.2	8.6	17.2	72.0	100	95
Size of firm with which respondent qualified						
Top 20	18.7	26.1	21.1	34.1	100	299
Medium	6.7	12.7	21.1	59.4	100	279
Small	7.5	13.1	23.7	55.7	100	305

Source: Postal questionnaire, see Appendix.

that at his small firm during his training there was the use of 'random statistical tables'. The firm of Longcrofts were, around 1970, using 'Random number tables and confidence levels'; while another respondent, who qualified in the early 1970s, described the sampling techniques used in his firm then as: 'Law of null hypothesis – acceptable percentage error.'

The first question on statistical sampling in an ICAEW examination paper appeared in the Final Audit paper of 1971 (November, Question 1); and from the 1970s on all the established textbooks devoted chapters or significant sections to statistical sampling. In 1972, for example, Lee, in the first edition of his popular book on company auditing, argued that:

> The quantity and quality of the tests [on a vertical 'checking in depth' basis] should be statistically determined from the initial review of the system in order that the auditor can take the results of the sample and draw reasoned conclusions about the total statistical population... the choice of the individual sample items should be carried out on a random sampling basis, using tables of random numbers.

Lee asserted, however, that the sample size would still be based on the auditor's judgement as to how much trust he puts in the client's system (Lee 1972: 47, 169, 170–71). In their 1978 edition, Spicer and Pegler supported the technique because: '...as the size of audits increases... the use of statistical sampling will act as a positive influence, enabling auditors to prove mathematically, and hence objectively, the definable degree of accuracy afforded by the tests they have executed' (Waldron 1978: 404).

The upward trend in the use of statistics in auditing in the 1970s is also reflected by our interviews. A former Deloittes partner remembers that: 'in about 1971/72 we all got into this statistical sampling and random checking, rather than checking everything. The testing became much more sophisticated. So that one could concentrate on what might be material' (Interview with Colvin). A Harmood Banner partner in the 1970s explained that:

> It is difficult to say back in those days why you tested 10 out of 100 items or 20 out of 20,000. It was just a gut feeling. You couldn't do the whole lot. ...But it would be very difficult to justify scientifically why you did those few and how you selected the sample. It wasn't until after the merger with Deloittes [1974] that some science was introduced into it and that came from the American end.
>
> (Interview with Patient)

Deloittes were probably the pioneers and most enthusiastic users of the technique in Britain, perhaps because of their American links with Haskins & Sells. McRae (1982: 171) identified this transatlantic influence on the matter generally, and found:

> In seven of the ten cases studied the pressure to use statistical sampling came from the United States branch of the firm. In another case the pressure came from Canada. In only two cases was the move towards adopting statistical sampling initiated by a British accountant.

Indeed, the usage of statistical sampling by members of the American Institute of Certified Public Accountants McRae (ibid.: 13) estimated to be about double that in the UK.

There is also a strong suggestion that the introduction of statistical techniques on any scale in Britain went along with, and was dependent upon, the introduction of computers in the 1970s. In the written descriptions of the sampling procedures used by respondents to our postal questionnaire the first mention of a 'computer based' technique was by a Price Waterhouse trainee who qualified in 1974. Indeed, this preceded the first note in a questionnaire response of the use of a fully fledged statistical sampling technique, CMA, by a Deloittes accountant and MUS by a Robson Rhodes accountant, who both qualified in 1975. This chronology, therefore, suggests strongly that statistical sampling and computers were being introduced in tandem in the early 1970s.

Yet the use of statistical techniques was still a minority activity in the early 1980s. Our 1970s figures in Table 4.1 are in rough agreement with McRae (1982: 13) who, based on interviews undertaken in the early 1980s, estimated that: 'approximately one third of large accounting firms made extensive use of statistical sampling, one third used the method on suitable audits and one third made little or no use of statistical sampling in auditing'. McRae concluded: 'Statistical sampling is not yet generally accepted as the standard method of audit sampling in the accounting profession' and 'much of the current usage is still experimental' (ibid.: 14, 179). Smith (1982: 141) of Arthur Young McClelland Moores discussed his firm's problems in implementing MUS, and noted that in the profession generally there had been 'not very much progress in terms of professional pronouncement, educational effort, or indeed general acceptance'. Writing in support of the technique, Sherer and Kent (1983: 69) noted:

> it is only recently that auditors have appreciated the value of statistical sampling methods for their work. Traditionally auditors have used *judgemental* sampling in their compliance and substantive tests and even today the use of statistical sampling is mainly to be found in the larger international firms.

As Table 4.1 shows, however, there was another doubling in the use of statistics in audits from the 1970s to the 1980s. While 32 per cent of our sample of trainees stated they used the technique always or often in the

1970s, over 60 per cent said they were doing so in the 1980s. Even more dramatic was the drop in those who stated they never used statistics: from about 40 per cent in the 1970s to 12 per cent in the 1980s. Again, as expected, Table 4.1 also shows that the use of the technique depended more on the size of the client than of the audit firm. Only 36 per cent of the total responses who mainly audited quoted companies said they sometimes or never used statistical sampling, whereas three-quarters of those who mainly audited small or medium sized companies gave this response.

The upward trend in statistical sampling in the 1980s was given a further boost by the accelerating use of computers, particularly personal computers (Interviews with Niddrie and Milne). McRae (1982: 14) predicted in the early 1980s that:

> The increased use of the digital computer for storing and processing accounting information is likely to have a major impact on the use of statistical sampling in auditing. This trend is already evident in California. The computer can perform statistical sampling and evaluation at an economic cost. Several statistical sampling software packages are currently available.

The accuracy of this forecast was confirmed by a senior partner at PW:

> Proper scientific sampling with random selection really started to be used in the beginning of the 1980s. Before then you had very clumsy access to random numbers and it was very hard work to do and therefore by definition wasn't done very much... Stats only really started to take off properly when you had the PCs and people had them on site to run their own programmes.
>
> (Interview with Brindle)

One practitioner told Higson (1987: 314) in the mid-1980s that: 'Without a computer to select the sample, manual selection could take an individual days to perform'. Manson (1997: 241) also concluded that 'statistical sampling is more likely to be feasible when the records are computerised'. And the fact that the use of statistical sampling was heavily dependent on computers was re-enforced by the written replies to our postal question-naire. Asked what methods of sampling were used, the frequent reply was that they were built into the '(PCAS) Personal Computer Audit Software audit programmes', and that the 'recommended formulas' in these packages were often used. Barras and Swann (1984: 39–40) found from their survey in the mid-1980s that:

> productivity gains are being realised as a direct result of the accoun-tants' own use of sophisticated audit software. Thus one firm claimed that the sample techniques used by their audit program allowed almost

ten times fewer transactions to be tested than previously. The example was also quoted of a large car firm audit, which, with the use of the latest statistical techniques, was cut down from three weeks to two days. However, in some practices, there is a sign of a return to more comprehensive checking methods in the audit; this has become feasible again because of the speed and capacity of the newer generation of computers, whose capacity is often under-utilised.

With regard to what statistical sampling techniques were used, Gwilliam (1987: 245) found that MUS

> is clearly the form of sampling which has gained the most significant acceptance among the major accounting firms for the purpose of regular audit use. Variants of MUS are currently being employed by Deloitte, Haskins & Sells, Arthur Young, Peat Marwick Mitchell and Touche Ross, among others.

A Deloittes partner stated in interview that by the 1980s they had put their faith in MUS:

> The sampling systems when they first came in were rather involved, but nevertheless they reduced the amount of work which one needed to do. And the final sampling system I worked on was one where having determined what the business did and where the risk areas were, you were able to do it on an actuarial sampling basis, so if you were looking at a profit and loss account, for example, where the totality was let's say £20 million you determine that everything over £2,000 would be looked at and with everything below that every pound had an equal chance of being picked up.
>
> (Interview with Milne)

Turley and Cooper (1991: 111) reported that 'while the need for individual judgement is recognised, and both statistical and judgmental methods are regarded as acceptable, the main emphasis is on promoting each firm's own methods'. This was confirmed by the written replies to the postal questionnaire. The large firms that did use statistics extensively tended to use their own in-house systems, which most commonly were varieties of MUS, although apparently CMA was still used at Touche Ross in the late nineties.

Finally, while our questionnaire and other evidence shows that by the 1980s a majority of auditors used statistical sampling always or often, it is worth attempting to determine what this meant in practice. The full statistical sampling methodology included not only the selection of samples but perhaps more importantly the interpretation of the results (Gwilliam 1987: 241). Yet even McRae (1977: 116, his italics), a strong advocate of the use of computers and statistical sampling in the audit, made the point in the late 1970s that: 'It is particularly important to grasp the fact that we are only using the computer... to *select* the sample. The actual auditing of the sample will be carried out in the normal way.' And Gwilliam (1987: 241) in his survey of research on auditing in the mid-1980s, concluded that: 'The use of statistical sampling techniques (as opposed to purely judgmental sampling, or the use of random number-based but unevaluated sampling) is still to be found on only a minority of audits in the UK.' In their review of the manuals of a sample of 21 audit firms in 1987, Turley and Cooper also reported that: 'Many of these methods are 'quasi-statistical... The firms' guidance, however, is often weak on the evaluation of sample test results' (Turley and Cooper 1991: 111). The leading auditors of the day interviewed by Higson (1987: 314–15) also admitted that interpreting any errors found was a problem. Rather bizarrely one partner felt that the 'statistical sampling process fell down when errors were discovered'. The written replies to our postal questionnaire also give the impression that the statistics were used more for the selection of samples than for the analysis of the results, and this was also the conclusion of Higson (1997: 211) and Humphrey and Moizer (1990: 227–8), who were told by one audit manager that: 'the way we do it tends to make it difficult to statistically extrapolate our results so we tend to have to use judgement always'.

The cynical replies of audit managers to Humphrey and Moizer's questions in the late 1980s indicate a lack of understanding of the techniques, which might in part explain why they were not more fully used. They concluded that: 'The audit planning activities of the managers were less scientific and rationalistic than the views commonly expressed in traditional auditing texts [and] audit manuals...' (Humphrey and Moizer 1990: 225). Managers were asked to explain the relationship between their sampling and the overall level of confidence to which they worked when arriving at their audit opinion. To most respondents this was not apparently so much a calculation as an act of faith. They expressed this in a variety of ways, including: 'We work to 95 per cent confidence. We are given figures (from sampling tables) that are supposedly statistically correct but to be honest I have not got a clue whether they are or not' (ibid.: 226). 'Sample sizes are set using a pre-set standard. If you are testing a key control, the sample is 72 invoices or documents. Why it is 72, I don't know – it is a statistical programme that we use.'

Perhaps because of these staffing problems, together with the practitioners' doubts concerning the use of statistics listed above, particularly the need for large samples in an increasingly cost conscious era, the 1980s saw a distinct cooling off in enthusiasm for statistical sampling. Maysmor-Gee *et al.* noticed a trend away from the use of statistical sampling between their surveys in 1976 and 1984 (reported in Higson 1987: 118). Indeed, based on a number of interviews with senior audit practitioners Higson (1997: 211) took an extreme view, concluding that, although:

> The 1970s saw the growth of statistical sampling and statistical approaches to auditing – recent developments mean that these have now almost been eliminated. Even with the reductions in sample sizes which occurred in the 1980s, firms would claim that there was an underlying statistical basis for their work. Now with most firms there is little pretence at a statistical approach to auditing.

Higson (ibid.) argued that in the early 1980s there was a swing away from reliance on internal controls towards analytical review and substantive testing of transactions, but:

> The rise of analytical auditing procedures during the 1980s also resulted in a justification for reductions in detailed substantive testing. The implementation of risk-analysis approaches continued to reduce the volume of testing' to the extent that, where 'a company had good internal controls and there was a good analytical review, then the auditor "may not do any tests of detail in many cases" ... increasingly "sampling is a test of last resort" '.

Manson (1997: 251) also, following the work of Loebbecke, accepted that although the use of sampling still remained important it 'in practice appears to have greatly diminished'.

This apparent retreat from statistics in auditing does not, however, accord with our questionnaire evidence. There was some evidence of a change of tack in some firms, since one respondent to the postal questionnaire noted: 'sampling was used in my first year (1991–2) at KPMG but was then superseded by analytical methods and selection'; and another respondent who qualified with a medium sized firm in 1996 had also recently gone over to 'analytical review techniques'. Indeed, Table 4.1 does show that the diffusion of statistical sampling slowed up in the 1990s, but there is no evidence of a decline in its use. About 60 per cent of the 1980s trainees said they used statistical sampling, always or often, but the technique continued to gain marginally in popularity, with 66 per cent giving that response in the 1990s.

Summary

Although a feature of the early bookkeeping audit was the attempt to check everything, clearly from the beginning this was impossible with larger clients like the railways and banks. Consequently from the first forms of sampling were used, the most popular of which were the block testing of all records in a period of time such as a month, stratified testing, related to the importance of the item; or a variety of other forms of random selection. These tests were conducted on the understanding that if mistakes were found this indicated a need for more intensive audit investigation. Although not unknown in the early years, testing in depth (following one transaction through all its accounting stages) became popular with the growth of the systems approach and the need for compliance testing in the 1960s. Although the theory was well understood in the interwar period the use of statistical sampling methods based on the laws of probability was not widely adopted until the introduction of computers in the 1970s. Never accepted by some major firms, two-thirds of audit firms used statistical sampling always or often in the 1990s, although it was far more used to determine the size of the samples than to interpret the results.

5 Internal control systems

Internal check

Like many (perhaps most) aspects of the process of auditing, the systems approach, despite its image of modernity, can in essence trace its origins back to the earliest professional audits; although again this fact has tended to be overlooked by historians. Lee (1972: 150), for example, stated: 'Auditing by means of an initial review of the company's internal control was first generally recognised as a feasible approach to the function in the 1920s and 1930s.' Yet British auditors were clearly putting some reliance on the client's internal systems long before then.

Some Victorian companies put in place a so-called 'internal check', which was a system of bookkeeping designed largely to prevent fraud. Commonly, responsibilities were divided among different individuals or departments so that they acted as checks on one another, making fraud difficult without collusion. Quilter's Parliamentary evidence in 1849 made clear that even at that stage railway companies 'ought' to have an internal check put in place by the chief accountant or chief cashier (Kitchen 1988: 27).

Early auditors made use of these systems in their work. The first edition of Dicksee (1892: 40, his italics) noted that 'not only will a proper system of internal check frequently obviate the necessity of a detailed audit, but it further possesses the important advantage of causing any irregularities to be corrected *at once*, instead of continuing until the next visit of the auditor'. The internal check was often the first item on audit programmes. In the preface to their first, 1908, edition of *Audit Programmes*, Spicer and Pegler (1908: n.p.) detailed what this involved:

> It will be observed that the suggestion that the Auditor should ascertain the system of internal check in operation has been repeatedly made . . . It is obvious that the system of internal check will vary according to the circumstances of each business, and of course in practice it is frequently more or less incomplete. . . . The practical importance to the auditor of an exact knowledge of any system in operation is unquestionable, as in

all large audits the work to be done by the Auditor will be in direct relation to the system of internal check employed.

The first edition of Spicer and Pegler's textbook in 1911 also put a heavy emphasis on assessing and then relying on the internal check.

> The amount of detail checking which the Auditor must perform before he can satisfy himself that no fraud exists, will depend to a great extent on the system of Internal Check in operation...He must not of course do this indiscriminately, and assume that because there is a good system of Internal Check in operation he need perform no detail checking whatever. He must test the transactions as exhaustively as the circumstances permit, and should he find anything irregular he will then make a complete examination.
>
> (Spicer and Pegler 1911: 6–7)

This passage almost certainly exaggerates the extent to which British auditors could rely on their client's internal systems, although the practice probably became more common in the interwar period, and indicatively the term 'internal check' first appeared on an ICAEW Final Audit paper in 1930 (November, Question 9). An interview with an auditor of quoted companies in the 1930s confirmed how the system worked in practice. 'Most of the audit work...was on a sampling basis. If the company's own controls were strong then the sampling would be limited. If they were weak then the sampling was much more extended' (Interview with Keel).

Internal audit

According to the first edition of Spicer and Pegler (1911: 26) 'the highest development of the principle of Internal Check' was the internal audit, where a company employed staff full-time to oversee that their bookkeeping and other systems were working properly – in effect to check their internal check. Internal audits therefore potentially assisted the external auditor even more than the internal check.

The pioneers of the internal audit in the UK appear to have been the public utility companies. The railways had internal audits by at least the 1880s, and in the 1888 ICAEW meeting, quoted earlier, Murray stated: 'Take the case of railway companies. We cannot there deal with details; we must be content with the internal audit, and to a great extent merely satisfy ourselves as far as we can as to the results' (quoted in Chandler and Edwards 1994: 87). Internal audits were also common in early gas companies. For example, the Imperial Continental Gas Association had by 1900 'a comprehensive system of internal audit, carried on chiefly by Inspectors of Accounts who travelled round the different Continental establishments'

(Hill 1979: 12; *Accountant* 12 November 1927: 645–56; see also 26 March 1921: 359–65; 25 August 1923: 267–74). Banks also were early users of internal audits. Bolton, at the 1888 ICAEW meeting, told how:

> a bank like Coutts' at the West end of London, resolved to have a thorough and complete audit of their own books, and for many years past only found that to be practicable by having all accounts kept twice over, so that the accounts that are kept by one set of clerks for the work of the bank, are kept by another set of clerks quite independently as for the audit of the work.
>
> (Quoted in Chandler and Edwards 1994: 85)

The local authorities also had internal audit departments by the interwar period (Wood 1976: 140).

Internal audits were also not unknown in early industrial companies in Britain. The first edition of Spicer and Pegler's textbook (1911: 26) stated that internal audit departments were found 'in businesses of any magnitude', but it is not clear what this meant nor easy to gauge how common internal audits became. They almost certainly increased in popularity in the 1930s (Interviews with Hewitt and Brittain), and an article by Sir Nicholas Waterhouse in 1934 stated that: 'a company with a large staff . . . should rely mainly on a proper subdivision of work and internal audit' (*Accountant* 27 January 1934: 124). Lawson's 1951 paper, quoted earlier, noted that in the 'largest concerns there is invariably an elaborate system of internal check amounting in some cases, to a full internal audit' (ibid. 6 October 1951: 306). In 1953, the ICAEW issued notes to guide external auditors in the correct relationship with internal audit departments because 'of the considerable number of organisations in which an internal audit is now in operation' (*Accountant* 15 August 1953: 208–10). An auditor of south Wales steel works in the 1950s said that some of the bigger companies would have their own internal audit departments (Interview with Evans); and in the late 1950s the *Accountant* believed that: 'In virtually every large organisation an internal audit department has been established' (*Accountant* 18 April 1959: 450). Not withstanding this evidence, however, even in 1975 a survey revealed that only 56 per cent of leading UK private sector organisations had internal audit departments (Chambers 1981: 21). Higson (1987: 316–17) found that in the 1970s and 1980s there was a significant increase in the number of companies with internal audit departments, although still 'only large companies have them'. They could constitute 'anything from two or three people whose job it is to count the petty cash, to a group of twenty people issuing reports to the board of directors'. Moreover, according to Higson, in the straightened times of the 1980s internal audit departments were being reduced in size and were looked upon as 'a relative luxury'.

Internal controls in America

American auditors were almost certainly in advance of the British in their reliance on their clients' internal systems. As we discuss later, from an early date American auditors focused on the balance sheet, and already by 1912 Montgomery (1912: 82, his italics) explained: 'If the auditor has satisfied himself that the system of internal check *is* adequate, he will not attempt to duplicate work which has been properly performed by someone else.' However, as we noted earlier, this was no more than the British textbooks were telling their readers, and Montgomery (1912: 80) admitted: 'as the organizations which have a complete system of internal check are very much in the minority, the auditor will most frequently have to undertake a detailed audit'.

Therefore it is not possible to say how much more in advance of the British in the audit of internal controls the Americans were before the First World War. However, they were clearly ahead by the interwar period and the presumption in Montgomery's 1934 textbook was that audit clients would have an adequate system of internal check. Internal audits were also developed earlier and more fully in the US, where: 'Many large corporations have auditing departments' (Montgomery 1934: 64–5). An Institute of Internal Auditors was formed in the US in 1941, and by 1949 it had over 1,000 members in 20 chapters (Montgomery *et al*. 1949: 53). Significantly, the first organisation for internal auditors formed in Britain in 1948 was the London Chapter of the New York Institute of Internal Auditors, and an Oxford summer school paper in 1947 noted 'that our friends in the United States who are, I think, in some ways ahead of us in accounting technique, are treating the internal audit almost as a separate profession' (*Accountant* 2 August 1951: 147).

Moreover, among many American companies by the 1940s the internal check had expanded into a wider range of procedures designed to 'safeguard the assets of the company, check the accuracy and reliability of its accounting data, promote operational efficiency, and encourage adherence to prescribed managerial policies' (Montgomery *et al*. 1949: 49). These wider systems were now called 'internal controls', the change of nomenclature from 'internal check' taking place between the 1934 and 1949 editions of Montgomery. By the latter edition the American auditor had the luxury of using their clients' extended internal controls, and not only auditing the income statement but also verifying each item in the balance sheet was also largely a matter of assessing the client's systems and only doing substantive tests where these were weak. Little had apparently changed by Montgomery's eighth, 1957, edition except curiously the internal check returns to significance as part of the internal controls whereas it had not been mentioned eight years earlier.

There were also significant audit innovations in America at this time. A 75 page appendix to Montgomery's 1949 textbook now gave model internal control questionnaires (ICQs) which interrogated management as to their control systems. These were detailed for five different types of client: Commercial and Industrial companies; Public Utilities; Banks and Trusts; Investment companies and Stock brokerage firms (Montgomery *et al.* 1949: 573–648). The ICQ for the first of these categories, for example, contained just under 200 questions (many in turn split into subsidiary questions) divided along the client's departmental lines or into each balance sheet item. A lot of the questions were of the old internal check nature, such as: 'Are all accounting employees' duties rotated?', but others were of an efficiency testing character, for example: 'Are expenses and costs under budgetary control?' (a question of course that would have meant very little to the average British audit client). Montgomery *et al.* (1949: 37–8) also gave a brief mention of flow-charts, which it said should trace the course of transactions around the company, and an equally brief description of 'selecting a number of transactions in each category and following them through the records', depth testing in all but name.

The rise of the systems approach in Britain

In contrast to the Americans, the British textbooks in the early 1950s were still describing the bookkeeping or detailed audit. Dicksee (Magee 1951), Spicer and Pegler (Bigg 1951) and de Paula (1951) were merely repeating their first editions in noting that the reliance on the internal check obviated the need to examine every entry in detail. There was no use of the term 'internal control', nor mention of flow charts or ICQs. Only in the fifties in Britain was the term and probably the practice of internal check generally expanded into internal controls, and indeed a question using the phrase 'internal control' did not appear in the ICAEW Final Audit paper until 1963 (November, Question 2).

Yet the American methods were well known in Britain. In Lawson's key 1951 paper, already referred to a number of times, the complete panoply of American inspired techniques was set out. He noted the frequent use in the largest British companies of the internal systems, where: 'The auditor can then rely upon a limited test of detailed transactions with a view to satisfying himself as to the effectiveness of the control exercised within the business itself' (*Accountant* 6 October 1951: 306). Lawson elaborated on the need for an investigation and statement of the client's internal system and, without calling them ICQs, stated that 'some practising members find it useful to have a standard form of questionnaire setting out the various points which must be borne in mind in this inquiry'. Finally, as we mentioned earlier, Lawson also described the practice of depth testing used by the auditor to 'satisfy himself that the system is operating effectively' (ibid.: 306). But to what extent was the approach outlined by Lawson being applied?

Table 5.1 While I was undertaking my articles/training, as the auditors we were involved in auditing the companies' own internal control systems...

	Always (%)	Often (%)	Sometimes (%)	Never (%)	Total respondents (%)	N
Decade qualified						
1920s/1930s	2.3	9.1	50.0	38.6	100	89
1940s	2.8	9.9	38.0	49.3	100	128
1950s	2.6	8.4	45.5	43.5	100	150
1960s	9.0	13.8	51.0	26.2	100	146
1970s	20.8	26.2	36.2	16.9	100	131
1980s	26.1	33.6	34.5	5.9	100	120
1990s	29.4	28.6	34.6	7.4	100	136
Respondent audited mainly...						
Quoted companies	29.7	36.7	26.5	7.1	100	155
SMEs	12.2	16.3	45.9	25.6	100	473
Sole traders and partnerships	4.8	3.6	42.2	49.4	100	83
Size of firm with which respondent qualified						
Top 20	20.0	26.8	36.8	16.5	100	280
Medium	12.6	13.8	46.6	27.1	100	247
Small	11.1	17.9	39.7	31.3	100	262

Source: Postal questionnaire, see Appendix.

As Table 5.1, which contains further results of the postal questionnaire, indicates, there was no particular trend in the use of the systems approach from the interwar period down to the 1960s. Around 11 per cent of respondents stated they always or often audited the client's own control systems during their training in the decades from the 1920s to the 1950s. It should be noted, however, that this is not an insignificant figure and, moreover, in the same period always less than half the respondents said auditing the client's controls was never part of their audits, confirming that testing internal controls was probably a feature of some British audits from the earliest years. Nonetheless, the approach was relatively infrequently used even in the 1960s when less than a quarter of trainees always or often used the procedure. This was despite the fact that as early as 1961 the ICAEW's statement on the general principles of auditing – U1 – had stressed the need for the auditor to base his audit work on a careful examination and assessment by depth testing of the system of internal control (*Accountant* 18 May 1963: 645). Perhaps tellingly, the term 'internal control questionnaire' did not appear in the ICAEW Final Audit paper until 1970 (November, Question 2).

The Coopers manual placed the emphasis of the audit squarely on internal controls, which it did not distinguish from 'internal check'. It stated: 'The detailed checking undertaken by the auditor should be kept to a minimum... The system of internal control in force in the client's office forms the foundation on which the audit must be based' (Cooper 1966: 1, 11).

The system was to be ascertained by means of an ICQ, ideally to be filled in by the client's management (ibid.: 15, 361–457). The internal control system should then be subject to depth testing, which were called 'procedural tests' rather than compliance tests. The extent of these tests would depend on the quality of the system found, and the nature and scale of the business; clients being categorised from A to E, as noted above (ibid.: 27). Based on the judgement of the audit manager the tests would comprise, 'ten to fifty representative items under each main aspect', for example, purchases or wages, for a week or a month (ibid.: 28–9). Each transaction selected should then, the manual stated, be checked exhaustively through its stages from origin to conclusion, the vouchers, records, authorities and other features of the internal control being examined at each stage (ibid.: 493). One Coopers partner in 1966 suggested that the balance of time spent in this type of audit was: one third taken up with the examination, evaluation and testing of the system of internal control, and two-thirds on the verification of balance sheet items (*Accountant* 7 May 1966: 563).

For the smaller companies with poor internal controls the Coopers manual indicated that the detailed audit of the bookkeeping was still the order of the day. This was to be done by 'vouching a proportion of the transactions recorded therein with supporting documents, vouchers and other evidence. A number of transactions should also be selected for verification in depth' (ibid.: 26). It is a point worth making, however, that the attempt by the Coopers manual to distinguish between a 'procedural' internal control type audit, and a 'vouching' bookkeeping audit was (like the 'detailed' and 'balance sheet' audits in the early editions of Montgomery discussed later) merely a matter of emphasis. Both required some testing of the underlying bookkeeping and internal control and both required an audit of the balance sheet.

There is nothing in the Coopers manual (as described earlier, it was in use in the firm from the late 1940s but continually amended until it was published in 1966) to indicate when the firm adopted their approach in practice, but it was in operation for the audits of their largest clients, like Unilever (the soap and margarine conglomerate and perhaps the third largest industrial company in Britain by value) in the 1950s (*Accountant* 26 October 1957: 474–7; Hannah 1983: 190). However, Coopers were at that time almost certainly in the vanguard in the use of the systems approach in Britain, although of course they were not the only firm using this technique. An auditor with Peats indicated that in audits of the bigger steel works of south Wales in the 1950s:

> some of them would have their own internal audit department, and our work would very much bear in mind the work they had done, and we would read their internal audit reports. That would cut down the work that we had to do, reduce our audit fee, and that's why of course they have their own internal audit.

> (Interview with Evans)

Nonetheless, an article in the *Accountant* (20 May 1967: 658–65) after the Coopers manual had been published excoriated the British profession for its slowness in modernising its procedures along systems lines.

This backwardness on behalf of some firms was also evidenced in our interviews. The partner in a medium sized Newcastle practice, who audited large quoted companies like the Consett steelworks in the 1950s, remembers that when they merged with Cooper Brothers in 1965 their systems approach came as news to him: 'when we joined Coopers it was apparent that the amount of ticking that had to be done to satisfy yourself was becoming an enormous burden and that you had to begin to rely on internal control' (Interview with Middleton). And clearly the late 1960s was the time of change for even large firms. A Price Waterhouse partner remembers: 'in 1969 there was a major upgrading in the way we did an audit. The old-fashioned audit programmes, which comprised of ticking and bashing, disappeared about then...We tended to do a lot of system checks, following bits of paper all the way through the system' (Interview with Heywood).

Interestingly, and not for the only time there is a general impression of muddle among the textbooks as they struggled to come to terms with the systems approach and graft it on to the time honoured methods. As we have seen, the Coopers Manual of 1966 gave a central role to the systems approach, as did a casebook on auditing procedures published by the ICAEW in 1971. There it was stated that the previous very large amount of vouching 'is rarely appropriate nowadays', and the casebook suggested that virtually the whole of audit work be directed at the client's control systems, together with a minimum of testing or verification and a review of the final accounts (Bird 1971: 15). These publications were well in advance of the traditional textbooks, however, and probably of current practice too. The last, 1969, edition of Dicksee stuck closely to the traditional audit, and gave only a brief nod to the recent innovations, stating only

> that there may be a generally lower level than before of detailed checking consistent with the system of internal control, but that auditors do have the responsibility of critically reviewing the internal control system. This is done by most auditors by the use of an internal control questionnaire.
>
> (Waldron 1969: 27)

De Paula was the most progressive of the textbooks but did not acknowledge the new departures until its 1976 edition, where it announced that since the last edition in 1970

> considerable changes have taken place in the auditing techniques used by many of the larger professional accounting firms in the UK, when undertaking the audits of companies, especially those large enough to

have developed their own internal control systems. These changes are of a sufficiently fundamental nature to warrant an extensive revision of the whole text.

(de Paula and Attwood 1976: ix)

De Paula then went on to detail the use of ICQs and flow diagrams, although not depth testing (ibid.: 29). Not until the sixteenth, 1978 edition of Spicer and Pegler's textbook, however, was the systems approach, including depth testing, put, in theory at least, at the heart of the audit process. Yet even then the bulk of their text was still given over to the 'vouch and post' audit, which 'starts with the books of prime entry and ends with the balance sheet, the sequence of checking following the order in which the entries are made' (Waldron 1978: 33–63, 91, 430).

Davis (1996: 6) dates the transition from what he calls the first generation of audits, or 'verifying transactions in the books', to the second generation or the systems approach, as taking place in the late 1960s. But probably the change among the generality of audits was only starting then. Our questionnaire evidence, set out in Table 5.1 indicates that while 11 per cent of respondents indicated they always or often used the systems approach in the 1950s, this had risen to only 23 per cent in the 1960s. Even in the 1970s less than half gave this response, and it had risen to 60 per cent by the 1980s. This trend was matched by a drop in respondents who never used the technique, from around 40 per cent or over in the decades down to the 1950s, falling to 26 per cent in the 1960s and 6 per cent by the 1980s. Again, Table 5.1 tends to indicate that the use of the technique had more to do with the size of the client than the size of the audit firm with which the respondent qualified. Nonetheless, on our evidence, the larger audit firms were still twice as likely to always use the procedure than small firms, probably a reflection of the fact that the large firms had larger clients. Turley and Cooper's (1991: 84) survey in 1987 also showed that, of the nine largest audit firms, eight used internal control evaluation on all audits and one considered it optional; of the manuals of 12 smaller firms, only four used internal control evaluation on all audits, while eight thought it optional or did not indicate one way or the other.

It also has to be pointed out that the systems approach never met with unanimous approval among practitioners in Britain. Turley and Cooper (1991: 14) thought that the systems approach as practised in the 1980s

> resulted in a large volume of flowcharting, evaluation of systems and testing, much of which was not well focused or necessary when seen in terms of the financial statement objectives of the audit, although it might have produced material for inclusion in the management letter.

Auditing systems, Higson (1997: 200) also noted, was costly and could lead to 'over-auditing', with a lot of work undertaken compared with the often relatively weak evidence gained. Therefore, Higson argued, the technique was never wholly relied on compared with substantive testing of the accounts themselves, which continued to be preferred by practitioners. This preference, combined with the fact that audit fees came under pressure from clients in the late 1970s and early 1980s creating a drive for efficiency and the need to save money, led, according to Turley and Cooper (1991: 15), to something of a retreat from the systems approach. Maysmor-Gee *et al.* indeed noticed a fall in the use of ICQs between their surveys in 1976 and 1984 (reported in Higson 1987: 119).

There is, however, little evidence for this decline from our questionnaire responses. As Table 5.1 shows, the upward trend in the use of the systems approach levelled off in the 1990s, from the 60 per cent of trainees using the technique always or often in the 1980s, to 58 per cent who did so in the 1990s; but this is well within the sampling error of the data (at the confidence level of 95 per cent the 58 per cent figure is accurate to within ±8 per cent). Checking internal controls remained a very common audit procedure.

Management letters

The end product of all audits, of course, is the audit report. This book is concerned with the techniques of the audit process and although clearly the audit report is part of the process it is a subject in its own right which could not be done justice here. However, at the risk of straying into the equally large and contentious topic of the purpose of the audit, we will look at one aspect of the audit endgame which has come to prominence in recent years – the management letter.

As with most aspects of the audit discussed up to this point, the management letter, while only taking a prominent part in the audit procedure in recent decades, in fact has in embryo at least a long history. Again, the management letter had its precursor in America. The American equivalent of the British audit report was in the early years called the auditors' certificate. This certificate became known as the 'short form' report and was attached to the published accounts and stated that the balance sheet in the auditor's opinion showed the financial position of the company. This certificate could also be lengthened to five or six paragraphs if the client specifically asked the auditor to certify, for example, inventories, depreciation or additions to plant etc. (Montgomery 1934: chap. 30, 1949: chap. 6). The American auditors' report as such became known as the 'long form' report and was a lengthy bound volume for the use of management. The long form report (which Montgomery argued should be interesting and readable) would also include the client's accounts but might also comment generally on the company's results, its overall financial position, as well as criticisms of its accounting and internal check. There might also be analysis of the client's financial situation by means, for example, of ratios such as the percentage of costs and expenses to total assets, or general data on the industry in which the client operated, often presented in graph form. The apparent reason for this lengthy type of American reporting was that the early audit was not compulsory for American companies and so auditors (who across the Atlantic were often called 'the profession of business advice') had to make themselves useful to their clients (Montgomery 1912: 7).

From the beginning professional auditors in Britain were, of course, also used to giving lengthy opinions to management on the general state of their company. Such reports among other things, as we have noted earlier, were commonly published prior to the floatation of a company on the stock exchange; for example, the reports on Bell Brothers, the steel company, by Robert Fletcher in 1874, and on the same company by Peats in 1900. British auditors had also occasionally given advice and made detailed written reports to clients over and above the audit when asked to do so; for example, the report to the directors of the Consett Iron company in 1877 on dividend policy during a down-turn in the iron trade (Consett Iron Company, Report to Directors, 30 June 1877; I am grateful to Prof Trevor Boyns for this reference).

Also, if in the course of the audit weaknesses were found in the client's procedures it made sense that these should be itemized and the client informed, often in writing. One auditor remembered writing such letters:

> We did that in 1934. It was one of the things that the partners insisted upon, and we were very much judged on the quality of what we wrote.... It was a letter that went out with the final accounts and the audit report. It might say: 'We think that your recording of petty cash is rather loose...'.
>
> (Interview with Passmore)

There was apparently at one stage some discussion in the ICAEW that the audit report itself was the best place for such comments, that is, to follow the practice of the US long form report. But in 1950 the past President of the Institute, Sir Harold Howitt, reported: '...we are resisting so much on the Council in our deliberations any suggestion that the auditors' report should go into the field of criticism of the management' (*Accountant* 13 May 1950: 540).

As Table 5.2 displays, a sizable minority, already around a third of firms from the interwar period down to the 1950s, sent out what we now call management letters at least sometimes. However, until the 1960s only 10 per cent or less did so always or often.

Increasingly, British firms took up the management letter which of course, since its prime function was to comment on control weaknesses, was concomitant with the growing importance of testing internal controls. One of the first explicit references to the management letter as such in the trade press appears in a description of Canadian audit practice in the late 1950s (*Accountant* 29 August 1959: 122). In a summer school lecture in

Table 5.2 While I was undertaking my articles/training, as the auditors my firm sent out management letters...

	Always (%)	Often (%)	Sometimes (%)	Never (%)	Total respondents (%)	N
Decade qualified						
1920s/1930s	2.7	4.0	26.7	66.7	100	75
1940s	3.4	6.7	29.4	60.5	100	119
1950s	3.9	5.2	31.0	60.0	100	155
1960s	11.2	12.6	46.2	30.1	100	143
1970s	30.0	24.6	29.2	16.2	100	130
1980s	43.3	36.7	18.3	2.5	100	120
1990s	54.4	27.9	15.4	2.2	100	136
Respondent audited mainly...						
Quoted companies	41.5	27.0	16.4	15.1	100	159
SMEs	21.6	18.6	30.6	29.2	100	494
Sole traders and partnerships	5.5	4.4	28.6	61.5	100	91
Size of firm with which respondent qualified						
Top 20	36.5	20.3	22.3	20.9	100	296
Medium	12.5	16.8	34.8	35.9	100	273
Small	15.8	15.1	28.5	40.6	100	298

Source: Postal questionnaire, see Appendix.

1960 Rae Smith of Deloittes stated that: 'Management has a right to expect that an auditor will report to them on any weak points he finds in a system of internal control', although 'any comments which an auditor makes in a report on deficiencies of control should not be irreconcilable with the report he makes on the accounts as auditor' (*Accountant* 29 October 1960: 553). A year later it seems to have been accepted that: 'The logical conclusion of any review of internal control is the management letter' (*Accountant* 7 January 1961: 6).

A significant advance in the use of management letters can be detected in the 1960s and the process of writing the letter became more formalised within firms. A retired senior partner with Peats related how the procedure worked in the 1960s: 'These [management letters] started to get developed from...lower grade ones which went to certain sections [in the client company], then you worked up to what was called the executive summary, which went to the actual board' (Interview with Grenside). As Table 5.2 shows, in the 1960s almost a quarter of trainees were now working in firms which always or often sent out management letters; about 70 per cent did so at least sometimes, while less than a third never did so. A Coopers auditor referring to the management letter thought that: 'In the 1960s, we were regarded as being pretty innovative as a firm in writing these' (Interview with Lainé); and a Whinney, Smith & Whinney partner confirmed that management letters at his firm 'came in the late 1960s' (Interview with Whinney). A PW man also remembered that by the late 1960s: 'It was standard practice to offer clients management letters.' But all was not straightforward, 'only 50 per cent of the clients wanted them. The others didn't want to spend the money' (Interview with Carty). This quote indicates that some firms specifically charged for the letter but this apparently was not the common practice (Cooper 1966: 16–19; Thornton Baker 1981: 323–7).

In the 1960s, the management letter also moved beyond mere comments on the client's internal controls into offering general advice. Again almost certainly transatlantic practice was ahead of the British. An American giving a paper to an ICAEW summer school in 1966 indicated that at his firm the managing partner had stated: 'It shall be our policy henceforth to furnish as part of our regular service to as many audit clients as possible, periodic reports to management analysing recent operations and results, and containing comments and recommendations designed to aid and improve the client's operations, productivity and profitability' (*Accountant* 27 August 1966: 257). In this period in Britain too, audit firms took a conscious decision to increase the value of their audits to their client's management and began to make a much greater attempt to understand all aspects of the client's business. An interviewee referring to the 1950s said: 'I remember when I first went to audit we never really got to grips with what the client was doing. We seldom went out of the audit room onto the factory floor' (Interview with Colvin). A future senior partner at Peats talking of the 1960s articulated the new emphasis:

> We all took the view that we should change significantly from just doing an audit to really trying to help the company to become a better company...people [auditors] became more expert in understanding particular businesses. The whole thing changed from the original days when somebody somehow wrote out an audit programme without really understanding the business. Now in later years you don't begin until you understand the business. There was...the development of quite long and quite detailed management letters pointing out the weaknesses of the business and areas where they could improve the business.... There was a far greater relationship with the client themselves. We got to a point where partners used to go to the client and just talked to them. With no audit going on, they would keep contact with these people to find out what they were doing. Try and help them with what they were doing, or give them advice.
>
> (Interview with Grenside)

By 1965, a journal article even suggested that it be made a statutory duty of the auditor to give clients advice on the general financial well-being of their company, although of course this has never been implemented (*Accountant* 6 March 1965: 309). In 1969, Harris, a leading partner with Price Waterhouse, in an article tellingly entitled: 'The Business Approach to the Modern Audit' exemplified this new change of emphasis and talked of the auditors' 'positive contribution to the improvement in financial controls and profitability of the client's business' by means of the 'internal control report' (*Accountant* 19 July 1969: 42, 74). Also Lee's book on auditing, in 1972, gave a full account, including the commercial aspects, of the management letter, which he said should not only comment on accounting and financial matters but also 'areas of managerial and operational activity within the company, often of a non-accounting nature, in which the auditor feels there could be increased efficiency and profitability – for example, improving storage facilities... minimising production material wastage' (Lee 1972: 40–1).

The Coopers manual, as already noted, gave management letters a key role in the audit and extensive coverage (Cooper 1966: 16–19), although it still referred to them as 'letters of weakness', as did the 1969 edition (Cooper 1969: 16). The 1981 edition of the manual, however, used the phrase 'management letter,' and in the full meaning of the term, since the letters 'should not be restricted to control deficiencies but may deal with a variety of financial and business matters of interest to the client, including trends in profitability, tax matters, etc., whether arising from the audit or otherwise' (Coopers & Lybrand 1981: 116).

The standard textbooks, however, were slow to acknowledge the management letter. There is no reference to the practice in either the 1968 edition of de Paula (1968) or the 1969 edition of Dicksee. By the 1970s, the textbooks to some extent woke up to the issue but they did not acknowledge the wider commercial role of providing advice which would improve the client's profitability. The 1976, fifteenth edition, of de Paula noted: 'It is now generally accepted practice for auditors to report to management on matters coming to their attention during the course of the audit', but the report was to be restricted to financial or accounting matters (de Paula and Attwood 1976: 25). The 1978 edition of Spicer and Pegler still only contained a cursory note that if the test of internal controls revealed weaknesses the client must be advised 'in a management letter or letter of weakness' (Waldron 1978: 120). In Woolf's first, 1978, edition he stated: 'it is normal for the firm to send to the client a letter of weakness (sometimes referred to as "internal control letter" or "management letter")' (Woolf 1978a: 145). But, as with the other textbooks, Woolf did not indicate that the management letter had moved on from merely commenting on the internal controls of clients, and he does not do so even in his 1997 edition, where indeed the term 'weakness letter' is still preferred (1997: 135). Moreover, an audit textbook like Gray and Manson (1989) made no reference to the management letter at all.

The management letter, of course, was not part of the statutory obligation of the auditor, and it is possible to read into the stance of the textbooks a reluctance to discuss the more overtly commercial aspects of the audit.

Perhaps for this reason too the first time the term 'management letter' appeared explicitly in an ICAEW examination was not until the 1989 Final Audit paper (December, Question 6).

Table 5.2 shows management letters in fact became the general rule from the 1970s. From less than a quarter of trainees' firms using them always or often in the 1960s, about 55 per cent of firms were doing so in the 1970s, and 80 per cent in the 1980s, by which time only 2.5 per cent of firms never sent them out. The trend in popularity of management letters continued into the 1990s, although the growth in their use, as the practice became almost the rule, levelled off significantly – to 82 per cent of firms using them always or often. Most marked in the 1990s was the growth, to well over half the sample, of firms who always sent out the letters. Table 5.2 also reveals that the incidence in the use of the management letter was again more to do with the size of the client than the size of the audit firm.

It is not immediately apparent why the increase in the popularity of the management letter took place when it did. An auditor with small provincial firms thought: 'It only became an integral part of the audit in the late seventies, although it was originally called a report not a management letter. It came from the Institute laying down standards' (Interview with Wilde). This must refer to the impact of standards in general, since the Auditing Practices Committee's Draft Guideline, *Reports to Management*, in 1986, was the first specific intervention on the question of the management letter by a regulatory body (Woolf 1986: 149–53). A more plausible explanation, which is discussed with regard to audit changes generally in the conclusion, is that the management letter was related to shifts in the commercial relationship between the auditors and their clients. An auditor with Deloittes noted in interview:

> It was only in the 1970s, when management letters started to become prevalent, that the auditing profession had to pull its socks up and realise an historical audit wasn't much good to the client unless we were able to justify it by making recommendations to the client as to how he could improve the financial performance of the business.
>
> (Interview with Colvin)

And as Woolf put it in his 1997 edition: 'The report to management could be the one constructive by-product of a service otherwise thought of as a necessary evil – a by-product for which the client actually sees value for money' (Woolf 1997: 144). Audit managers told Humphrey and Moizer (1990: 231–2): 'the traditional audit product was not valued by client management', and that 'Auditing was no longer just concerned with credibility assessment, but was also about serving a more advisory role'; 'financial directors were no longer looking for just an audit report, but for people who understood the business and could come up not just with "control errors" but also with "fairly good business ideas" '.

Summary

From the beginning professional auditors used for some of their evidence their client's internal checks, that is, the arrangement of their bookkeeping to prevent staff fraud, and its fullest extension – the internal audit – where the client's own staff checked the company's organisation. In Britain however only the largest and well run companies, such as the railways, other public utilities and banks, would have these systems. In America they were more advanced, and by the 1940s auditors there put a heavy reliance on testing their client's internal controls, which now covered all aspects of a company's organisation, using ICQs, flow charts and depth testing. Because of the backwardness of British companies this systems approach did not become dominant here until the 1970s, and in contradiction to the views of some commentators it still remained a popular audit procedure in the 1990s. Along with the development of the systems approach came the management letter, pointing out weaknesses in the system. Written comments had always been issued to clients in some form but in the 1970s this became the rule, and indeed extended to also giving management general advice on increasing their profitability.

6   The balance sheet audit

Problems of definition

As Woolf (1997: 129) in his textbook put it: 'It is natural for every discipline to develop its own terminology and auditing is no exception. There is, however, a degree of confusion arising from differences in usage.' Nowhere is this more the case than with regard to the so-called 'balance sheet audit'. We noted earlier in the context of the systems approach, that the textbooks and perhaps the profession in general were in some confusion in grafting the apparently American inspired techniques onto the standard British bookkeeping audit. The biggest confusion, however, was reserved for the treatment of the balance sheet audit, a term which was, and probably still is, used loosely in Britain, with no clearly agreed definition; an impression which, like the other examples of ambiguity, does nothing for the general credibility of the auditing process.

As we have noted, American auditors put a greater reliance on auditing the balance sheet earlier than the British. The first edition of Montgomery in 1912 distinguished between first, the 'detailed audit', which it said was concerned with 'the verification of the routine bookkeeping' and was clearly identified with the traditional or English audit. The second type of audit was the implicitly more progressive, American, 'balance sheet audit'. This, Montgomery (1912: 82) explained, as we outlined in the previous chapter, involved an audit of the internal check and then required the auditor: 'to verify the assets and liabilities, and to make such an analysis of the Profit and Loss Account as will enable him to certify that it has been properly stated'. In fact, however, since both the detailed and the balance sheet audits involved testing the internal check, and both of course audited the balance sheet, the distinction between the two was only one of emphasis. And, as we noted above, Montgomery (1912: 277) accepted that before the First World War even American companies' control systems were not good enough for the auditor to avoid a detailed audit in the majority of cases.

However, by the fifth, 1934 edition, the detailed audit had been dropped and Montgomery could state that: 'Most modern audits, although they include the examination of certain cash transactions, have as their ultimate purpose the verification of the balance sheet and its related income account' (Montgomery 1934: 18). Indeed, out of the 32 chapters to Montgomery's 1934 textbook only two are devoted to the verification of the income account. Montgomery explained: 'When a balance sheet audit is undertaken, it is assumed that an adequate system of internal check is in force' (ibid.: 41–2). 'The verification of the income account can hardly extend beyond tests and scrutiny' (ibid.: 477–8); and 'the tendency during recent years has been to belittle the importance of finding errors in books of account and to magnify the advantages of concentrating on the search for fraud and the verification of the balance sheet' (ibid.: 27).

To the Americans then the balance sheet audit was a type of audit which could be distinguished from another type – the detailed audit. The British however gave the term 'balance sheet audit' a variety of meanings. Often the term is used in the American sense where 'balance sheet audit' implied the character of the whole audit; one based on internal control testing and asset and liability verification. This was the meaning taken when the 'balance sheet audit' was apparently first mentioned in Britain – in the *Accountant* in the early 1940s. There it was defined as a procedure: 'effected in the case of large corporations whose internal system is good and where it is possible to rely to a large extent on work done by the corporations' own internal audit staffs' (*Accountant* 12 April 1941: 279). This was also the meaning given by Lawson in his 1951 paper.

> In recent years there has been an increasing tendency towards what is loosely known as the 'balance sheet audit'. The expression is, of course, used to cover more than the mere verification of assets and liabilities which had always been part of the normal auditing procedure. The essential distinction between the detailed audit and the balance sheet audit is one of approach. The detailed audit starts with the books of prime entry and ends with the balance sheet, whereas the balance sheet audit starts with the verification of assets and liabilities and probes back to original entries and vouchers where the auditor considers that necessary.
>
> (*Accountant* 6 October 1951: 307)

Equally frequently, as in the Coopers manual, the phrase 'balance sheet audit' was used as simply meaning the part of the audit which is concerned with the balance sheet (Cooper 1966: 489–90). Sherwood, in an article in 1972, however, muddied the water further by putting a slightly different construction on this definition, stating that:

> It has long been recognised that an audit divides naturally into two parts, each of which is complementary to the other: (i) the final audit, now known as the balance sheet audit and (ii) the interim audit, best defined as a review of the transactions between successive balance sheets.
>
> (*Accountancy* April 1972: 18)

This usage was followed by Innes *et al.* (1981: 9–11) who described the typical audit in the early 1980s as: first the systems audit via compliance testing; second the transactions audit by vouching, both parts were interim and conducted during the year. Then finally there was the year end or balance sheet audit supplemented by a final audit review.

Woolf's 1978 textbook compounded the confusion. His definition of the balance sheet audit was that it started with the balance sheet and worked back to the underlying records, and was appropriate for large well run organisations with strong internal controls, and where an interim audit had already covered basic tests of routine procedures. This was in line with other definitions of the balance sheet audit and would seem to describe the audit common in Britain in the 1970s. But Woolf went on to assert that it was not popular in Britain and that it 'is more common in the USA' where they concentrate on the balance sheet rather than the profit and loss account, whereas 'the reverse has traditionally characterised UK audits' (Woolf 1978b: 142). Exactly the same wording was used in Woolf's sixth, 1997, edition. But then, almost incredibly, as if the definitions were not muddled enough, Woolf added:

> The term 'balance sheet audit' is also used to describe audits at the 'small end of the spectrum', in which the system of controls is unreliable, the records sparse and rudimentary, and hence undue reliance has to be placed on management assurances...the burden of testing falls on the 'end results'...'Do the figures make sense?'
>
> (Woolf 1997: 132)

The rise of the balance sheet

In fact, leaving definitions aside, as we noted above, the extent to which auditors pay attention to balance sheet items, as opposed to the client's transactions or systems of control is only a matter of degree. Both traditional and present day audits paid and pay attention to the client's internal check or controls and audit the balance sheet to some extent. As we have seen, in the generality of audits early British auditors had to direct their work to the transactions in the profit and loss account because as likely as not they were also making up the accounts, if not doing the bookkeeping. Interestingly, this was somewhat paradoxical in view of the fact that legally, unlike the balance sheet, a profit and loss account did not have to be submitted to the shareholders until the 1929 Companies Act, and did not have to be audited until the 1948 Act (Freear 1977: 18–19).

However, as with many apparently recent audit processes, a focus on the balance sheet in some audits dates back to the dawn of the professional audit. Where they were faced with a pure audit of a large well run client the early British auditors like their American counterparts realised that checking transactions was less important than verifying balance sheet items. In the 1888 ICAEW meeting discussed previously, Murray indicated that for the largest companies, where they could not hope to check everything, the focus should be on the balance sheet. 'Take the case of a bank' he said, 'what are we to do there? We must limit our examinations very much to the balance sheet' (Chandler and Edwards 1994: 87). A Price Waterhouse partner interviewed, recalled of the 1950s, that the audit: 'would have been quite focused on the balance sheet. The broad underlying theory being that, if you get two balance sheets right, the difference between the two would show up in the profit and loss account. So rather than audit the profit and loss account to death we concentrated on making sure the balance sheet was right' (Interview with Stacy).

Nonetheless, our evidence is that the auditor's concern with the balance sheet increased in the 1960s and 1970s, but again, as with the definitions, there was an apparent muddle in the textbooks and perhaps in the profession generally as to the direction of the trend. Some argued that the balance sheet was becoming a relatively less important part of the audit as a result of the rise of the systems approach. Harris in his article in 1969, already discussed above, took this line. Detailing the systems based audit he wrote: 'the concept of the audit has changed in that the examination of financial and internal controls ranks at least equally in importance with the traditional approach which has been to place the main emphasis on a balance sheet audit' (*Accountant* 12 July 1969: 42). This view was confirmed by de Paula, which textbook, although it had referred to the balance sheet audit in passing in its 1966 edition (de Paula 1966: vii), dropped any mention of it in the 1976 edition. Indeed, de Paula must have thoroughly confused, not to say misled, audit students of the 1970s, asserting that the balance sheet was now of reduced interest to the auditor:

> changes in audit practice have been directed towards the procedural audit, that is to say, the review of transactions between successive balance sheets, rather than the audit of the balance sheets themselves. What has emerged has been the 'systems audit' in which the auditor seeks reassurance as to the validity of financial data produced by an accounting system.
>
> (de Paula and Attwood 1976: ix)

But Spicer and Pegler, in their 1978 edition, flatly contradicted de Paula. They emphasised the growing importance of the balance sheet audit to which it devoted a chapter, if one uncomfortably inserted into a text, as we have said, still largely devoted to the bookkeeping audit. Spicer and Pegler took the American/Lawson view of the balance sheet audit, which '*starts* with the verification of the items appearing in the balance sheet and involves only such examination of original entries and vouchers as the auditor feels to be necessary'. This was to be accomplished by checking the system of internal check with depth testing (Waldron 1978: 432, 441, his italics).

Indeed the evidence is that the trend in the *typical* British audit was, from the 1950s on, a shift in emphasis away from the profit and loss account and towards more work on the balance sheet, and this went hand in hand with the growth of the systems approach. Our interviews give many indications of this. Typically, an accountant recalled that when Coopers became auditors at GKN, the steel makers, where he worked in 1960: 'The biggest change was probably their emphasis on a balance sheet audit...they placed a lot of emphasis on stocks' (Interview with Davies). We can quantify this change to some extent by focusing on the treatment of two balance sheet items – stock and debt.

Stock

As we discussed in the first chapter, the early British auditors rarely if ever went beyond their clients' books and other records, and this certainly applied to the checking and valuation of balance sheet items like stock. After 1896 auditors could point to the judgement in the Kingston Cotton Mill case, where, as Spicer and Pegler (1914: 174) noted, the:

> Court held that an Auditor is not a valuer; that it is not his business to take stock; that in the absence of suspicious circumstances he is entitled to rely upon the representation of responsible officials; and that he is not guilty of negligence if he accepts that certificate of such persons as to the value of the Stock-in-trade.

Spicer and Pegler did maintain that the Kingston Cotton Mill judgement did not mean that stock should not be audited; the auditor should ascertain that the stock-taking was adequately done, and should cast the stock-sheets and test the valuations (ibid.: 175). How the valuations were to be tested however was not made explicit. Regarding stocks, Dicksee (1904: 215) considered it 'essential that the extensions and additions be re-checked... and...to be satisfied as to the soundness of the principle of valuation adopted'.

But there was general agreement in the profession that the auditor was entitled to take the assurances of the client's management. The early editions of de Paula (1917: 85), for example, on the attitude of the auditor to stock stated: 'there is no certain means by which he can verify the existence of this asset...he is bound to rely very largely upon the internal checks in this connection, and upon the certificates given by management'. It was quite common at the turn of the century for the auditors to state in their audit reports that the stocks had been certified by the management. In our survey of 232 audit reports in 1900, stock was mentioned in 17 per cent of cases. Typical comments were: 'The Stock in Trade has been taken by your staff in the ordinary way, and is certified by the Works Committee of the Board as being at below cost'; or 'The Stock is taken and certified by the Chairman and Managing Director.' In 1920, a sample of audit reports of similar size to that of 1900 yielded 21 per cent of companies where the auditors stated that they had taken the stock as certified by the companies' officers. But thereafter, for reasons not immediately apparent, this practice declined, and by 1935 in a similar sample of companies in only 7 per cent of audit reports was stock mentioned in this way.

Yet some auditors went much further than taking management's say so. There is evidence that occasionally the auditors did the stock-taking themselves: a service on offer to the client for a fee like any other. For example, in 1900, T.W. Read & Co, the auditors of the Liverpool Grain Storage and Transit Co. Ltd, noted in their audit report: 'We have also half-yearly independently taken the Stock.' One auditor interviewed recalled stock-taking at a hospital in the 1920s (Interview with Sanders). Some auditors also physically checked the stock if only on a sampling basis, which is perhaps the meaning of this audit report by Peats on the accounts of Bell Brothers, the iron and steel makers, in 1901: 'The Stocks have been certified by the Officials of the Company. The Stocks of Stores have been included in the above Balance Sheet at book values, but these Stocks have been verified at various times during the year by survey' (Bell Brothers Ltd, Auditors Report, 14 March 1901, held in British Steel archives. I am grateful to Prof. Trevor Boyns for this reference).

As with all aspects of the audit there was a wide diversity of practice regarding stock, even within the same firm. One trainee in the 1940s remembering stock audits said:

> these would vary tremendously. In some cases there would be a very casual look at the stock, getting some of their stock books and just checking some of the calculations and test checking some of the prices. But some of them would be very detailed. We would take a section and just take the whole thing apart. We'd find the method whereby prices were established, then we'd do some physical stock checks. We'd do a lot of record ticking on whatever stock records system they had, and that would vary from company to company. It was not really a statutory requirement of an audit, the clients would specify what they wanted us to do.
>
> (Interview with Kenwright)

The early auditors also on occasions attended a client's stock-taking. As Table 6.1 reveals, according to our questionnaire survey only 43 per cent of auditors never attended stock-takes even in the 1920s and 1930s, and a clear majority attended at least sometimes. The procedure, however, was obviously not the rule; only 13 per cent of articled clerks always or often attended stock-taking in the interwar period. An article in 1936 (*Accountant* 11 April 1936: 576) argued a point auditors made many times,

Table 6.1 While I was undertaking my articles/training, as the auditors we attended the clients' stock taking...

	Always (%)	Often (%)	Sometimes (%)	Never (%)	Total respondents	
					(%)	N
Decade qualified						
1920s/1930s	3.6	9.5	44.0	42.9	100	84
1940s	3.8	13.0	47.3	35.9	100	131
1950s	3.1	21.3	42.5	33.1	100	160
1960s	19.2	23.3	38.4	19.2	100	146
1970s	35.4	27.7	29.2	7.7	100	130
1980s	48.3	39.2	12.5	0.0	100	120
1990s	60.1	31.9	5.8	2.2	100	138
Respondent audited mainly...						
Quoted companies	46.4	30.7	16.3	6.6	100	167
SMEs	25.5	27.3	30.3	17.1	100	503
Sole traders and partnerships	5.3	8.5	44.7	41.5	100	93
Size of firm with which respondent qualified						
Top 20	36.0	26.4	24.7	13.0	100	303
Medium	19.8	23.4	34.5	22.3	100	287
Small	18.9	23.4	34.5	23.4	100	306

Source: Postal questionnaire, see Appendix.

that they were not technically qualified to evaluate stock, and must either call in an expert ('a solution rarely resorted to' for financial reasons), qualify their report, or 'accept the verbal or written assurance of the trusted official'. The auditor's lack of qualifications for the role was pungently made in interview by an accountant who was auditing in the 1930s:

> I can remember one particular client was a leather manufacturer and he kept skins in pits. It was a horrible smelly place. I had to go and try to find out how many skins he had got there, and he would just tell me. I couldn't get in and physically count them...I had to ask him to sign a certificate about the stock and that was it. So although we did attend some stock-takes, there often wasn't very much point.
>
> (Interview with Palmer)

Another article in 1938 argued:

> Auditing procedure ordains a less rigorous examination of stock than of any other item in the balance sheet. This is due mainly to the inherent difficulty of verifying such an item, and to the immunity given to the profession in this respect by the well known and much quoted judgement in the *Kingston Cotton Mills* case.
>
> (*Accountant* 2 April 1938: 447)

However, the writer saw a middle way and advocated where possible a testing of the stock by a 'thorough investigation of a selection of items, in company with a responsible official of the audited concern'.

The practice of attending stock-taking increased in the 1950s. By this time a new factor in the situation was the 1939 McKesson and Robbins case in the US which had involved a massive management fraud, based in part on fictitious stocks which the auditors (Price Waterhouse) had not physically checked (Chatfield 1977: 135–7; Cochrane 1979: 178; Baxter 1999: 157–74). As Lee (1988: xviii) has stated:

> There was little auditing beyond the accounting records prior to the 1900s...and there was little attempt made by auditors at the physical verification of assets and liabilities...The McKesson and Robbins case in 1939 in the U. S. changed all that however.

Following quickly on from the case, the American Institute of Accountants reported to their members that 'corroboration of inventory quantities by physical tests should be accepted as normal procedure', and where practicable stock-takes should be attended as 'generally accepted auditing procedure' (*Accountant* 24 June 1939: 851). On top of the American Institute's dictat, in 1941 the Securities and Exchange Commission (the US regulatory body set up in 1934) found Price Waterhouse at fault in the McKesson and Robbins case, and also placed attendance at stock-takes (and the circularisation of debtors) as central to the American auditors' duties (*Accountant* 16 August 1941: 85–6). Interestingly, Montgomery *et al.* (1949: 207–8) thought the observation of inventory taking 'was followed by many public accountants for years' prior to the McKesson and Robbins case.

By the 1950s the attendance at stock-takes was normal practice in the US; but this was not the case in Britain (*Accountant* 12 January 1952: 53). A future head of Arthur Andersen recalled that the American firm attended stock-taking in Britain in the 1960s, and implied that the firm was advanced in this regard compared with their English rivals (Interview with Plaistowe). And this US leadership was confirmed by another retired accountant:

> The Americans went into far greater depth than we did, and even now I don't think we have gone as deep as they do. In 1959–60, I was involved with a take-over of a company in marine caulking...After the take-over I had to meet the auditors of the new company who were shocked that I hadn't done very much on the stock...Then it came out that in America they would have had chemists in. [Then] we came to do far more stock checking, sending chaps down on the final day to check the count, a lot more than we used to in the old days.
>
> (Interview with Jones)

The McKesson and Robbins case in fact had initiated a lively debate in Britain as to whether auditors here should follow the American lead. In favour of stock attendance, one correspondent argued that since auditors test everything else 'there was no reason whatever why a test check of the stock should not form part of the normal audit programme' (*Accountant* 5 July 1941: 5). When another correspondent made the standard objection that the auditor was not competent to value stock, the reply came back that the objector 'will probably find he can count tables, motor cars, or even bags of dried chemicals as well as the next man' (*Accountant* 12 July 1941: 18). In 1949, a lecturer to the ICAEW summer school noted:

> The practice of attending to observe the making of physical tests, now adopted by some auditors, should not, however, be discouraged; in fact this has proved to be useful in many instances...they enable the auditor to be satisfied beyond reasonable doubt that the accounting procedures laid down, including the system of internal control, is in fact faithfully followed in practice.
>
> (*Accountant* 20 August 1949: 198)

Most British opinion however was against attendance. Stanley Dixon (who went on to become the first chartered accountant working in industry to become ICAEW President in 1968–69) in an article in 1950 wrote: 'No auditor, for instance, could physically inspect the stock at the hundreds of branches of the chain stores to be found in almost every city' (*Accountant* 3 June 1950: 627). And another article in 1951 returned to the familiar theme: 'There seems to be widespread fear in this country that, if the American procedure were introduced here, the auditor's attendance at stock-taking might involve him in responsibility for matters requiring a technical knowledge which he cannot possess' (*Accountant* 6 October 1951: 311).

The textbooks tended to toe the party line. Dicksee's 1951 edition remarked on the McKesson and Robbins case and on the US practice of stock-taking attendance, but made no recommendation that this procedure should be followed in Britain (Magee 1951: 166). The 1951 edition of Spicer and Pegler was definitely against the practice, reaffirming that: 'The auditor cannot be expected to verify the existence of each item of stock by actual inspection' (Bigg 1951: 176). The textbook went on to discuss the increase in the US in the observation of the taking of inventory, and noted:

> This view has attracted a certain amount of support in this country, and many auditors do, in fact, carry out some sort of a test check of the physical existence of stock. It is, however, pertinent to question the practical value of such a procedure, having regard to the auditor's unfamiliarity with the diverse types and quantities of articles included in the inventories.
>
> (Ibid.: 178)

As Table 6.1 shows, attendance at stock-taking by auditors was slowly on the increase in Britain down to the 1950s, by when about a quarter of audit trainees did so always or often. But there was still a wide diversity among firms. Many auditors interviewed asserted that physically checking stock or attending stock-taking was common in their firms (Interview with Davies). Colourful stories included those from an accountant who trained with Mellors, Basden & Mellors in the 1940s:

> Before my time, the firm audited Pimms, the drinks people, and they would only allow the senior partner to look at their inventories, to protect Pimms' secret formulas. The lower level [audit] staff were not allowed to see these things. I also remember one boot and shoe whole-saler where I made the mistake of checking the tiny tots shoes on the top shelf, tipping them on the floor and then having to try to put them all back up again in pairs.
>
> (Interview with Hewitt)

A further memory was of:

> my old principal telling me back in the fifties, if I went to a certain place to observe a stock-take don't forget to ask for a ladder. I said, 'What am I going to need a ladder for?' He said, 'You are going to climb up each of those stacks and look down the middle and see if it is empty.'
>
> (Interview with Haddleton)

Another interviewee, as an articled clerk training in the City in the late 1950s, recalled:

> Right from day one I can remember going for physical stock-taking. For January 1st or December 31st, it was regarded as absolutely essential you never went on holiday at that time. And very often you were involved with stock counts at more than one company on the same day. You had a team of people with some going to one place and some going to another and you popped in a day later to see if they had followed it up.
>
> (Interview with Patient)

But our interviews with accountants practicing at the time also confirmed that stock attendance was not the usual practice at many firms in the 1950s and 1960s. A partner at Cork Gully thought: 'We didn't physically attend stock-taking until well into the 1960s' (Interview with Fabes); while another remembered, 'stock attendance started in the middle to late sixties' (Interview with Mordy). One interviewee recalled that in his medium sized firm: 'It wasn't till fairly late in my career that the accountant would be expected to attend a stock-take in person. This came about very much as a result of audit manuals being published in the 1970s' (Interview with

Boothman). In a speech in 1958, Cooper Brothers' Henry Benson said only that 'it will become a routine practice of auditors in the future to watch the physical stock-taking carried out by the company's officials' (*Accountant* 4 October 1958: 418). Benson's own firm were not insisting on the practice since the Coopers manual stated only that the observation of physical stock-takings should normally be carried out annually in the case of all American owned clients, but in the case of other clients it should be done periodically, usually once every three years; with weak clients, annually, or large clients – annually at different locations (Cooper 1966: 134). The second edition of the manual in 1969 was still unclear as to the desired frequency of attendance, and did not make the practice mandatory for their auditors, noting merely that: 'the best method by which the auditor can satisfy himself as to the effectiveness of the application of the client's stock-taking procedures is by observation' (Cooper 1969: 145).

Through the 1950s, however, lecturers at the summer schools or student societies, the trade press, textbooks and the Institute itself swung round towards urging attendance at stock-taking on the English profession. A lecturer in 1957 reported:

> Attendance at the time of physical inventory-taking is becoming more and more common [although] it must be clearly understood that an auditor is not an engineer, a chemist or any other kind of technician nor can he be an expert valuer. All the same, by being present at the physical stock-taking, he gets a general impression of the way the stores are managed and this will help him to form an opinion of the degree of reliability of the stock sheets... another precaution which we adopted was occasionally to take a sample of the liquid in a tank and send it off for analysis to a chemist.
>
> (*Accountant* 2 November 1957: 509)

The 1957, twelfth edition, of de Paula (1957: 126) stated: 'there has been a growing practice for auditors in this country to adopt the American procedures... many, including the writer, are of opinion that all auditors would be well advised to adopt this new practice'. By the 1969 edition, Dicksee claimed that the American view on attendance 'is also the prevailing view of the profession in the United Kingdom' (Waldron 1969: 175).

The textbooks took their cue from the recommendation of the Institute, and stock was an issue on which the professional bodies pushed their members perhaps a little ahead of practice. A speech in 1957 to the Seventh International Congress of Accountants by the then president of the Society of Incorporated Accountants and Auditors argued that: 'best practice does require some steps to be taken to verify by visual means the existence of the stocks listed on the stock sheets wherever this is possible and practicable without technical knowledge to do so' (*Accountant* 21 September 1957: 346). The ICAEW's U2, Statement on Auditing, on 'Stock-in-trade and

Work in Progress', issued in 1962, laid down: 'That the auditor should *in appropriate cases* attend the physical stock-taking by the company's officials to satisfy himself that the stock-taking is properly done and the system of internal check is in effective operation' (*Accountant* 18 May 1963: 645, my italics). Moreover, the first report of the International Study Group (formed in 1966, comprising representatives of the ICAEW, the Scottish and Irish Institutes, and the leading US and Canadian bodies, as an aid to the international harmonisation of accounting practice) found: 'In America, the attendance of the auditor as an observer at physical inventories is virtually mandatory... In the United Kingdom, [it] is not obligatory but it is coming to be recognised as highly desirable (*Accountant*, 27 January 1968: 98–100). Headquarters reinforced their enthusiasm for the practice in 1968, when U2 was amended to read:

> *wherever it is practicable and stock-in-trade and work in progress is a material factor* in the business, the auditors should satisfy themselves as to the effectiveness of the client's stock-taking procedures by observation on a test basis of these procedures whilst the stock-taking is in progress.
> (*Accountant* 19 April 1969: 550, my italics)

A year later, the Council of the ICAEW issued a fresh Statement on Auditing (No. 11) to the effect that: 'In most circumstances' attendance was the best method of stock verification (ibid.).

Interestingly, an ICAEW examination question in the Final Audit paper in 1969 (November, Question 7) suggests that the consensus in the profession was that the practice remained an option for auditors, albeit a highly recommended one; whilst the wording of a question in 1972 (November, Question 7) suggests that in the space of three years attendance at stock-taking had become the norm. Certainly by the 1970s the textbooks were emphatic on the issue. The 1976, fifteenth edition, of de Paula advised that regular attendance at stock-taking 'should now be regarded as an essential feature of an audit' (de Paula and Attwood 1976: 200); and the 1978 edition of Spicer and Pegler (1978: 186) similarly argued that: 'Stock is frequently one of the larger items in a balance sheet and for this reason alone, the auditor should attend stock-taking.'

The growing practice of stock attendance in the 1960s and 1970s is confirmed by Table 6.1. Evidently, while only a quarter of trainees attended always or often in the 1950s, this figure had risen to a little over 40 per cent in the 1960s, and by the 1970s it was almost two-thirds. Interestingly, this increase was almost entirely due to the growth in the numbers who always attended, possibly indicating that the practice was being written into the audit programmes for the larger clients. Viewed another way, a third of trainees in the 1950s never attended stock-taking, while only 8 per cent never did so in the 1970s. By the 1980s attendance had become almost universal; 88 per cent always or often attended, and not a single respondent said they never did so.

And the upward trend continued, if at a slower rate. By the 1990s, 92 per cent of trainees always or often attended their client's stock-taking.

Finally, it must also be noted that, not only because of attendance at stock-taking, stock verification and valuation in general took up an increasing amount of audit time. Chan *et al.*'s (1993: 768) interviews with partners in the Big 6 firms in the early 1990s indicated that with some clients, especially those in high technology industries, the effort spent in auditing inventories could take as much as 25 per cent of audit effort, although this was probably the upper bound among audits generally.

What brought about this increased interest in stock? We will return to the question of the causes of process change in more detail in the concluding chapter but several points which specifically relate to stock can be made here. The Americans clearly lead the way, and US subsidiaries operating in Britain insisted on the practice of attending stock-takes. But there were not that many American firms operating in Britain to have made a crucial difference to audit practice here. Moreover, the American influence was not the decisive factor on British practice since stock attendance was mandatory in the US by 1950, whereas it was not the rule in Britain for two or three decades later. It seems, again, that the British were adopting the measure at their own pace for their own reasons.

One factor was that as part of the growing importance of the taxation on profits, the 1960s saw the Inland Revenue take a much greater interest in the valuation of stock as a major determinant of company profits, which meant that to some extent the auditors had to follow suit (*Accountant* 27 January 1962: 90; Wilson 1995: 202–3). Another factor was possibly the 1967 judgement in the case of Thomas Gerrard & Son Ltd, which found the auditors negligent in not detecting the inflation of stock levels by the company. The judge indicated that standards with regard to stock were now expected to be more stringent than those laid down in the Kingston Cotton Mill judgement (*Accountant* 24 June 1967: 834–5; Waldron 1969: 315). The Gerrard judgement must have reinforced the auditors' growing interest in stock but equally, coming in the late 1960s, could not be said to have initiated it. Finally, further clues as to the reasons for the enhanced importance of stock in the audit come from Table 6.1, which shows that stock-taking attendance was more determined by the size of company audited than the size of audit firm. This seems to argue that since audit clients were growing in size this was a factor in the growth in stock-taking attendance. Yet it is not immediately apparent why stock attendance is a practice more suited to larger rather than smaller clients, and we will return to this issue in the last chapter.

Circularising debtors

As with attending stock-taking, circularising debtors – asking them to confirm in writing their debt to the auditor's client – is not a recent innovation. Various articles in the *Accountant* in the 1890s had argued for circularisation, but the practice was not generally taken up (Chandler and Edwards 1994: 111, 144, 154). Reference to the practice as appropriate in specific investigations for fraud, if not in a routine audit, is also to be found in the 1925 edition of Spicer and Pegler (1925: 569); and to circularise or not to circularise was sporadically hotly debated in the trade press. An article in the 1920s noted:

> Now, it is a recognised practice with professional auditors to circularise debtors for the purpose of verifying the amounts shown by the ledgers to be due, and whilst it may be a fact that certain debtors ignore the request for such information; even so, the procedure provides such a safeguard as cannot lightly be ignored by the auditor.
>
> (*Accountant* 27 November 1926: 738–9)

This assertion provoked a fierce response, exemplified by the correspondent whose objections to the view that the procedure should be considered 'recognised practice' included the point: 'I deal with businesses where the number of accounts runs into thousands. Who bears the costs of circularisation?' (*Accountant* 2 December 1926: 806).

The *Accountant* conceded in an editorial that:

> communication with debtors is useful in the case where dishonest practices have definitely been traced to a member of the client's staff... [but] communications between auditor and debtors are always likely to be regarded as an extraordinary form of audit test.
>
> (*Accountant* 18 December 1926: 853–5)

In 1939, a correspondent asked for advice on the practicalities of circularisation (*Accountant* 8 July 1939: 51). A number of straightforward instructional replies were forthcoming, including helpful standard forms of letters to debtors, but with a *caveat* that the letters might be misinterpreted 'as a sign of financial difficulty and inquiries as to the possibilities of a liquidation [of the audit client] usually follow' (*Accountant* 15 July 1939: 81–2). Others resisted the imposition of more responsibilities onto the auditor, and an editorial in the *Accountant* (14 June 1941: 438–9) observed: 'We repeat our hope that the positive duty of communicating with debtors, as part of an ordinary audit, will never be laid down as an obligation of English auditors.' Another correspondent agreed and pooh-poohed the idea: 'Imagine writing to the "debtors" of the Midland Bank or Imperial Chemical Industries – what a fan mail for the auditor' (*Accountant* 9 August 1941: 77).

Table 6.2, detailing the incidence of the practice based on our questionnaire, shows strikingly similar results to Table 6.1, on attendance at stocktaking, in that of those accountants training in the interwar period half circularised debtors at least sometimes.

Our interviews with accountants revealed the now familiar diversity of experience. A number of respondents discussed how they circularised

Table 6.2 While I was undertaking my articles/training, as the auditors we circularised debtors...

	Always (%)	Often (%)	Sometimes (%)	Never (%)	Total respondents (%)	N
Decade qualified						
1920s/1930s	2.4	3.7	43.9	50.0	100	82
1940s	9.2	10.8	37.7	42.3	100	130
1950s	4.5	15.3	47.1	33.1	100	157
1960s	16.3	17.7	42.2	23.8	100	147
1970s	33.3	22.5	35.7	8.5	100	129
1980s	47.5	30.8	19.2	2.5	100	120
1990s	29.0	42.0	23.9	5.1	100	138
Respondent audited mainly...						
Quoted companies	40.9	27.9	17.7	13.5	100	167
SMEs	18.0	23.9	38.3	19.7	100	411
Sole traders and partnerships	4.2	4.2	45.8	45.8	100	93
Size of firm with which respondent qualified						
Top 20	24.3	30.2	30.2	15.3	100	303
Medium	20.0	17.2	37.2	25.6	100	287
Small	19.6	18.6	35.9	25.8	100	306

Source: Postal questionnaire, see Appendix.

debtors on audits in the 1930s (Interviews with Chapman and Keel); it was how one auditor said she discovered a fraud at the beginning of the Second World War (Interview with Burgess). Others stated they did not undertake the practice in the 1930s (Interviews with Edey and Passmore) or 1940s (Interviews with Ainger and Carter), while an accountant training with a small firm recalling circularising in the late 1940s and early 1950s stated: 'I think we did occasionally, or a section of them [debtors], but I don't think the response was awfully good' (Interview with Muir).

The procedure of circularising debtors then was well understood from the start of the professional audit but was not generally thought necessary. In his 'state of the art' lecture on auditing to the 1951 summer school, Lawson distinguished between a 'positive' confirmation, a request to the addressee to reply whatever the status of his account with the client firm, and a 'negative' confirmation, where a reply was only requested if the addressee disputed the sum involved or denied a debt existed (incidentally, according to the Coopers Manual 1966: 268, the negative method was the one used most extensively in the US). Lawson went on:

Generally the positive method is more satisfactory but it is hardly practicable to adopt this in such businesses as retail stores where there are a
vast number of individual accounts. In this country it is not the general

rule to circularise debtors, though this is done to a limited extent...the 'positive' method cannot be fully effective unless a very high proportion of replies is received. For this reason the system is more effective when applied to businesses where there are relatively small numbers of accounts with large balances such as the accounts of stockbrokers and merchant bankers.

In the case of industrial companies it may be useful to obtain confirmation of some of the larger accounts.

(*Accountant* 6 October 1951: 308–9)

Like attendance at stock-taking the circularisation of debtors was also given a boost by transatlantic events, where, again following the McKesson and Robbins case in 1939, the American Institute of Accountants declared that the practice should be 'generally accepted auditing procedure' (*Accountant* 16 August 1941: 85–6). Whereas in 1934 Montgomery (1934: 152) noted that the practice was the exception rather than the rule, by 1949: 'Confirmation of receivables by direct communication with the debtors has been generally accepted auditing procedure for some years' (Montgomery *et al.* 1949: 152). The British necessarily became subsequently involved since as one ex-senior partner with Price Waterhouse explained, whereas in the 1930s they did not circularise debtors: 'it was a growing thing because we had a lot of work for US companies or their subsidiaries' (Interview with Duncan).

However, other than becoming essential in audits for American companies, the impact in Britain of McKesson and Robbins was not dramatic (*Accountant* 20 May 1967: 658–62). An article in 1958 still stated: 'Postal verification of debtors is not a widespread practice in the United Kingdom, but it is occasionally encountered in large undertakings – particularly those with American affiliations, thanks to Messrs McKesson and Robbins' (*Accountant* 2 August 1958: 132). The writer also noted that in his experience there were problems with the technique. He reported, for example, that due to the failure of the debtors circulated to understand the purpose of the exercise one reply received stated:

'Next time you ask me to check your accounts, please enclose a fee'; and one old lady, to her considerable distress, mistook the verification request for a solicitor's letter, and there was an illiterate who asked the local salesman to sign the form for him...Others ignore the forms completely, but hang on to the reply-paid envelopes until they next have occasion to write to the company on any other matter – possibly months or years later. This deplorable practice appears to be particularly common amongst small farmers.

Despite these problems, as Table 6.2 shows, whereas a half of those respondents training in the interwar period stated they never circularised debtors, only a third replied in this fashion in the 1950s, and less than a quarter by the 1960s, when over a third stated they always or often did so. A significant jump in the practice took place in the 1960s, and as some indication of its growing importance debtor circularisation was first explicitly mentioned in an ICAEW Final Audit examination paper in 1965 (November, Question 5). Again interviews with those auditing at the time confirm the timing of the increase. 'When I was articled we never circularised debtors, but I had to in my first audit with CG [Cork Gully] in the early 1950s. But probably it did not become standard practice until the 1960s' was one response (Interview with Fabes). Another interviewee agreed it 'was not a practice that was seriously taken up until the 1960s' (Interview with Wilde). It was common in one respondent's medium sized City firm in the early 1960s (Interview with Patient), while a Whinney, Smith & Whinney partner thought that: 'It was probably from about the mid-60s that we used to circularise debtors' (Interview with Whinney). At Price Waterhouse by the late 1960s: 'it was a standard practice. In those days we would circularise about 100 debtors on each assignment' (Interview with Carty). According to an article in the *Accountant* (20 May 1967: 658–62) the procedure was seen mainly as an 'effective way of testing internal control systems', which was also the role seen for it in the ICAEW's Statement U7, on the verification of debtor balances by direct communication, issued in 1967. Interestingly, the statement noted only that it 'is an established practice in some countries, and its use in the United Kingdom is increasing' (*Accountant* 17 June 1967: 802).

Unlike a number of auditing techniques Coopers did not lead the way on this issue. A senior partner of the firm recalled of the late 1940s and early 1950s regarding the circularisation of debtors: 'I don't think that was normal at that time. It wasn't a Coopers innovation. I think it was required on doing American audits. I can recall doing it in the fifties, one or two written confirmations of various things' (Interview with Hobson). The Coopers Manual of 1966 merely stated: 'In the United Kingdom, confirmation of receivables by direct communication with the debtors is not usually carried out'. However, it should 'be carried out on all audits emanating from the United States (Cooper 1966: 267–8). No change was made to these instructions in the second edition (1969: 307) of the manual.

The textbooks were also slow to advocate the circularisation of debtors. For example, the 1957 edition of de Paula, which identified the technique as an 'American audit procedure', regretted that:

> Except in cases of suspected fraud, this check is not commonly practised in this country. The writer is of opinion, however, that the profession should seriously consider adopting, as standard audit practice, the direct verification of a proportion of the debtors' balances. It is, without question, the only really effective check upon the total of book debts appearing in a balance sheet.
>
> (de Paula 1957: 60)

In the 1966 edition of de Paula (1966: 58), the technique was described as 'not commonly practised in this country', and the 1976 edition still stated: 'Except in cases of frauds this check is not universally practiced.' That edition asserted however that it was a procedure the British 'are unwise not to adopt, as standard audit practice', and went on to describe the process in some detail (de Paula and Attwood 1976: 207). By the sixteenth, 1982, edition, however, de Paula dealt with the matter far more thoroughly, and model negative and positive confirmation letters were given (de Paula and Attwood 1982: 288–92). The technique was also now fully treated in the 1981 edition of the Coopers manual which stated: 'In the United Kingdom it is common practice to obtain confirmation of debtor balances by direct communication with selected debtors' (Coopers & Lybrand 1981: 289–93).

Table 6.2 confirms the timing of the growth in the practice of obtaining confirmations from client's debtors. Whereas, as we have said, a third of trainees in the 1960s stated that they always or often undertook this task as part of the audit, this figure rose to 56 per cent in the 1970s, and 78 per cent by the 1980s. The numbers never circularising debtors in the 1980s had collapsed to insignificance; down from a half of interwar qualifiers who never did so. Again the application of the practice was highly dependent on the size of the client, and very little on the size of the audit firm. Significantly, however, and unlike any of the other audit techniques on which our respondents were questioned, the use of confirmations actually fell significantly in the 1990s. Only 71 per cent of the 1990s trainees said they circularised debtors always or often, largely due to a big drop from 47 per cent to 29 per cent in those saying they always did this. Firms seemed to be using confirmations less, and were to some extent becoming more selective in their use.

The reasons for this most recent trend are probably to be found in the weaknesses of the procedure frequently noted above. Perhaps the major problem was the poor response rate. Another respondent who qualified with a medium sized London firm in the 1960s told us he: 'always considered those awful routines of circularising debtors to be a total waste of time. The debtors never replied' (Interview with Spens). This weakness was confirmed by the first edition of Woolf (1978b: 177), which stated that: 'Many audit firms use certain external confirmations so extensively that they have developed standardized formats for the purpose...Despite the low response rate (mainly due to computerised records) this is still a common practice.' The one and a half page treatment of the subject is repeated almost word for word in the 1997 edition (Woolf 1997: 200–1). The seventeenth, 1986, edition of de Paula also said: 'It is a potentially powerful technique, its major limitation being that increasing numbers of customers fail to cooperate by responding to confirmation requests' (Attwood and Stein 1986: 217). A further problem was the accuracy of the responses. Hatherly (1980: 126–7) reported an American experiment which deliberately circularised bank customers with incorrect balances and found only 46 per cent detected the error, and a similar 'negative' circular raised only an 18 per cent detection rate.

Its seems clear therefore that reduced response rates in recent years, perhaps exacerbated by cost pressures on business generally, as well as inaccurate responses and complications caused by computerisation, has led to audit firms relying less on the circularisation of debtors. Nonetheless, as Table 6.2 shows, the practice is still always or often carried out by almost three-quarters of audit firms.

Summary

Although even in the nineteenth century with larger clients auditors placed considerable reliance on the balance sheet, the typical bookkeeping audit focused on transactions and largely took the word of management with regard to balance sheet items. Across the Atlantic, by the interwar period, the main audit effort was on the balance sheet together with the client's internal controls. And, although in terms of definition and its importance 'the balance sheet audit' caused confusion in the British profession, the US style focus on the balance sheet increased in Britain after the Second World War. The significant growth in the importance of the verification of assets and liabilities particularly from the 1960s on can be measured by the increased practice of attendance at the client's stock taking and sending out written debtor confirmations, both of which had become the rule by the 1980s. The circularisation of debtors however was a declining practice in the 1990s due to poor and inaccurate responses and the pressures on costs.

7 Computing and the audit

Early accounting machinery

The greatest change in the way professional external company audits were conducted since they began was brought about by the technological revolution embodied in the electronic computer. Interestingly, as with the audit changes discussed so far, there was no overnight transformation since computers themselves were introduced by audit clients slowly over several decades and, moreover, they were preceded by mechanical data processors. One auditor interviewed noted this lack of a complete break with the past: 'Everybody thinks the computer has arrived all of a sudden and revolutionised the thing. Way back before the [Second World] War we had punched card machines – Hollerith, Powers-Samas. You could do much the same operation. It just wasn't so fast' (Interview with Goodwin).

The most basic of these early office machines was the comptometer, which was simply a manually operated mechanical adding machine whose primary advantage was to take the drudgery out of casting, but some machines could also subtract, multiply and divide (*Accountant* 2 February 1924: 177; Campbell-Kelly 1989: 7–8; Jones 1995: 166 and plate 58). The leading make was the American, Burroughs machine, and it was first used widely in Britain in the 1920s on large audits which could justify the cost of the machine and of the (invariably female) operator.

The more advanced data processing machines could store and manipulate data and involved mechanically punching holes in cards, one card representing an individual transaction. The cards were then sorted based on the position of the holes, and the results were then tabulated into printed totals or balances. First invented by Herman Hollerith in America in the 1890s, the two main producers in Britain were the British Tabulating Machine Company, who marketed the Hollerith machine, and Powers-Samas (*Accountant* 12 September 1925: 403). The machines could handle complex data and were ideal for processing information from invoices, statements, wages or stock records, and were often called ledger-posting machines after their major function. Even in 1925 they were capable of quickly producing a trial balance (*Accountant* 12 September 1925: 405–6; Bigg and Perrins, 1971: chap. XI). The punch card machines were still a novelty in Britain in the 1920s, but were widely adopted subsequently (the Midland was the first bank, for example, to mechanise its accounts in 1929; *Accountant* 2 February 1929: 133; 7 August 1937: 198). The Hollerith and Powers-Samas machines were described in Dicksee in 1928 (1928: 56), and a question on the difficulties posed for auditors by mechanised accounting first appeared in the ICAEW's Final Audit paper of 1937 (May, Question 3). An article in the late 1930s noted that: 'To-day, so fast is mechanisation growing, that mechanised accounts are becoming the rule rather than the exception' (*Accountant* 20 March 1937: 416). Spicer and Pegler's, 1951, tenth edition devoted some time to: 'the systems of accounting by the use of machines, which are being utilised to an increasing extent in all but the smallest businesses' (Bigg 1951: 112). These mechanical tabulating machines continually improved in performance, and were indeed only ousted as the most common office data processors by the electronic computer in the 1970s (Campbell Kelly 1989: chaps 1–9).

Early on, many in the profession realised that mechanical tabulating machines could be of advantage to the auditor. The benefits were set out in an article in the late 1930s. Machinery, it was noted, had already meant for auditing that: 'more time is now spent on the final accounts in an attempt to interpret their meaning. This means that less time must be spent on the preliminary audit and this has been allowed by mechanisation'; 'it is a farce and waste of time – as well as an insult to your intelligence – to check every-thing' (*Accountant* 20 March 1937: 418–19). The 1951 edition of Dicksee noted that the machines 'produce ledger accounts with automatic accuracy, once the original transactions have been correctly punched on the cards' (Magee 1951: 65–6). Spicer and Pegler in 1951 also argued that machines: 'make it unnecessary for the auditor to check in detail the individual postings, although a certain amount of test-checking may be desirable (Bigg 1951: 114). Or, as an article in 1952 put it: 'an auditor may reasonably reduce his tests of 'posting' pure and simple whilst extending, or not reduc-ing, his scrutiny of original documents and data, and of ledger accounts' (*Accountant* 22 November 1952: 613).

Yet evidence that auditors were floundering somewhat even with these early mechanical accounting machines comes from a review of Dicksee's, 1945, sixteenth edition, where the textbook's editor is criticised for only devoting two paragraphs to mechanisation, in view

> of the difficulties arising and the necessary changes in audit practice when the auditor discovers that a considerable part of the records are prepared on typewriters, or may even be represented by a drawer full of cards with holes punched in them in various positions. The lack of guidance as to the responsibility of the auditor in such cases is one of the outstanding deficiencies in professional literature at the present time and calls for discussion and considered judgement.
>
> (*Accountant* 8 December 1945: 286)

The main problem was the one which was to be accentuated with the widespread use of the computer two or three decades later, namely the difficulty in following what was to become known as the audit trail (the facility to trace the paperwork for individual transactions through each bookkeeping stage). An article by Coulson, a partner in Barton, Mayhew & Co, argued that machinery

> tends to the taking in of information in large quantities and the production of an output in summarised, analysed and sub-summarised form, with little or no visible link between the documents in which the original information was contained and those in which the final output appears.
>
> (*Accountant* 22 November 1952: 611)

De Paula (1957: 24) noted that the machines meant 'a number of bookkeeping operations have been dispensed with, such as writing up sales and bought day books and the keeping of bought ledgers'. Dicksee, in 1951, thought that: 'While the use of mechanical methods does not in any way alter the principles of auditing, their application may in some respects become more difficult.' For example, where invoice figures were posted straight to the ledgers, and journals were not used, the auditor must vouch the original document with the entry in the ledger, and tracing ledger entries back to invoices could be difficult. However, 'many ledger posting appliances include automatic safeguards' against wrongful posting; and they should also, Dicksee advised, be tested by sampling (Magee 1951: 65–6).

In fact, the solution to the problems had been to some extent set out in an article in the *Accountant* (20 March 1937: 418–19) in the late 1930s, which advocated that the system of internal control could be checked by, for example, seeing that different clerks performed separate operations, in the manner of manual bookkeeping. The auditor should then have the effectiveness and reliability of the machine demonstrated to him, and prove the machine by seeing how it handled test calculations and deliberate mistakes. This was the procedure, of course, remarkably similar to that worked out for coping with the electronic computer thirty years later.

The coming of computers

Crude electronic computers (often called in the early years electronic data processing systems or EDPs) were commercially available by the mid-1950s. Stoneman (1976: 20) estimated there were 12 computers installed in the UK by 1954 and 306 by 1960. Estimates of numbers, however, vary. One source has the UK with 389 computers in 1962, third in world usage behind the 9,337 in the US and 472 in Germany (McRae 1964: 42). Stoneman (1976: 20) puts the 1962 figure for the UK at 620. Whatever the figure, however, it was apparently safe for a practitioner to conclude in 1961 that: 'The amount of genuine experience of auditing large and medium-sized computers in this country can, therefore, be fairly stated to be insignificant' (*Accountant* 14 January 1961: 321). And a future partner who trained with Price Waterhouse in the mid-1960s recalled: 'When I started auditing there weren't any IT [information technology] systems' (Interview with Brindle). In the 1960s, however, the installation of computers was growing rapidly (Kelly 1987: 9). Price Waterhouse, for example, calculated that their clients had 60 computers between them in 1963 and 275 four years later (Jones 1995: 294). Stoneman (1976: 183) estimated that there were 1,424 computers operating in the UK by 1965; 5,470 in 1970, and 10,983 by 1975.

It was only in the late 1960s, therefore, that computers became a really significant factor in auditing, and this can be gauged by activity in the Institute. A PW partner described going on the first course on computers put on by the ICAEW in 1963: 'it was a little bit like an army course I went on about navigation by astronomy where we never went out at night; at the Brighton course on computers, we never saw computers, we just talked about computers' (Interview with Hewitt). By the late 1960s, however, the Institute was better organised to meet the challenge. In 1969, it organised the first residential course to deal specifically with the problems of auditing computer systems, and also issued two separate Statements on Auditing: U14, 'Internal Control in a Computer-based Accounting System', and U15, 'The Audit of Computer-based Accounting Systems' (*Accountant* 25 January 1969; 11 December 1969: 806–12; 18 December 1969: 855–64). Published as a booklet in 1970, the latter discussed the controls members should expect to find in clients' systems, and gave a checklist for assessing clients' computer applications (*Accountant* 26 March 1970: 471). The first question on electronic computers and auditing appeared in the 1967 Final Audit paper (November, Question 3).

Our interviews leave no doubt that the late 1960s was when computers became a major factor in the audit. As the auditor quoted above remembered:

> Things began to happen in the 1968 or 1970 period, when Price Waterhouse started doing its own internal accounts on computer. I think that inventories and debtors were being dealt with by computers in the late sixties in the Courtauld subsidiaries, and by the mid-seventies quite a number of family companies had moved along in that direction.
>
> (Interview with Hewitt)

A future senior partner with KPMG also reported: 'my first encounter with IT was in 1968–9, on the first computer audit course I went on organised by Peats. It was with systems known as CRAM, which were notoriously unreliable' (Interview with Sharman).

The computers of the 1960s and 1970s were the large and relatively expensive mainframe computers, which only sizeable organisations could afford or justify the outlay on. They were inflexible and cumbersome in that data to begin with was usually still input via punched cards, and they were also unreliable and by today's standards relatively weak. For example, an early audit package in the 1970s was designed to run on computers with memories as small as 14 K (McRae 1977: 120), or millions of times smaller than a present day desktop computer. The next major landmark in computing technology was the rapid innovation in the 1980s of personal computers or PCs, which probably had an impact on accounting and auditing greater than the mainframes. Developed simultaneously by the American companies, Apple and IBM in 1979–80, as is well known, the PCs were, as the name suggested, small enough to sit on everyone's desktop. They rapidly achieved storage and calculating power greater than the largest early mainframes, and by 2000 over 500 million had been sold world-wide (Carr 1985: 36; *Observer* 12 August 2001). Crucially from an auditing point of view the PC brought computing within range of the smallest client.

What impact then did the arrival of the mainframe and then the PC have on the audit? The accounting profession was relatively quickly onto the benefits and problems that computers were likely to bring, given their vastly greater power compared to the previous mechanical accounting machines. A prescient writer in 1952 argued that: 'I do not think anyone today can prophesy how fast progress will be nor to what extreme ends these almost human machines will be developed' (*Accountant* 23 February 1952: 191). Indeed, he felt accountants should take a leading role in the introduction of the new technology. 'One of the most important factors in speeding up development is that members of the profession should know and understand the capabilities of accounting by electronics and should educate the business world in it'. An editorial in the *Accountant* in 1956 was also spot-on: 'the electronic computer will probably be the greatest influence on accountancy since the invention of double-entry book-keeping in the fifteenth century' (*Accountant* 3 November 1956: 449). De Paula also (1957: 25) noted:

> These computers differ from the forms of mechanisation hitherto encountered chiefly in their power and speed, which enable them to carry through accounting processes right from the initial recording of a transaction to its ultimate impact on all relevant accounts – without many intermediate records, calculations, and entries which are necessary in more conventional accounting processes. This must inevitably present a completely new set of problems for the auditor ... much of the auditor's checking of mathematical accuracy may become superfluous. On the other hand the auditor's duty of vouching the correctness of entries at the first moment of their presentation to the accounting process might increase.

But de Paula in 1957 talked rightly in terms of future developments, and ignored computers in the rest of the textbook.

Many of our interviewees were upbeat regarding computers since their innovation meant apparently there was now no need to worry about arithmetical accuracy. One accountant explained that with computers: 'one assumes usually that the books tend to balance themselves. The columns do tend to add up' (Interview with Shaw). 'Used intelligently the computer can serve to make the audit less tedious' was how another respondent put it (Interview with Kemp). It also: 'enabled accounting systems to be set out and consistently applied' (Interview with Hardcastle).

Another initial reaction to computers from auditors was fright. An article in the *Accountant* in 1961 voiced the view that: 'Most auditors are terrified at the thought of a computer' (*Accountant* 14 January 1961: 40). McRae in 1964 found: 'The general feeling seems to be that the computer is an additional cross to be borne by an already overburdened profession' and that a client installing a computer 'invariably caused a great deal of consternation, and in a few cases something verging on panic' (McRae 1964: 159). One interviewee agreed and found them 'absolutely terrifying: a) because I didn't understand computers; and b) because nobody seemed to know how to audit a computer' (Interview with Middleton). Initial meetings with the machines could be traumatic:

> I can remember we would do a complete audit on a business in east London which supplied chemicals. They had huge stock, very small items but there were millions of them, and they maintained this computer and we had to try and audit the thing.
>
> (Interview with Sharman)

Another accountant working in a small Sheffield practice in the 1970s admitted:

> I wasn't computer literate at first but became knowledgeable about the advantages and limitations of computers through experience. We still prepared the accounts for all of those firms. One firm in particular which had computerised their records was in great difficulty as a consequence and I had to devise a manual back-up system which was successful in restoring order to chaos.
>
> (Interview with Burdett)

Auditing 'around' the computer

The main debate within the profession was whether to audit 'through' or 'around' the computer. Auditing 'through' the computer required the auditor to acquire computing competence enough to be able to question themselves the quality of the programming and processing undertaken by the machine. The audit 'around' or 'black box' approach to computer auditing 'effectively relied on verifying input and output and on reconciling the two...without investigating too closely the actual processing patterns of the computer' (Gwilliam 1987: 308).

To begin with, probably out of a necessity born of ignorance, audit 'around' was the preferred procedure. A partner with Whinney, Smith & Whinney talking of the 1960s confirmed:

> I think we were really auditing around the computer rather than through it. I don't think I ever audited through a computer...looking at the construction of the programme. If you look at the input and say, well what comes out at the other end is what you expect to come out, then you are really auditing around it rather than through it. Although, towards the end of my time [1987] we were running enquiry programmes in clients' computers.
>
> (Interview with Whinney)

A PW partner in the 1960s and 1970s also reported: 'for a long time people audited around the computer...You took what went in and what came out again and built the bridge between the two' (Interview with Carter).

The main problem with computerised accounts from the auditor's point of view was that, to a far greater extent than with the previous accounting machinery, the auditor lost the audit trail. However, auditing 'around' the computer was assisted in the early years by the auditor retaining the ability to follow the audit trail to a certain degree by asking for print-outs from the computer at the various accounting stages. In that way, the computer could simply be viewed as the instrument by which conventional records were produced, and auditing 'around' remained possible (Woolf 1978b: 334). Another interviewee articulated this view, remembering auditing a grocery company around 1960 and:

> going into an air conditioned room full of machines with huge tape reels that contained all their customer accounts and ledgers. I remember being amazed and a bit overawed by the whole thing but I realised that it was only like a large ledger and contained the same information, although you could flick through the pages of a ledger and audit it as you went. But once I realised that you could get these machines to print you off a ledger if necessary and check them the way we always had, I began to realise that they were just a tool.
>
> (Interview with Chapman)

The professional wisdom in the early years of computers was, therefore, that the auditor could successfully audit 'around' the computer. The process was set out in an article in 1958:

> Adequate checks can be devised without the auditor having to become a skilled programmer. It would be unwise in any event for an auditor to rely on such programming knowledge as he can acquire without also employing the other checks which should be available.
>
> (*Accountant* 6 September 1958: 281)

In the course of an address in 1960 to chartered accountants and British Computer Society members A. W. Howitt also followed this line, stating that: 'it is not essential that any auditor should be able to programme or operate *any* computer';

> an auditor is entitled to insist upon certain checks being provided in the system, and can ask for certain facilities to be provided. Rigid control of the input data is necessary. The main problem is 'Where does the auditor stop?' He must take a certain amount on trust. It is in arriving at decisions on these points that he exercises his auditor's skill.
>
> (*Accountant* 16 July 1960: 92; 14 January 1961: 40)

Howitt remarked that one well known firm faced with one of their first audits of a computer installation sent their staff on a programming course. This was unnecessary, he argued. Auditors did not need to be programmers since, as accounting firms were the leading consultants when it came to computer installations, they had the in-house expertise if they required it.

Some textbooks also supported auditing 'around'. The 1969 last edition of Dicksee did its best to ignore computers, and unabashedly stated that throughout the book it still 'assumes that the records are maintained on "traditional" lines, by means of books, whether hand-written or prepared by accounting machines working on double-entry principles' (Waldron 1969: 370). The textbook gave only a two and a half page treatment of the computer and clearly assumed the auditor would audit 'around' the machine. It did include a suggested ICQ for EDP systems, and stated that

> auditing such a system then involves the auditor in following what we frequently call the audit trail, i.e. a testing journey through the system along the route of a specific example to see if the system does work correctly...it is unlikely that the programming knowledge of the auditor will always be high enough to enable him to test the machine program except by putting information in and observing the results...It is, therefore, recommended that if any doubts arise...the auditor should call on the services of an expert.
>
> (Waldron 1969: 372)

It was also generally realised that auditing 'around' put increased reliance on the client's internal controls. As one auditor put it, 'if you've got computerised systems, you're testing the effectiveness of the system, and you are relying to a great extent on that' (Interview with Niddrie). As early as 1957, an article noted that the growth in the use of computers was going to go hand in glove with the systems approach:

> It is already clear that conventional auditing techniques, already the subject of earnest re-examination in the audit of large businesses, will be of little use in the audit of an electronic data processing system. ...The

external auditor will have to base his opinion, to a great extent, on his examination of the system of internal control and on his evaluation of the work performed by the internal auditor.

(*Accountant* 13 July 1957: 34)

Another article in 1958 also remarked:

Normally an organisation which converts to E.D.P. will be large enough to arrange a sound system of internal check.... Unless the system of E.D.P. is well-designed and incorporates an adequate internal check the auditor's task may prove to be one of extreme difficulty.

(*Accountant* 12 July 1958: 47)

A PW partner thought computers themselves:

meant that you had to think more about controls because it is not quite so easy to put ticks on a computer. So control over computers has pushed us yet more into thinking about the way that things are managed by the client, with us coming along to see whether that client has got a system that is likely to hold up.

(Interview with Stacy)

Another interviewee summed up this change:

It means that you swing around from transactions to systems. The more that goes into a black box and the more mystery and mystique that there is the more you require expertise to be satisfied that the system is working...I don't think computers have changed the fundamental recording of transactions or the fundamental judgement that is required at the end of the process when you tot the figures up and you look at the final set of accounts.

(Interview with Patient)

Testing the system of course was also important where the auditor worked 'through' the computer.

Auditing 'through' the computer

The audit 'around' the computer was increasingly challenged by advocates of the audit 'through' approach; and they seemed to gain the upper hand in the late 1960s. McRae was a strong supporter of auditing 'through' the computer and frowned on the black box approach. He noted that the 'popular argument in favour of ignoring the computer when auditing an EDP system is that, in the past, the auditor has seldom attempted to look into the mechanics of punched card machinery'. McRae's answer was that auditors *should* have looked into the punched card system, and that anyway the electronic computer was 'a different kind of beast' (McRae 1964: 160). He thought that it was unfeasible for the auditor to check the writing of the programs themselves, but advocated the use of sample jobs to test the system, audit in depth using statistical sampling by taking say a random 1 per cent sample and following it through the system using an audit trail of printouts, and also using the computer with the auditor writing a programme himself to extract exceptional items (McRae 1964: 175–81; McRae 1977: 107). McRae, went on to make the most vigorous case up to that date for the detailed audit of computer programs themselves when he wrote in 1966:

> Auditors must learn to systematize the audit of the suit of computer programs in much the same way as they have systematized other aspects of auditing. The program is an integral part of the system and in auditing any highly-automated procedure it is necessary, as all authorities agree, to concentrate on checking the system. Although this does not mean that input-output can be ignored entirely.
>
> (*Accountant* 25 June 1966: 807)

Audit 'through' also found a strong supporter in Anthony Pinkney, the Cooper Brothers partner and author of, *The Audit Approach to Computers*, published in 1966 (*Accountant* 7 May 1966: 561). Pinkney challenged the prevailing wisdom that the auditor did not need expert knowledge of computers:

> I do not believe that an auditor can make an intelligent assessment of a computer system unless: a) he is an expert in conventional systems of internal control, i.e. he must be a good auditor; b) he has the ability to superimpose on this a reasonable technical knowledge of computers. To obtain this knowledge, I think he must have some experience in the writing of computer programmes so that he can appreciate both the capabilities and limitations of the computer.
>
> (Ibid. 14 May 1966: 600)

Pinkney (1966: 14) argued that there were three audit approaches to computers. First, was the view that there was no need to 'review the system of control within the data processing department and normal audit techniques can be used without alteration'. Second, the auditor could insist on the maintenance of an audit trail by means of print-outs, combined with an examination of controls inside and outside the computing department; and third, since the insistence on an audit trail was increasingly unreasonable, came the testing of controls and the use of special audit techniques inside the computer itself. Favouring the third option, Pinkney (1966: chaps 3–6) set out the procedures which were to become standard for auditing 'through'. They included: the use of ICQs for evaluating the internal controls; procedural tests of the system, for example, tracing transactions from input data to final print out where the audit trail could still be followed; while for the future he correctly prophesied greater use of test-packs – running dummy transactions through the system to see if it worked properly; and finally the use of the auditor's own programs to assist in balance sheet verification.

The first edition of the Coopers manual came out in the same year as Pinkney's book, and since he was a Coopers man he is likely to have had an input into the manual. The manual considered the application of computers in audit procedures in a separate chapter and at some length (Cooper 1966: 220–39). It stated that one 'approach is for the auditor to ignore the existence of the computer', but it quickly dismissed this as a possibility and instead set out a detailed ICQ appropriate for computer departments, which included making an informed assessment that the correct computer programmes were being used, and then using test packs 'still at an early stage of development' to run through the system to test it worked properly (ibid.: 230, 234). By the 1969 second edition of the Coopers manual, in a greatly extended chapter on the subject, talk of ignoring the computer had disappeared, and now the auditor was instructed to use computer programs, either written himself or general purpose programs,

> to read and examine files of data at high speed, thereby providing access to information otherwise not easily reviewed... [and] carry out audit tests that have not previously been practicable or to reduce the time spent on such tests in a conventional system.
>
> (Cooper 1969: 270)

The two main methods of auditing 'through' the computer, namely test packs and running the auditor's own programmes in the client's computer, were probably American innovations. Running tests through the computer had possibly been first recommended in an article in the American, *Journal of Accountancy*, in 1963, written by Boni, the former chairman of the American Institute's committee on electronic accounting. He advocated auditors using what he called 'test decks' on the computer:

> Accountants... should devise in readable computer language, a list of (dummy) transactions for the computer to process. The list should be selected to test the handling of transactions and the effect on end results, covering every possible means of breaking down a programme... To know the built-in checks the auditor should be involved in the initial steps of systems design, and he must probe the system in depth.
>
> (*Accountant* 19 October 1963: 491–2)

Also by the mid-1960s in the US computer programs were available especially written to meet the auditor's requirements for auditing 'through' the computer:

> Programs can be written to select items randomly in cases where the auditor wishes a test to include a representative cross-section of transactions in an account with a printout of the selected items in the form necessary for the auditor's purpose.
>
> (*Accountant* 3 September 1966: 288)

These computer audit packages were introduced in Britain from the late 1960s; and at the ICAEW's residential course in 1969 Deloittes', J.B. Faris, outlined the design of an audit programme of procedural tests constructed from the answers drawn from an ICQ (*Accountant* 25 January 1969). One of our interviewees, a partner with Peats, talked of the growing use of computer audit programs: 'in the early seventies we started to use what we called System K970, it was the first computer-based auditing package' (Interview with Sharman). McRae (1977: 119) listed five (two British and three American) programmes available, including ASK 360 developed by Thomson McLintock and Whinney Murray, apparently

> the first programme in Britain, developed by auditors for auditors. It was designed to examine most magnetic files maintained on an I.B.M. system 360–370 computer ... to extract from the files the exact information the auditor needs to examine in detail, in order to tackle the audit.

Another, AUDITAPE, was developed in the US by Haskins & Sells: 'It incorporates one unique feature and that is the detailed statistical sampling programme incorporated in the package. This uses the monetary unit sampling technique which makes the selection of an item proportionate to its value' (ibid.: 124). One drawback with these systems was that they had to be designed for particular makes of computer. For example, AUDITFIND developed by ICL's software branch in conjunction with Peat Marwick Mitchell, Price Waterhouse and Thomson McLintock, would only run on ICL machines (ibid.: 120).

In passing, the rise of auditing 'through' computers had implications for the organisation of the audit firms' workforce. An article in 1969, argued that computers would

> entail a big change in the education and training for the auditing profession. Accountants will require a much greater knowledge of mathematics and of computer techniques than ever before. The profession in Britain is slowly moving round to a recognition of this need, although the professional examinations still only cover these subjects at an elementary level.
>
> (*Accountant* 8 November 1969: 619)

As one PW partner in the 1970s and 1980s put it:

> all firms have had debates about whether you have separate computer
> audit sections and you send that team out and they look at the com-
> puter because the audit staff don't know an awful lot about computers,
> to saying that: 'No, we don't want specialist computer staff, everybody
> ought to be able to handle it'. And it's swung back and forth. As we
> have got further into the computer age, so it's less and less common to
> have computer auditors who are just computer boffins. Generally
> speaking now everybody has to know about computers and computers
> are part of their training. It's only very fancy situations where you have
> got, say, big databases accessed from different points where you need
> to get an expert to come along and work alongside you.
>
> (Interview with Stacy)

In contrast to the 1969 edition of Dicksee, other British textbooks were
reasonably well abreast of computing developments, and indeed were usually
advocates of audit 'through'. Already the 1966 edition of de Paula devoted
a chapter to computer auditing, and noted that: 'In the early days of
computers it was, perhaps, natural that auditors should try to mitigate their
lack of knowledge and experience of computers by auditing "round the
computer"...there may still be occasions when this approach is used'
(de Paula 1966: 67–8). Now, however,

> the auditor must face up realistically to the problem of obtaining the
> necessary knowledge of computers and their method of operation...
> he has got to acquire sufficient knowledge and experience to be able
> to recognize a well-organized computer system and to diagnose the
> symptoms of inefficiency and ineffectiveness.

'This is not to suggest that it is necessary for him [the auditor] to become
an expert, or even a competent programmer but he must learn the rudi-
ments of the science'. De Paula gave a model ICQ for computer systems,
and advocated, for example, the vouching of error printouts and the use of
test packs or 'simulated transactions on the appropriate media which can
be used to test all the programme controls' (ibid.: 80). However, the use of
test packs were 'not used as much as might be expected' because of their
tendency to alter the client's own data (ibid.: 81). By the 1976 edition of
de Paula and Attwood (1976: chap. 6), and the 1978 edition of Spicer and
Pegler (Waldron 1978: 420–1), detailed schedules for auditing 'through' the
computer were fully set out, and the approach had clearly won out, at least
in theory. In practice too Crump found in 1981 that, of 64 accounting firms
who replied to his survey, 22 said they had little or no involvement with
computers, and of the rest (which contained 12 out of the top 15 firms)
85 per cent said they checked that the system specification for each

application was complete and in line with the client's documentation; 61 per cent used test packs; 56 per cent used their own audit programs, and 72 per cent used off-the-shelf packages (*Accountancy* October 1981: 68).

According to Gwilliam (1987: 308–9), auditing 'through' the computer became the preferred method because of advances in the computer's capabilities, and because of the increase in the auditor's responsibility for the detection of internal control weaknesses and fraud, following well known computer based frauds, such as the Equity Funding case in the US which came to light in 1973 (see also Woolf 1978b: 353–65). Woolf (ibid.: 341) also argued, like Gwilliam, that audit 'around' was made unacceptable by the improvements in computer technology. The increase in computer speeds in the 1970s had meant that comprehensive print-outs slowed the process up and therefore became uneconomic. Reliance was now placed by management upon the 'exception reporting' principle, whereby only accounts which required action, for example, debtors whose credit limit had been exceeded, ever saw the light of day. In this circumstance the audit trail was lost and auditing through the computer became necessary. This should be accomplished, according to Woolf, by the use of ICQs to test the systems, test packs and computer audit software (computer-assisted audit techniques or CAATs), such as Deloittes' AUDITAPE program, to interrogate the client's computer. Interestingly, Woolf's chapter on the computer in his 1997 edition differed very little from his first, 1978, edition (Woolf 1997: chap. 11).

However, there are strong suggestions that audit 'through' did not triumph completely in practice. Pound found that although auditing 'around' was 'not highly regarded' in 1978, that was not to say it was not frequently still used in practice (Gwilliam 1987: 308). Moreover, the 1978 first edition of Woolf (1978b: 296–7) gave the profession something of a broadside on the issue:

> Despite the enormity of the transformation which electronic technology has wrought in data processing methods...there is still a dangerous and widespread reluctance on the part of the profession to acknowledge that the presence of computers does radically alter
>
> (a) the way in which accounting data is recorded;
> (b) the way in which such recording must be controlled and authenticated;
> (c) the training needs and attitudes of the staff responsible, at both management and technical levels; and
> (d) the way in which the process and its results must be audited.
>
> This attitude of burying one's head in the sand, of hoping that if auditors continue to ignore computers they (i.e. the computers, not the auditors!) may go away...[is] an attitude regrettably reflected in the majority of auditing texts...we are in fact faced by something totally different from anything previously encountered.

Indeed, in 1980 it was still possible for Hatherly (1980) to write a book on the audit evidence process without mentioning computers once, and an article in 1982 by Gwilliam and Macve, based on talks to researchers in eight international accounting firms, repeated Woolf's scepticism of computer auditing in practice, and concluded that still: 'Some firms consider...a perfectly satisfactory audit can be carried out "around" the computer' (*Accountancy* November 1982: 121).

There were solid reasons for the lack of wholesale acceptance of audit 'through'. Turley and Cooper (1991: 37) found that firms who did audit 'through' the computer encountered poor computer literacy among the audit firms' partners and staff, and their inability to cope had caused problems. In 1987, Gwilliam reported that the use of CAATs was

> limited to the reduction of audit costs by means of extracting data from client files, e.g. for statistical sampling purposes, and for checking calculations and totals...[and] field auditors are not usually sufficiently competent to run such programs successfully and may be over reliant on assistance from either the client's staff or the firm's own computer auditing specialists.
>
> (Gwilliam 1987: 311)

Also, regarding the use of dummy test data, Gwilliam (ibid.: 313) reported their 'widespread application has been reduced by certain limitations'; it was apparently time consuming, required considerable expertise, may corrupt the client's real data, or be subverted by the client's staff anyway. Finally, both Barras and Swann (1984: 24) and Turley and Cooper (1991: 37) found great problems arising from the incompatibility between the systems of the client and those of the auditor.

Turley and Cooper (1991: 37) reported that despite massive investment in the 1980s by audit firms in PCs 'real progress had been slow'. There had been 'many "false dawns" and unfulfilled predictions'. Computers had often only meant mechanising existing tasks not developing new techniques, such as the automation of the whole audit process. Computers were often used less for audit techniques, such as the interrogation of the client's files for identification of exceptions, or for sample size calculations, or sample selection, and more for administrative tasks such as word processing, or accounting tasks such as striking trial balances (ibid.: 38). Higson (1997: 205) also confirmed that even in the 1990s audit 'around' was very much alive and kicking:

> very few firms were working on the development of expert systems. Computer-assisted audit techniques (CAATs) tended to be used only on the very largest clients when there was no other practical way of conducting the audit; however the use of sophisticated CAATs seems to be fairly limited...the general tendency appears to be to audit the

controls around the computer system and then analyse the output, rather than auditing through the computer.

Manson *et al.* (1997: 255) also found that the widespread interest among firms in audit automation (such as in planning the audit, calculation of sample sizes, the recording of time spent on audit tasks or the drafting of management letters) only dated from the early 1990s, but again IT tended to be used more for the administration of the audit than the audit process itself.

Nonetheless whether the auditors went around or through them computers represent the biggest single change in the professional audit since it began, and the most profound change in the labour process of the auditor, particularly the trainee at the sharp end of the work. Their work changed from ticking the entries in a ledger to clicking a computer mouse. Moreover, our interviews conducted in the late 1990s with the leaders of the major audit firms, perhaps for obvious reasons, were decidedly upbeat about the computer based audit. Arithmetical accuracy was not now an issue, and the timing of the audit had been transformed. As one current leader of the profession put it:

> These days accounting systems are right because the IT systems...are so accurate. Not only that but they are very reliable and totally consistent and work on time. In the old days you never knew quite when the accounts were going to come out. Now, the first run will be produced at 8:45am Tuesday 14th July and then it will be on the screen. Bang, it will be right: it will add up. So that changes very much the way in which you audit and those systems and their implementation are what you concentrate on. Also, because of IT systems you can audit at any time...Because the systems are continuously producing accurate numbers the importance of year-end numbers is far less.
>
> (Interview with Brindle)

Another of our interviewees related how the auditor's computer now worked closely with the client's system:

> Technically, since the early eighties, we've had direct access into clients' own computer systems. We now live in their systems, auditing. Our people from locations around the world validate information and transmit it over the same network to us, using the client's system. The increasing ability to download information from your client's system onto your system and then manipulate it to do any sort of testing that you want to is very cost effective.
>
> (Interview with Sharman)

The concept of working papers has apparently in many cases become a misnomer. As another contemporary leader said: 'it is not just computers replacing the working paper files; our [audit] programmes are designed with the aid of a computer, within a computer. So you now have tailored programmes for the client' (Interview with Scicluna).

Computers and the audit in the future

Interestingly, some leaders interviewed in the late 1990s sketched revolutionary computer-led change in the future, whereby companies would supply continuously updated accounting data, and the year-end audit would be a thing of the past. As the head of Price Waterhouse explained, company accounts will be: 'all on the computer screen via some form of net which will continue to be audited as you go along. And that's not very far away.' (Interview with Brindle). At KPMG: 'it is quite feasible that in the next 15 years, historical audit will be replaced by contemporaneous audit... we will be doing audits as the reports are written. We've invested a huge amount in researching this, $50 to 60 million, this year' (Interview with Sharman). At Coopers the view was:

> The capacity of IT to deliver information has totally transformed auditing. The Institute and the Stock Exchange give awards every year for the best annual report, but whether we will have this celebration of historical data in five years time, I don't know. The real users of this data want it very fast and the technology is there... There are a lot of people in my profession who are working on it and the investment in technology to provide the assurance necessary with real-time systems is the next stage.
>
> (Interview with Lainé)

At Arthur Andersen the future role of the auditor had also been mapped out:

> We are moving towards an era when companies will have public databases of most of the financial information that investors require. The question that investors will want answered is 'How reliable is that database? Who is looking at the controls over it? Who is testing and sampling it?'
>
> (Interview with Currie)

This brave new world has not however come to pass at the time of writing.

Summary

Although they had their precursors in mechanical data processors which came in the 1920s, the coming of electronic computers in the 1960s represented the biggest change in the way the audit was conducted since the start of the professional audit. The job literally went from ticking entries in ledgers in the 1960s to, by the 1990s, clicking the mouse on a PC. At first, largely out of ignorance, the auditors tried to audit 'around' the computer, paying attention only to the input and output of the machines or attempting to follow the audit trail with printouts. In the 1970s however this procedure became less tenable as machines became faster and more powerful and auditors had to come to terms with auditing 'through' the computer, or using test packs to run dummy data through the system and introducing the auditor's own software to interrogate the computer – so-called 'computer-assisted audit techniques'. However, many problems remained, including the lack of skill of the audit staff and the incompatibility of the client's and the auditor's systems; and although many leading auditors sketched a future of continuous and contemporaneous electronic auditing in fact even auditing 'around' the computer is still not a thing of the past.

8 Risk, materiality and analytical review

The retreat from the systems approach which, as we discussed in Chapter 5, Turley and Cooper (1991) and Higson (1997) thought they had discovered in the 1980s and 1990s, was linked, they argued, to a corresponding rise of the audit techniques which involved the assessment of risk, the concept of materiality and an analytical review of the evidence. However, the historian must be at his most cautious when discussing these concepts or techniques since, unlike for example vouching, testing or attendance at stock-taking, they involve little or no physically verifiable activity. They are approaches to the audit activity and are possibly, it might be argued, merely a state of mind, or even a form of words – perhaps a *post hoc* justification for doing less audit testing. This was indeed apparently the view of a leading auditor, one of Higson's interviewees, who thought 'the whole thing is about reducing substantive testing – justifiably' (Higson 1997: 210).

The concepts of risk, materiality and analytical review are closely related but they are treated (relatively) separately here in the interests of clarity.

Risk assessment

In America, the concepts of risk and materiality in auditing, which had not explicitly appeared in the 1934 edition, were firmly established at least by the seventh edition of *Montgomery's Auditing* in 1949. The textbook noted how: 'In the performance of field work the auditor must keep in mind the elements of materiality and relative risk. The exercise of due care implies greater attention to the more important items in the financial statements than to those of less importance' (Montgomery *et al.* 1949: 13). 'If a total is composed of a large number of small items there is less risk of material error than when the total is composed of a few large items' (ibid.: 45). By the 1957 edition, Montgomery (Lenhart and Defliese 1957: 50) was arguing that:

> the financial soundness of a business has a bearing on the degree of risk the auditor may safely assume . . . the newly organised business struggling for a foothold, or the established business fallen on hard times, may

endeavour to postpone write-offs, adopt less conservative accounting policies, and conceal pledging of assets and creation of liabilities.

Of course, again, even in Britain the idea that some clients and some areas of the client's business carried a greater risk of things going wrong, and therefore should attract greater audit attention, was as old as auditing itself. If not given the precise term, even in those early days audits were often planned on the basis of inherent risk. This is implicit in Pixley's oft quoted principle, enunciated in the 1880s, that: 'the auditor must be entirely guided by his experience as to what he can take for granted, in fact, anything he does take for granted is at his own peril' (quoted in Chandler and Edwards 1994: 155). Awareness of risk as a factor was discussed by respondents to our interviews and the postal questionnaire. For example, one respondent wrote of his firm's method of sampling in the early 1950s as: 'Non-statistical, based on appraisal of risk, value and volume, together with evaluation of internal controls.'

But the early awareness of risk was nothing like the full-blown auditing concept it was to become. Risk was probably beginning to be established as a more conscious focus of the British audit in the 1970s. In Sherwood's article in 1972 he discussed using questionnaires to ascertain the risks or weaknesses in the client's system, and of designing tests in the light of materiality (*Accountancy* April 1972: 18–20; October 1973: 17–22). Lee (1972: 168) too noted: 'The less confidence he [the auditor] has about the system, etc. the greater will be the degree of risk he will be undertaking by not verifying every transaction, entry or record.' Yet, still these uses of the word did not imbue 'risk' with the weight of functional meaning it later acquired, and none of the textbooks of the seventies, Waldron 1978, de Paula and Attwood in 1976, nor Woolf's first edition in 1978, mention risk as a factor in the audit. Innes *et al.* (1981: 12) talk of the scrutiny of 'high risk items' but it was not in anyway central to the audit. Hatherly (1980: 30–1), in his book on the audit evidence process, discussed risk briefly in the context of its inverse relationship with the levels of materiality and in sampling, but did not analyse the different types of risk, and it was certainly not the focus of the audit process.

Risk assessment as a fully fledged concept was a creature of the 1980s. Even in America, the 1975 edition of Montgomery (Defliese *et al.* 1975) did not place any more emphasis on risk than previous editions, but the 1985 edition stated that in the whole audit strategy: 'The auditor's assessment of overall audit risk is of primary importance' (Sullivan *et al.* 1985: 203). The textbook analysed the different types of risk (discussed in the section on analytical review below) and offered mathematical formulae for calculating overall risk (ibid.: 226–40).

The British were not far behind if at all. According to Higson (1997: 206): 'Most firms moved towards a risk-based approach in the late 1980s'; but it was probably earlier than that. The first ICAEW examination question explicitly dealing with areas of risk appeared as early as the 1981 Final Audit paper (December, Question 1). Indeed, the various editions of Woolf's booklet, *Current Auditing Developments*, which discussed topical auditing issues for the benefit of examination students, probably precisely dates the rise of risk as an audit 'technique'. The first edition, published in 1978, contained no mention of the concept, while the third edition in 1982 had a section devoted to:

> Risk-based auditing...the phrase recently coined to cover the present search for an audit approach which reconciles the apparently irreconcilable objectives of (a) minimising professional risk, while (b) guaranteeing full fee recovery on every assignment. The risk-based approach is therefore designed to avoid over-auditing in low complexity (and hence low risk) situations, and under-auditing in high complexity situations respectively.
>
> (Woolf 1982: 93)

Woolf offered the popular but none too scientific, '80/20' rule, which asserted that 80 per cent of the auditor's work contained only 20 per cent of the risk of things going wrong. On this basis audit firms apparently allocated their lower grade and cheaper staff to the routine work, leaving the 'partners and others on high charge-out rates to concentrate on the judgemental areas which conversely account for 80 per cent of audit risk...and form the basis of most litigious matter' (ibid.: 93). Auditing then, according to Woolf, focused on error prone areas and high value items chosen on the basis of some level of materiality determined by '(a) the auditor's assessment of overall reasonableness (based on analytical review of the draft accounts), and (b) his assessment of the internal controls in force' (ibid.: 93).

The notion of risk very rapidly assumed popularity as an important component in the British audit in the 1980s, and interviews with the leaders of the top firms in the late 1990s emphasised the weight put on the concept and the heavy burden it carried in the overall audit methodology. For example, the head of Arthur Andersen went as far as to say: 'all the business now is about risk assessment' (Interview with Currie).

In its full flowering the risk based audit directed work at areas which were perceived as having the greatest risk of three types of error: first, those inherent to the nature of the client; second, the likelihood that the client's system of internal controls would not detect error; and third, the possibility that the audit, by means of substantive tests of detail and analytical review, would not detect those errors missed by the internal control system (Turley and Cooper 1991: 16; Manson 1997: 235). According to Manson (1997: 237) it is the first type, inherent risk, or judging the clients and the market they operate in, which distinguished it from existing procedures: 'The risk-based approach can be seen as an extension of the systems-based audit. The main difference between the two approaches is that the risk-based approach specifically recognises and requires the auditor to assess inherent risk.'

Manson (ibid.: 237) recognised though that 'there is often an interrelationship between inherent risk and control risk'.

The emphasis on risk went together of necessity with a greater emphasis on planning the audit. This planning was over and above that in the audit programme, and was embodied in an 'audit planning memorandum' drawn up by the audit senior. The memorandum had elements of strategic planning, involving the use of the concepts of risk and materiality, audit work planning, time scheduling and personnel planning (Humphrey and Moizer 1990: 225). As one manager put it: 'Good planning removes the potential for cock-ups.' A PW partner reported that they 'have placed a great deal of emphasis on planning an audit. So before you actually start the work, you decided what are the risk areas, and what could go wrong. Then you decide how you can tackle them, and what audit tests are necessary. Also, what items are unlikely to go wrong, and therefore the work can be reduced in those areas' (Interview with Carty).

Attempts were also made to use statistics to assess risk. Deloitte, Haskins & Sells were apparently using a statistically based risk model, also used by a number of other firms, in 1982 (Gwilliam 1987: 190). Leaders of the major audit firms asserted an almost scientific basis to risk assessment. A partner at Peats thought the technique was now 'very, very sophisticated' (Interview with Sharman). Gwilliam (1987: 10), however, was unimpressed with the statistical methods of assessing risk, and concluded:

> it is unlikely that, other than in exceptional circumstances, any real credence can be placed upon the results, in strict quantitative terms, of the models as currently used. It is also true that actual users of the quantitative models, i.e. the field auditors, appear to have a relatively limited grasp of the underlying concepts.

Manson (1997: 251) noted ten years later: 'it is unlikely that any of the more sophisticated mathematical modelling associated with risk discussed in academic journals...will find general acceptance in audit practice'.

Most risk assessment was left to the auditor's judgement, rather than any more objective criteria. Even in America Montgomery (Defliese *et al.* 1990: 189) had retreated from the position of its 1985 edition which had attempted mathematically to calculate risk, stating:

> it may not be practicable to objectively quantify certain components of audit risk because of the large number of variables affecting them and the subjective nature of many of those variables. Accordingly, many auditors do not attempt to assign specific values to risk factors.

In Britain, of the 21 firms surveyed by Turley and Cooper (1991: 61), 15 included risk in their audit methodologies, but only four applied a mathematical formula for its assessment; others used descriptive models, or simply recognised the general concept with the assessment of risk left to the individual auditor's judgement. Indeed, the lack of formality was often seen as a virtue of risk assessment. Humphrey and Moizer (1990: 225) found among audit managers that:

> In discussing the judgemental nature of the audit process, a theme common to all interviews was that the flexibility of audit work had increased in recent years. This was seen to be as a result of the introduction of risk-based audit approaches. The use of standardised forms and questionnaires was stated to have been reduced in several firms and whilst some managers spoke of a tendency to follow what was done last year, the emphasis was much reduced.

Yet again, of course, it should be noted that judgement is what auditors have always used, if perhaps in a less explicit way. So, as we discussed earlier, there is room for scepticism as to whether the vogue for risk assessment represents a change in audit technique as such.

What brought about this emphasis on risk in the contemporary audit? Manson (1997: 234–5) argued that the risk-based approach came in first 'to curb increases in fee levels' combined with 'maintaining or indeed improving the quality of audit work'. This supports Humphrey and Moizer (1990: 229) who found that audit managers thought risk analysis had been introduced for two reasons. First, 'as a way of enhancing the effectiveness of the audit in detecting material errors'; getting away from the formal form-filling procedural approach, and more towards 'understanding the business'. The second reason was the pressure on fees requiring the audit methodologies to become more efficient. Quotes from the practitioners Humphrey and Moizer (ibid.: 230) interviewed included the views that: 'As the market place becomes more competitive, we have got to do cheaper audits, do them quicker'; and 'the pressure on time caused by fees has forced people into sitting down at the outset and thinking about what extra things they can cut out without affecting audit quality'. Our interviews also emphasised the commercial reasons for the change. The PW partner, quoted earlier, said that the purpose of directing audits to areas of greatest risk was 'to make your ultimate fee commercially sensible to the client' (Interview with Carty). Another respondent put a slightly different slant on the matter arguing that:

> the move towards risk-based audits which is very much in vogue at the moment, is all designed to make the audit more meaningful, to reduce the tedium and to add value to the audit for the client, because I think it's fair to say at the moment the vast majority of clients feel that the audit is something that is imposed upon them by statute. They regard it as a financial burden and they suffer it, they don't want it.
>
> (Interview with Kemp)

Materiality

As with risk, informally auditors had been using the underlying principles of materiality from earliest times. In America Montgomery (1934: 28) argued in the 1930s that: 'So long, therefore, as small errors in calculations, extensions, etc. do not, relatively speaking, actually affect the balance sheet or earnings, time should not be wasted on such adjustment'. And the term 'materiality' was being used explicitly in the US in the 1940s; that is: 'if the effect of the client's practice is not material in relation to the figures shown in the financial statements, there is usually no need for an exception in the auditor's report' (Montgomery *et al.* 1949: 68).

Of course we noted in Chapter 4 that British auditors from an early date were in the habit of using stratified testing or giving more attention to the largest items in the accounts, which meant they were implicitly employing the materiality (and risk) concept. Moreover, Taylor and Perry's (1931: 9) textbook, for example, noted that test checking of large businesses could be 'confined to more important matters'. The first published usage of the term 'material' in the English accounting context, however, came in an early ICAEW Recommendation in the 1940s, which (advocating uniformity in the treatment of accounting principles from one year to the next) stated: 'any change of a material nature, such as a variation in the basis of stock valuation or in the method of providing for depreciation or taxation, should be disclosed if its effect distorts the results' (Bigg 1951: 285). Also the eighth schedule of the 1948 Companies Act, regarding the classification of items in the accounts, stated: 'where the amount of any class is not material, it may be included under the same heading as some other class' (ibid.: 286). Interviews with auditors working in the 1950s also reveal that the concept of materiality was in use explicitly by that date. An interviewee described his first job on the Unilever audit after moving from Spicer and Pegler to Coopers in 1958:

> There was a fairly senior manager above me and that was so different. I used to keep on going in to say: 'Look I've found a mistake of principle'. And he would say, 'How much is involved?'. And I'd say: 'Seven or eight thousand pounds'. 'Not material!'
>
> (Interview with Denza)

Materiality as an explicit auditing concept, therefore, preceded that of risk, but in the 1960s its use seems to have accelerated. The Coopers manual of 1966 used the phrase 'material variations' regarding accounting figures, and gave the firm's auditors the instruction that 'excessive time should not be spent on items which are unimportant' (Cooper 1966: 32). In 1968, the ICAEW Council's statement on the 'Interpretation of "Material" in Relation to Accounts' was published (*Accountant* 27 July 1968: 116–17), and a number of articles on the issue also appeared in the *Accountant* around that time. One contributed by an American CPA discussed the research that the Americans were conducting to establish criteria for levels of materiality (ibid. 12 October 1968: 477–8).

But although the concept was known its practical application seems to have been patchy. The notion of materiality passed the 1969 edition of Dicksee (Waldron 1969) by, and although the concept is briefly mentioned in the fifteenth, 1976, edition of de Paula, in the context of the evaluation of the materiality of weaknesses in the control system, the term is not defined (de Paula and Attwood 1976: 59). Not until the sixteenth edition of Spicer and Pegler, in 1978, does a British textbook do this: 'a matter is material if its non-disclosure, mis-statement or omission would be likely to distort the view given by the accounts' (Waldron 1978: 233). It is probably safe to say, therefore, that although it must have been implicit in the auditor's work from the first, and its currency increased in the 1960s and 1970s, the establishment of materiality as an explicit audit technique does not come fully into its own until the 1980s, along with risk and analytical review.

The key issue with regard to materiality was how to determine, given the huge variation in the size and nature of the clients, at what monetary level an error became material in any particular set of accounts. Spicer and Pegler in 1978 offered no guidance, but the later editions of Woolf indicated that firms took a base, usually total turnover (or gross assets in the case of a bank; some firms took profits), and produced tables of a range of turnovers and then gave the percentage figure within each range at which an error would be considered material; the larger the turnover the smaller the percentage. For example, a client with a turnover of £50,000 might have a materiality limit of 4 per cent or £2,000; one with a turnover of £5 million would take 1 per cent or £50,000 as being material (Woolf 1997: 169).

The extent to which firms applied such formulae in practice however was again variable. Lee found that out of 21 firms in the UK in 1984, seven had no materiality guidelines, and of the rest only 10 provided specific quantified criteria for application in practice (Gwilliam 1987: 224). Also, for those using formulae the materiality limits could be adjusted; for example downward if in the view of the auditor the assessment of the internal controls and the analytical review suggested weaknesses (Woolf 1997: 171). Indeed, what set the percentages in the first place was, according to Woolf (ibid.: 168), 'unavoidably a matter for the audit partner's judgement'. As the Audit Practices Board's, Statement of Auditing Standards on materiality in 1995 made clear: 'Materiality is a subjective issue' (ibid.: 168). And how the materiality limits were arrived at was apparently a mystery to the grass roots auditors. 'Don't ask me how we arrive at 3 per cent of turnover as an overall materiality figure. It is a statistical figure provided by the audit manual' was how one audit manager replied to Humphrey and Moizer (1990: 227). Lee found that the consensus among practitioners was that materiality was 'a matter of expert judgment of circumstances' (quoted in Higson 1987: 116). As with risk, Turley and Cooper (1991: 71) reported that: 'Almost universally, considerable emphasis is placed on the role of judgement in the determination of individual materiality levels.'

Analytical review

Again, alongside risk and materiality the Americans apparently led the way with the concept of analytical review. Montgomery (1934: 477–8) was suggesting in the 1930s that: 'The verification of the income account can hardly extend beyond tests and scrutiny which consists largely of analyses and comparisons with prior periods.' By 1949, Montgomery *et al.* (1949: 34) was arguing that: 'A review of comparative figures, actual and budgeted, ratios, and trends assists the auditor in planning his audit examination.' And in 1950, a list of auditing methods drawn up by the American Institute of Accountants included 'analysis and review' (Myers 1985: 53). Little had changed with regard to the concept in Montgomery's eighth, 1957, edition, (Lenhart and Defliese 1957) but according to the ninth, 1975, edition, (Defliese *et al.* 1975) analytical reviews now played a prominent part in the American audit, and the appropriate review for each aspect of the audit is extensively discussed in the textbook. The importance of analytical review in America at least predates that of risk.

In Britain the formal use of analysis came later but of course, as with the two concepts dealt with earlier, analytical review, one definition of which was an 'assessment of whether the figures in the accounts make sense' (Gwilliam 1987: 419), has been a function of the process since the beginning of the professional audit. The good auditors from the first took notice of whether the accounting figures overall made sense. The Kingston Cotton Mill case indicates that auditors in the 1890s looked at changes in the gross profit percentage and the stock/turnover ratio of their clients for signs of irregularities in the accounts (Chandler 1996: 22). Patrick, a practising Scotch accountant, writing at the turn of the century thought: 'the principal should devote his best energies to the scrutiny of results and of general principles' (Brown 1968: 321). Auditors at that time would also compare the reported figures with the previous year's results. It was common practice for railway accounts to give the previous year's results alongside the current figures for comparison. The Midland's accounts contained this feature as early as 1860 (Midland Railway, half-yearly account, 30 June 1860). By 1935, 62 per cent of our sample of quoted companies had adopted this procedure, and including in the accounts comparisons with the previous year became compulsory under the 1948 Companies Act (Arnold and Matthews 2002: 8).

A leading PW partner who trained in the 1950s indicated his firm were using their working papers for the purposes of analytical review then, and emphasised that:

> Today's audit involves a lot of analytical review, understanding what is in the balance sheet, what's in the debtors, what's in the work in

progress. Reviewing it and looking for the soft spots, using your judgement and so on. That process would be very similar today to what it was when I started. What is more sophisticated today is risk assessment.

(Interview with Stacy)

Coopers had systematised the analytical approach by the 1960s, since another interviewee reported that the firm in that period:

began to be more interested as to why certain things had happened; why the figures turned out the way they did. They invented the term 'performance indicator', which I think now is used pretty well throughout the profession and the business world. We decided to home in on performance indicators, and we got very strong on it and issued all sorts of technical circulars around the firm. We were then beginning to try to really understand what the figures meant.

(Interview with Livesey)

The Coopers manual indicated the firm were computing data such as gross profit as a percentage of turnover or the ratios of debtors or stock to turnover, and looking for 'any special circumstances explaining material variations in these figures' (Coopers 1966: 19).

British auditors, or the best of them, had, then, always analysed the client's results to some extent. The textbooks, however, were quiet on the issue until the 1970s. Even then they did not use the term 'analytical review' explicitly, as they were doing across the Atlantic, and described little more than the auditor's well established review role. In 1971, the casebook on auditing procedures published by the ICAEW put virtually the whole burden of audit work on the client's control systems with apparently a minimum of verification if these were found to be sound. However, they did suggest 'a review of the final accounts' at the end of the audit, described as:

a review in the light of all the circumstances, on the basis of judgment and common sense, of the accounting principles applied, the validity of the figures and the method of presentation of them...one method which is worth using is a comparison of this year's figure with the last year's and enquiry into any significant changes. The auditor should also bear in mind the country's economic climate in reviewing the profit figure: the reason why profits have slumped in a year of boom may reveal some unusual item of fraud.

(Bird 1971: 15)

The fifteenth edition of de Paula and Attwood (1976: 211) discussed a profit and loss account review, regarding which they said procedures in Britain 'are not well disciplined and often fall short of the standards applied for instance in North America'. The auditor is urged by de Paula:

> to stand back from these [audit] routines and assess the information he is given with critical objectivity...test management's explanations of any unusual features therein by comparison with the previous period and the forecast out-turn for the period under review.

The 1978 edition of Spicer and Pegler stated that the audit programme would include, for example, comparing the gross rate of profit with the previous year and explaining any material changes (Waldron 1978: 444). Yet the first edition of Woolf merely notes:

> Although it is possible to attempt to 'formalize' the informal through the usual media of programmes, checklists and other documentation... none of these rigid frameworks can substitute for the sixth sense which the skilled auditor gains from many years of experience in analysing the accounts of a wide variety of business concerns...Audit work on the final accounts involves a good deal more than the direct or indirect verification of specific assets and liabilities. It is equally important that the accounts, in themselves, should be seen by the auditor to 'make sense'.
>
> (1978b: 173, 212)

Only in later editions of Woolf (1997: 215) did the actual term 'analytical review' come into use.

The vogue for the formal use of analytical review as a consciously specified technique in its fully worked out form came in in Britain relatively rapidly in a matter of a few years, and can be dated (as with risk assessment) to the late 1970s, early 1980s, by when the concept was common currency. The first explicit use in Britain of the term 'analytical review' was found in an article in 1979 on audit evidence. The writers used the phrase to refer to evidence gained from: 'Comparison with previous years, analysis of trends and ratios and of external factors affecting the business' (*Accountancy* September 1979: 120). By 1980, Hatherly (1980: 35–9), in his book on audit evidence, gives a more or less full exposition of the technique, including the gathering of data from the wider economy, the client's industry and competitors, the application of regression analysis and the use of the review 'in determining the scope of detailed tests'. Gwilliam (1987: 13) reported that by 1982 accounting 'firms generally are heavily committed to analytical review as an integral part of the audit, from initial planning through to completion'. The spread of computing also assisted analytical review calculations (Higson 1987: 269). McRae (1982: 36–41) studied the audit manuals of five large firms in that period and found the audit procedures were basically similar: first, analytical review; second, procedural (i.e. systems) evaluation via sampling in depth and compliance sampling; third, substantive testing; and finally the evaluation of the results.

In the mid 1980s, Higson (1987: 307) detected in interviews with the partners of the leading firms that, as well as an overall rapid growth in its use, there was a trend towards using the analytical review in the planning stage as well as just an end of audit check. The 1995 Audit Practices Board's, Statement on Auditing Standards (SAS) on 'Analytical procedures' stressed the importance of applying the procedures at the planning as well as overall review stages, and ran through the procedures used in practice, which were: a comparison of the current year results, budgets and forecasts with the previous year; comparisons with competitors; the comparison of ratios, for example, turnover in relation to doubtful debt provision; the use of management accounts. Any apparent distortions and inconsistencies should, the SAS suggested, be followed through (Woolf 1997: 219–21). Analytical review should also be used in conjunction with, and not as a substitute for, substantive testing.

As with a number of other audit concepts we have previously discussed, to some extent there is a lack of precision in the use of the term, and certainly there was a variety of different procedures involved in analytical review in practice. As Gwilliam explained:

> The term analytical review is wide ranging in nature and encompasses a variety of audit procedures including at one end of the spectrum 'eyeballing' financial statements for reasonableness as a final audit check, and, at the other, the use of sophisticated quantitative techniques at an early stage of the audit so as to incorporate the knowledge gained thereby into the design of substantive testing plans. ...the relatively informal procedure is commonplace on virtually all audits, whilst the use of more quantitative methods is much less frequent.
>
> (1987: 272)

These quantitative methods were predictive models which used regression analysis; that is, taking data from previous years to predict what the current year's figures should be, identifying variances and unexpected change, and thereby assessing the likelihood of error. In the late 1970s, for example, Deloittes apparently used the STAR in-house model, which used step-wise regression analysis developed by the US firm, Haskins & Sells, introduced in 1971. STAR was also linked in with the use of statistical sampling, and it was claimed to have been used 30,000 times in worldwide audit engagements (McRae 1982: 160; Gwilliam 1987: 273; Higson 1987: 105).

However, regression analysis would seem to have been little used. Gwilliam (1987: 13) found that: 'When it comes to using formal procedures (in particular multiple regression models) the [audit] firms are generally less enthusiastic'. By the mid-1980s 'slow progress' was being made (ibid.: 419–20). Analysis was

> usually simplistic 'reasonableness' tests based on comparison with previous year figures or, on occasion, information about other similar

firms. The development of more sophisticated models...has not led to their widespread audit application. The reasons for this are varied but appear to include: the difficulties of constructing satisfactory predictive models for individual firms; the difficulties of identifying when variances need investigation; the lack of suitable data on which to base such models; and lack of familiarity with, and confidence in, such techniques amongst audit personnel.

(Gwilliam 1987: 13)

Only one firm had a model that could be described as in general use, while 'in the great majority of audits subjective judgements (based on a variety of sources of evidence) have to be made' (ibid.: 193). Moreover, in their 1989 textbook, Gray and Manson (1989: 256) place most emphasis on the use of ratios and deal with regression analysis in only three lines; while Woolf in his 1997 edition ignores it completely as does the 1995 SAS. Gwilliam (1987: 13) thought regression analysis was used more in the US, yet Montgomery's eleventh, 1990, edition made no mention of it (Defliese *et al.* 1990).

Indeed, it is clear that analytical review in practice was always a highly subjective exercise (Higson 1987: 306). Writing in the mid-1990s, Davis (1996: 6), a partner with Coopers & Lybrand, thought that analytical review, the third stage of his historical model of audit approaches (after the verification of transactions and the systems approach), had given way to the fourth stage or 'investigatory audit'. To Davis this involved: 'audit people making judgements about people', since: 'The whites of their eyes test is worth hundreds of words in an audit programme.' Higson (1997: 201, 208) also claimed in the 1990s to have found a switch among auditors to concentrating analysis on the control environment, a 'top down approach...how managers manage the business'; or 'the audit of motivations'. On the other hand Manson (1997: 240) summed up the situation as follows:

> Analytical review procedures are considered one of the least costly forms of testing to perform but there is some evidence that auditors do not consider them particularly effective and therefore tend to rely more on tests of detail to provide them with the necessary assurance.

Summary

Around 1980 auditors adopted a number of new 'techniques'. They began in a formal way to assess the risk involved in an audit in terms of the inherent characteristics of the client, the risk that the client's internal procedures would not pick up any problems and the risk that the auditor's own work would not detect weaknesses in the client's system. More audit effort would then be directed to the perceived weak areas. A second concept that gained currency in the 1980s was materiality, in that audit effort was only directed at items of sufficient value to significantly affect the accounts. Finally, also around 1980 auditors began to formally use analytical review to plan the audit work and review the results. The analysis involved, among other things, comparisons with the client's previous years' results, or those of other companies in the same business, and an analysis of key ratios between accounting items. Again, if unexpected items were found more audit work was indicated. However, it must be noted that all three of these techniques had been implicitly used by auditors since the dawn of the professional audit, and although they all had objective statistical techniques attached to them these were little used, and the age-old auditor's tool – subjective judgement – was mainly relied on in practice.

9 Conclusion

Audit changes since Victorian times

In the previous chapters we have detailed the transformation in British auditing techniques which have taken place over more than a century. In fact, these changes are largely confined to the last 40 years, since prior to the 1960s the professional audit had altered little since its inception. This bookkeeping audit had a number of characteristic features. Although called an audit the work in Britain typically also involved making up the client's books. This was the case to the extent that for most clients the main purpose of the audit was for the auditors, to a greater or lesser degree, to do their annual accounting. This so-called audit work could involve making up the books entirely (often from incomplete records), closing off the ledgers, casting the columns of figures and striking a trial balance, drawing up the profit and loss account and balance sheet, and then signing them off as having been audited. The auditor could be required to pick up the job at any stage in this process: at what stage being largely determined by the competence of the client's own accounting staff. Relatively little of the auditor's work in Britain, even down to the 1960s, was what they called 'pure audit'; that is, being handed a completed set of accounts, the accuracy of which they then checked; or in other words the theoretical and indeed statutory meaning of an audit.

Of course, even if the auditors were also making up the books, the auditing or checking process still had to be conducted as they went along. The typical bookkeeping audit then consisted of armies of articled clerks vouching transactions, checking postings from one ledger to another and casting columns of figures. Frequently in smaller clients all the transactions of a client were checked; long and tedious work. Although it is impossible to give an accurate break down, most man-hours in the bookkeeping audit were spent in this checking of transactions and postings in the day books and ledgers, far less time and effort was spent on verifying the assets and liabilities in the balance sheet. With regard to the balance sheet, key documents might be checked, but often, as was the case with stock valuations, the word of management would frequently be taken as sufficient evidence.

Moreover, so mechanical was the process that little thought went into planning the audit, often no written programme was followed, or working papers kept, and little attention was paid to the nature of the client's business.

The bookkeeping audit was transformed from the 1960s on and this is clearly illustrated in Figure 9.1 which graphs a crudely averaged proportion of respondents to our postal questionnaire who replied that they used the six techniques, detailed in Tables 3.1–6.2, always or often during their training. As can be seen, there is a clear break in trend, in that change up to the 1950s was slow, while after that the take-up of our selected audit methods was relatively rapid and sustained down to the 1980s. In the 1950s, less than 15 per cent of firms used our selected techniques, always or often, whereas by the 1980s the proportion was almost three-quarters. Interestingly, the graph is given an 'S' shape, familiar to students of techno-logical change (Griliches 1957: 502), by a falling off in the rate of diffusion of the techniques in the 1990s. This could be due to the usual explana-tion that the situations in which the techniques would be most viable were becoming exhausted; or that commercial or other factors were now changing, thus making the continued innovation of the techniques less appropriate. We will return to this issue later.

The major changes from the 1960s can be summarised as follows: first, the practice of also doing the books and drawing up the client's accounts declined. The auditors of public companies (and most private companies of any size) were not now drawing up their client's accounts and this is also graphed in Figure 9.1. Although auditors might still have had a major say

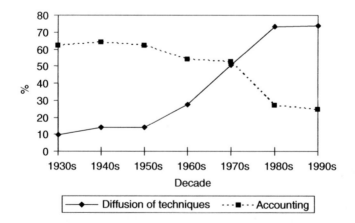

Figure 9.1 Diffusion of audit techniques and provision of accounting services.

Sources and notes: The diffusion of techniques is an average of the percentage of com-bined responses to Tables 3.1–6.2 who replied that they always or often used a technique in each decade. Accounting is the percentage of responses in Table 2.2 who replied that they frequently drew up the accounts of their clients in each decade.

in the form and presentation of their clients' accounts, for the most part audits were 'pure' audits. Second, from the 1960s the checking of accounting transactions was proportionately much reduced. Even for the smallest clients the auditor did not check all the records, as was common in the bookkeeping audit. The auditor now increasingly had to resort to testing a small sample, which was often chosen, but less often assessed, using relatively sophisticated statistical techniques, so called substantive testing. Third, audit evidence was also likely to come not from checking actual transactions but from testing the client's own internal system for controlling their business, so called compliance testing; often involving the use of questionnaires and the construction of flow charts. Fourth, the focus of the audit investigation shifted from the profit and loss account to the balance sheet; from verifying transactions to verifying assets and liabilities. As a result, the auditor was more likely to be involved, for example, in attending stock-taking and obtaining third party confirmations. Fifth, more work, particularly the testing of transactions and systems, was now likely to be conducted in interim audits during the financial year, leaving the year end for balance sheet verifications. Sixth, more planning went into an audit and the relatively strict following of audit programmes and manuals became the norm. Seventh, the amount of permanent documentation associated with the audit increased, including in addition to programmes, questionnaires and flow charts, the formal accumulation of working papers. Eighth, just as the bookkeeping audit was closely associated with an unofficial aspect of the audit, namely accountancy, so the audit acquired a role also outside its statutory function concerned with helping the client improve their business, and embodied in the management letter. Finally, by far the biggest change in the audit process was the use of computers, which became an essential aspect of almost every audit, not excluding the smallest of jobs.

Some of these changes made since the 1960s came under question or were superseded themselves in the 1980s. Auditors, since around 1980 spent more time before and after the gathering of audit evidence in understanding the client's business and the markets they operate in, and in assessing the company's comparative performance, in a process known as analytical review. As part of and simultaneously with this relative innovation, the areas of focus in the audit were increasingly determined by a technique known as risk assessment and guided by the associated concept of materiality. Most audit investigation now became directed at areas of the client's business deemed most prone to major error which was significant to the bottom line of the accounts. These post 1980s changes have usually been at the expense of the amount of testing of the actual accounting records and systems, and in the process auditors have been encouraged to use subjective judgement rather than follow rigid prescribed processes or objective techniques such as regression analysis.

As part of our postal questionnaire, respondents were asked to write in what they thought had been the most significant changes in the process of auditing during the time-span of their careers. The wording of the replies was analysed, and the results are reported in Tables 9.1 and 9.2. Interestingly, as Table 9.1 shows, about a third of the words or phrases used in the answers were not strictly concerned with the audit process or how the audit is conducted, but mentioned: accounting issues, audit regulation and a collection of other matters including for example the growth of competition among accounting firms, fee pressure and litigation.

Of the two-thirds of words and phrases used directly relevant to the audit process, as can be seen from Table 9.2, by far the most frequently cited

Table 9.1 Most significant changes in the process of auditing during career (all replies)

	N	%
Process	910	65.5
Regulation	226	16.2
Other	254	18.3
Total	1,390	100

Source: Postal questionnaire, see Appendix.

Table 9.2 Most significant changes in the process of auditing during career (process only)

	Pre-1960 (%)	Post-1980 (%)	Total (%)
Computers	20.8	19.2	19.4
Internal controls and audit	10.7	13.4	11.3
Documentation, programmes etc.	9.6	5.5	9.8
Statistics	7.0	3.1	5.9
Balance sheet verification	9.0	2.4	5.7
Analytical review	2.0	10.3	5.2
Risk	0.3	11.6	5.0
Detailed checking (less)	6.2	2.7	4.8
Testing (less)	1.1	9.2	4.6
Sampling	5.4	1.7	4.0
Ticking (less)	3.1	4.5	3.3
Management letters and client relations	6.8	3.4	2.9
Business focus	1.7	1.7	1.8
Technical (more)	1.7	0.7	1.7
Judgement	1.4	1.0	1.7
Materiality	1.1	1.0	1.7
Accounting (less)	1.7	0.0	0.9
Other	10.4	8.6	10.5
	100	100	100.2
N	355	292	901

Source: Postal questionnaire, see Appendix.

change was computers; almost twice as often as the next most important – internal controls. The rest of the factors mentioned also contain few or no surprises, although when the replies are divided into those from the pre-1960 and post-1980 qualifiers, the earlier group emphasised the growing importance of documentation, the balance sheet and statistics more than the later group, who in turn highlighted risk, analytical review and the reduction in testing. Also worthy of note is that, for both vintages of auditor and in total, if responses mentioning the decline in 'detailed checking', 'testing' and 'ticking' are amalgamated they would rank as the second most important change. Clearly the profession feels, perhaps fears, that evidence gathering, the heart of the audit process, is increasingly neglected.

A number of further points should also be made here. One significant aspect of the history of the changes in the audit, which we have frequently noted in the narrative earlier, is that apparent innovations were never completely original. What are perhaps generally regarded as recent innovations in auditing turn out to have a surprisingly long pedigree, and many if not most of these changes are merely a difference in emphasis within the audit rather than a complete break with the past. Almost without exception, the changes in practice, which were to apparently transform the audit process in the 1960s, were present in some audits in some form from the beginning. For example, some firms followed strict audit programmes from the start, and kept working papers of sorts; while, as important as it was, the Cooper's audit manual was not the first. More importantly, it was never possible, even in the 1880s, to check all the records in companies of any size, particularly the railways, the other public utilities and the financial institutions, so they already involved the auditor in testing by sampling. Testing the client's system of internal controls also had its precursor in testing the internal check, which auditors had also placed some reliance on since the start of the professional audit. Equally, the changing emphasis on the balance sheet clearly was just that; while some audit firms too had always attended some of their client's stock-taking, and would sometimes seek third party confirmations. Auditors had also always given advice to their clients, and where they found weaknesses in their bookkeeping or the internal check pointed this out to them, on occasions in writing – the forerunner of the management letter.

As for the 'state of the art' analytical review and risk assessment techniques of the 1980s and 1990s, to some extent the partner or principal in the bookkeeping audit had always directed their auditing of large clients to what they considered the weakest areas in their system, and indeed compared one year's results with the previous year and analysed key ratios. Relatively clever statistical techniques are associated with analytical review and risk assessment, but what is known of their application in practice indicates that greater emphasis, rightly or wrongly, is still placed on the auditor's judgement, which again is only what auditors from the start had prided themselves on exercising. Finally, computers too had their progenitors in the mechanical accounting machinery common in the 1930s, which to a lesser extent posed similar problems for the auditor to the electronic computer.

These examples of the precocious use of techniques later to become the rule gave the audit historically its further characteristic feature – a relatively wide diversity of practice between firms. Some firms did their client's accounting, others did not; some used audit programmes, some used none; some attended stock taking, others never did; some firms used statistical sampling techniques, others specifically ignored them, and so on. Higson (1987: 128) found 'great diversity in the methods adopted in just about every area of the audit' and this almost certainly continues to the present day. This variety was based on the preferences of the firm's partners but most importantly it was based on the wide range of their clients, particularly regarding their size and the professionalism of their management. Indeed, for this reason the bookkeeping audit still survives to some extent today. As can be seen from Table 2.2, even in the 1990s a quarter of our respondents to the questionnaire stated that they frequently also drew up their clients' accounts, and this practice is clearly identified across the whole period as being most common with smaller clients. Although for those auditing quoted companies the accountancy role had all but disappeared, there remained in the 1990s a large constituency of small concerns (who since 1994 had no legal obligation to be audited but might opt for an independent professional review, Woolf 1997: 338) where the auditors still 'did the books'; where the focus was on the transactions in the profit and loss account, and where in other words elements of the old bookkeeping audit were still very much alive.

Following on from this the point should also be made that in charting change we are not discussing the quality of the audit. We are not arguing that the bookkeeping audit was better or worse than the audit practised today, or that the changes that have taken place represent the concept of 'progress', much derided by recent writers on accounting history (see e.g. Power 1992: 40; Merino 1998: 606). The bookkeeping audit which was the rule down to the 1960s was simply different to the majority of audits today.

One final comment should be noted. This is essentially a history book and unfortunately despite a considerable amount of research effort on the audit, there is no detailed or quantified evidence as to how the audit is conducted at the present time. For example, Woolf (1997: 171) assessed the relative importance of the auditor's tools in the 1990s as follows:

> Internal control, if sound, may provide the auditor with one-third of the assurance sought; another third may be obtained from analytical review, assuming these show the draft accounts to be reasonable. The remaining third, in all cases, must be sought from substantive testing of transactions and balances.

Yet there is no mention of risk assessment in this analysis and clearly a more precise breakdown is required. Paradoxically we can be more confident on what auditors were doing a hundred years ago than we can be of their job today since much of the recent evidence is contradictory and conflicts with our own data on the 1990s. Further research effort is needed, for example, to determine how much substantive and compliance testing is being conducted, to what extent and how are statistical sampling procedures being used; what exactly is the role of and procedure for using analytical techniques and risk assessment, and how does all this fit in with the use of computers? A contemporary research programme, were one to be undertaken, should not only include what the firms' manuals or senior partners say is, or should be, done, but (as we have tried to do here in the historical context) what the junior auditors at the practical end of the process are actually doing. The recent and continuing audit failures would seem to make this research a valuable exercise.

We turn now to explaining the timing and nature of the changes in auditing techniques plotted in Figure 9.1.

Theories of technical change in the service sector

Unfortunately, the historian will find little helpful theory when looking to explain technical change in a profession, unlike the mass of theorising with regard to technological change in manufacturing (see e.g. Mansfield 1962; Salter 1969; Rosenberg 1982; Freeman and Soete 1997). The main reasons for this, apart from the fact that traditionally industry has been given more attention than services, probably stem from the fact that there are significant differences in the process of change in a professional service compared to that in industry. The most important of these differences is that, with the recent exception of IT developments, the changes in auditing techniques did not require significant capital investment and therefore, crucially, the scrapping of old plant. The economist's capital theory, which is at the heart of innovation theory in manufacturing, is therefore of no assistance.

There has, however, been some discussion regarding innovation in the service sector. Silber (1983: 89–95), for example, has argued that innovation in financial services in the US in the 1970s and 1980s was designed to lessen the financial constraints imposed on firms, particularly by government regulation. Pearson (1997), in analysing change in the British insurance industry between 1700 and 1914, identified a range of causal factors: technical change in the rest of the economy; the conservatism of the corporate culture in insurance firms; the cost associated with the inherent uncertainty of the business; legal or regulatory obstacles and the market structures in the insurance industry. Unfortunately, these efforts and others, for example by Podolski (1986), do not amount to theories of technical change in the service sector to compare in terms of depth of analysis with that for industrial invention and innovation. Moreover, the writers on services have focused almost exclusively on product innovation, whereas the history of technical change presented in this book is that of the process of auditing not its product. The audit product (leaving aside the arguments as to whether the audit delivered protection against fraud or a verification of the accounts; and also excluding discussion of the changing services ancillary to the audit such as accounting or management consultancy) has largely remained the same. The product of the audit is an opinion on a set of accounts embodied in the audit report which, give or take a few words, is in essence the same today as it was a hundred years ago.

We are therefore talking here exclusively about service sector process innovation for which there is no accepted theory. There is, however, much in the narrative in the previous chapters to suggest the main factors involved in the changes that took place in the audit process in Britain in the last hundred years or so. And while our conclusions may not amount to a theory of technical change in services they might go some way suggesting lines of enquiry into change in other services.

We will look first at two factors which did not have a major impact.

The regulatory system and the purpose of the audit

At first glance, since the audit was defined to some extent by legislation, case law and later regulation by the professional bodies and other organisations, it might be supposed that these had an impact on audit techniques. Silber (1983) and Pearson (1997) found that regulatory and legal factors were a mainly constraining influence on product innovation in the financial services sectors. However, as is well known the regulatory forces in accounting tended to follow not lead best practice (Edwards 1989: 212), so audit regulation probably only had a marginal effect at most on audit practice, encouraging some firms to come into line; or in other words on the speed of diffusion of some techniques.

The Companies Acts to some extent laid down the duties of the auditor, but statutory law never made any stipulation as to how the audit should be conducted. The wording of the Acts was always couched in very general terms; for example, the 1900 Act merely stipulated that the auditor had to make a report on the balance sheet, stating whether it showed a true and correct view. In the case of the 1948 Act, the auditors also had to state whether proper books of account had been kept, that the company was complying with the various aspects of the Acts, and state what loans to officers of the company had been made, if these were not disclosed in the accounts (Bigg 1951: 213–14, 276, 303). The 1967 Companies Act went a little further than the 1948 legislation in requiring that the auditors 'carry out such investigations as will enable them to form an opinion' on the adequacy of the books of account and their agreement with the balance sheet and profit and loss account. But, commented de Paula: 'The auditor must decide for himself in each case what steps are necessary' (de Paula and Attwood 1976: 251–2). The Companies Acts of the 1980s were no more prescriptive of the auditors' work than their predecessors (Woolf 1997: 288–9). The EU directives and, for example, the 1989 Act were concerned with the qualifications of auditors, their independence, the quality of the audit, the form the audit report should take, and the disciplining of auditors, but they said nothing on how the auditor was expected to conduct his or her work (ibid.: chap. 9).

As to case law, although, as we have seen, many legal judgements set out to some extent what was expected of the auditor they seldom went into how he was to accomplish the task. Judgements did not go beyond, for example, the bare declaration of the judge in the London & General Bank case of 1895, that the auditor should ascertain the true financial position: 'By examining the books of the company' (Spicer and Pegler 1914: 199). As we noted, in one instance, the Kingston Cotton Mill case concerning the checking and valuation of stock, the judge merely seemed to confirm (and approve of) what the auditors were already doing (or not doing). And, moreover, when for example the Gerrard judgement indicated that more was expected of the auditor in respect of the auditing of stock in the 1960s, it was also merely reflecting changes that were already underway. In 1976, de Paula was advising its readers that the upshot of previous case law amounted to the prescription that: '(1) An auditor must carefully examine his client's system of accounting and of internal control and must test it with vouchers and original records and make proper inquiries. (2) He must verify the existence of assets as far as is reasonably possible'. But de Paula concluded: 'the principles of case law are in several directions conflicting' (de Paula and Attwood 1976: 265); and, it might be added, were not specific as to technique. Subsequent judge-made law, although it continued to affect, for example, the liability (or lack of it) of auditors to third parties, as in the Caparo case of 1990, could also not be said to have had any bearing on audit techniques (Woolf 1997: 377–9).

Professional regulation, probably had more impact than the law. The ICAEW's Recommendations, which it started issuing from 1941, did not of course tell their members how to audit, but, for example: gave them a model audit report; advised how depreciation should be treated; stated the principles governing the valuation of stock – but not whether the auditor should attend stock-taking (Bigg 1951: 142–5, 219). The Recommendations with regard to auditing gave way to Statements on Auditing in 1961, which, as we have noted at points throughout the narrative above, gave strong guidance on a number of key issues such as: internal control (1964), verification of debtor balances by direct communication (1967), working papers (1969) and issues to do with computing (1969) (de Paula and Attwood 1976: 268). These however were not binding on members.

The ICAEW auditing statements were replaced by the auditing standards of the Auditing Practices Committee, first published in 1980, and which were superseded in turn by the Statements of Auditing Standards of the Auditing Practices Board (APB), set up in 1991 following the Companies Act 1989. The APB had the brief: 'to advance standards of auditing and associated review activities...and provide a framework of practice for the exercise of the auditors' role' (ICAEW 2000: 5). It quickly set standards on most aspects of the auditor's work, and, moreover, compliance was mandatory on pain of the practitioner having their right to conduct audits withdrawn (Woolf 1997: 18–19; ICAEW 2000: 5–7). In addition there have been attempts to control audit quality by organisations such as the Joint Monitoring Unit, which visits firms to check on the standard of their auditing (Woolf 1997: 358). It is impossible to be precise as to the effect on audit practice of this regulatory activity, but the present day more prescriptive regulations, like their predecessors, probably had only a marginal impact. This was because, as before, the SASs were couched in quite general terms, and they never initiated technical innovation. Most firms interviewed by Higson (1987: 299) were of the opinion that the standards' 'major impact was on terminology, rather than on audit procedures'. To Woolf (1997: 16), the SASs were merely 'the codification of contemporary audit practice and procedures...[and] indicators of best practice'. The heads of the major firms we interviewed also maintained, probably accurately, that all the regulation did was bring smaller firms up to what they considered to be their own high standards (Matthews and Pirie 2001: 435).

Finally, it is worth noting that it could be argued that the purpose of the audit might have had an impact on how the audit was carried out. Although historians disagree on the precise timing and reasons for the change, there seems to be a general consensus that in the first half of the twentieth century the purpose of the audit switched from the detection of fraud to the verification of the accounting statements (Lee 1972: 23–6, 1979: 161–2; Edwards 1989: 268–9; Chandler *et al.* 1993: 454). The switch to statement verification it might be suggested could account, for example, for the shift in audit emphasis away from transactions and the profit and loss account towards the balance sheet. The main reason for thinking that the change in the purpose of the audit from fraud detection to accounting verification was not an agent of process change, however, is a matter of timing. Both Lee and Chandler *et al.* argue that the switch was completed by the 1930s, whereas as can been seen from Figure 9.1 the main changes in process did not take-off until the 1960s.

Computers: the exogenous factor

As we have said, the biggest change to the audit process was the introduction of the electronic computer. This conclusion is not withstanding the computer's mechanical forerunners since its capabilities clearly exceeded qualitatively and quantitatively the punch-card machines. The introduction of the computer, however, requires no explanation from the historian of the audit. It was an exogenous technological change which, as we described in Chapter 7, the auditors, no matter how much they might at first have tried to avoid it, simply eventually had to come to terms with as best they could.

An aspect of the IT revolution, however, which is worth re-emphasising is its impact on other audit techniques – what students of technological change in manufacturing call 'spin-off' effects (see e.g. Trebilcock 1969). One such impact was that it became easier for clients to do their own accounting, until by the 1990s even the smallest of concerns could manage this on a PC. Computers, therefore, were a major factor in reducing the need for the auditor to do their client's accounting. Second, because computers are more difficult to check and interrogate than manual systems, this reinforced the change in audit emphasis towards assessing the client's own internal controls. The audit 'around' the computer, which was the first approach to the new technology, promoted the use of, increased reliance on and generally went hand in glove with, the systems approach. Nor was this reliance greatly altered when audit 'through' was increasingly used. Third, computers also reduced the need for arithmetical precision by the auditor, indeed it abolished the old skill of casting columns of figures, and generally took the mundane drudgery out of the audit (although in many cases mechanical processors had achieved this much earlier). It also must have, although this is unquantifiable, increased the productivity of the auditor. Finally, linked to this point is the fact that the spin-off effects are most clearly seen in the impact of IT on sampling. There, we have argued, the growing popularity of statistical sampling owed almost everything to the spread in the use of computers from the 1970s on. Analytical review was also at least partially assisted by computers.

But of course computers were not the only factor transforming the audit. As can be seen from Figure 9.1, rapid change was underway prior to the IT revolution, and we turn now to an analysis of the influences bringing about this change.

The American audit and its influence in Britain

Another common theme of our narrative has been the influence of the Americans on UK auditing techniques. Apparently without exception British auditing innovations (and/or their nomenclature) over the last hundred years originated in America. These American innovations make a formidable list: working papers, sampling, statistical sampling, substantive and compliance testing, the balance sheet audit, internal control, internal control questionnaires, flow charts, attendance at stock-taking, circularisation of debtors, short-form and long-form reports, materiality, risk assessment and analytical review. The question obviously arises as to whether these American innovations were directly responsible for their introduction and its timing into Britain. In order to answer this question and in turn explain changes in the British audit we must first take something of a detour and look at the history of auditing across the Atlantic, although unfortunately the history of the American audit is as in need of even more research effort than the British.

Interestingly, recent research indicates that internal audits in railroad companies, undertaken by their own bookkeepers, overseen by audit committees, and designed to root out fraud, date in the US from the 1820s, probably prior to anything like it in Britain (Previts *et al.* 2001). By the 1840s, external audits by professional accountants were instigated by shareholders' audit committees, and their reports were often published along with the rail companies' annual accounts (Boockholdt 1988: 70, 74). The concept of the fully independent audit, however, probably did not take off in the US until the 1870s. It was patterned on the British audit, which was said to have been in advance of American practice, and was indeed often performed by visiting British accountants (ibid.: 77; Moyer 1988: 3; Matthews *et al.* 1998: 244). Chatfield argued however that the British took the bookkeeping audit to the US without much regard to the differing conditions there. To the British: 'The attest function as they saw it depended mainly on verification of bookkeeping detail. Even in large companies this might include examining all cash payment vouchers and checking every footing and posting' (Chatfield 1977: 126). The purpose of the British audit, wrote Chatfield, was to look for frauds which had commonly, unlike in the US, led to the collapse of companies in Britain. To Chatfield then: 'There were valid reasons in Britain for the "detailed audit" approach. Bookkeeping error was very common; detailed checking was often needed to correct ledgers which had been out of balance for months or even years. Staff embezzlement was also common' (ibid.: 126). In effect, we can now see that what Chatfield had identified was that in Britain the auditors did their client's books, whereas in America this was usually not called for, although they usually drew up the final balance sheet.

Unsurprisingly, the American audit soon took on its own character, and the apparent contrasts with the British audit were fully set out in Montgomery's (1912: 8–10) first edition. Already the detection of fraud and error had been dropped as the main purpose of the American audit in favour of the verification of the financial position of the company for the benefit of the owners, managers, bankers and investors. As a result, as we suggested in Chapter 6, Montgomery favoured the more progressive 'balance sheet audit' over the traditional British 'book-keeper audits', although before the First World War the American audit remained detailed and was perhaps still not that dissimilar to the British. But by the interwar period, in its emphasis on the balance sheet and reliance on the client's internal controls, American practice had significantly diverged from the British. Indeed, the English accountant, Arthur Lowes Dickinson, who had first hand experience in both countries as a partner with Price Waterhouse, claimed in 1932 that 'the US profession had progressed to higher standards than those obtaining in Britain' (Edwards 1976: 302).

It has been argued by previous writers that the American audit took a separate direction from the British for three main reasons. First, according to Moyer (1988), in America accountants had a 'distaste' for the book-keeping audit because they faced a different legal framework. America had no equivalent to the British, 1900 Companies Act, so that the American auditor did not have clients who had a legal obligation to be audited. The lack of legal compulsion, Moyer (ibid.: 127) claimed, had two effects: the American auditor had to make himself useful to the client, and he had to keep down the cost of the service. It is possible that the early American auditors needed to please their clients more than the British, and perhaps the US long-form audit report was the result. As for the need to keep down costs, Moyer (1988: 126) argued: 'from the first the American audit had to justify its expense to proprietors and corporate directors...Expensive checking of managerial stewardship was costly in comparison with per-ceived benefits, and a substitute for the detailed audit was sought'. As Montgomery (1934: 64–5) remarked: 'Employment of a large corps of juniors, engaged for weeks in checking routine transactions which, in the opinion of the management, have been safeguarded by every conceivable device, will not impress the management as a good investment.' The need for savings, Moyer (1988: 128), thought meant that the Americans used sampling and an appraisal of the client's internal control system from an early date.

There are certain problems, however, with putting the legal framework at the heart of transatlantic differences in the audit as Moyer does. As we have seen, the British auditors also advised their clients as part of their audits, and whether the American auditors needed to offer their clients a cut price audit compared to the British will have to wait for evidence on the relative audit fees in the two countries. But there is a general weakness with the legalistic argument, in respect of the American auditors needing to make themselves more useful and cheap to their clients than the British, because to some extent it can only apply to the pre 1930s period. In 1933, the New York Stock Exchange introduced an audit requirement for all companies seeking a listing, and under the terms of the Securities and Exchange Act, 1934, in practical terms the audit became compulsory for listed companies in America (Tricker 1982: 55; Mitchie 1987: 34, 169, 197, 264, 272). Yet this new compulsion did not seem to have any impact on either the purpose or the method in US audits, which is some indication that the lack of the requirement had not been crucial prior to 1933 (Montgomery *et al.* 1949: 5; Chatfield 1977: 132–3; Cochrane 1979: 178; Zeff 1979: 209). Moreover, although from the 1930s onward British and American audits of stock exchange listed companies were on a similar legal footing they continued to diverge significantly in practice, with the Americans still appearing to lead the British. There is another way in which the regulatory systems in the two countries were important however and we will return to this issue later.

The second explanation for the contrasts between the UK and US audit, it has been argued, was the nature of their respective capital markets. Whereas in Britain even relatively small companies sought outside non-bank finance, and something like 13,000 companies were quoted on the London Stock Exchange in 1900, in the US bank finance was the rule, and before the First World War relatively few of even the largest manufacturing companies were quoted on Wall Street (Howitt 1966: 40–2; Cottrell 1980: 124; Jones 1981: 50–2; Kennedy 1987: 124, 133; Edwards 1989: 201–2). Therefore, according to Littleton (1981: 24–5), in America: 'The strongest motivating factor [for the external audit] seems to have been the need of creditors, particularly banks, for dependable financial information as a basis for their extension of credit.' Moyer (1988: 127) also argued that the American audit 'was built on bankers' need for reliable financial data about loan applicants'. The auditors were often employed by the creditors, and the demand for this type of audit in America was boosted by the merger movement between 1895 and 1905, when the promoters of amalgamations like J. P. Morgan needed verification of balance sheet items (Chandler 1977: 186; Littleton 1981: 27; Tricker 1982: 55). The need to satisfy bankers in America therefore 'strongly fostered "balance sheet audits"' because the ability to repay short-term loans could be judged by the relationship between current assets and current liabilities (Littleton 1981: 31). The nature of the capital market probably explains some of the early differences in the Anglo-Saxon audits, but again these differences persisted down to at least the 1960s by which time the transatlantic capital markets and the demand for audits were relatively similar.

The third and probably most significant reason for transatlantic divergence in audit practice was the size of the respective clients. A number of writers have alluded to the greater size of American companies as a factor in the nature of their audits (Lee 1972: 24, 1979: 161; Chandler *et al.* 1993: 456), but the true implications of this disparity have not been fully analysed.

American companies were on average larger than the British from an early date, although in recent years a new orthodoxy among business historians, based on the work of Wardley (1999), and Schmitz (1993), down-plays the difference in size. Wardley and Schmitz's evidence is deficient, however, since, for example, both their lists of the largest American companies in the pre-First World War period omit some of the biggest concerns. In fact, the disparity in size between British and American companies can easily be demonstrated, and goes back to the railways, where in the nineteenth century American railway companies had on average ten times the mileage of track of the British (Wilson 1995: 39). This size differential was also reflected in manufacturing concerns. For example, in 1903 US Steel was the largest industrial employer in America with 168,127 workers

(Wardley 1999: 107). The largest UK manufacturing company in the same period, Fine Cotton Spinners and Doublers, had approximately 30,000 workers; and the largest British steel company comparable to US Steel, Guest, Keen and Nettlefolds, employed 21,710 (an eighth the size of its American counterpart). In 1912, measured by market value, US Steel was two and a half times the size of the largest UK company, J & P Coats, and the difference was even greater among the lesser companies (Schmitz 1993: 23). The 45th largest US company (American Locomotive) was over four and a half times bigger than the equivalently ranked British company (Whitbread). Moreover, the disparity in the size of clients of British and American auditors persists, or has even widened slightly, down to the present day. In 2000, the largest US company by market value (Microsoft) was almost three times larger than the largest UK (part Dutch) company (Royal Dutch Shell); and the 45th largest American company (Wells Fargo), was about five times larger than the 45th ranked British company (Hays) (*Financial Times* 2000: 7–11).

America's biggest companies were larger than their British equivalents, but there was an added reason why American audit clients were larger than British clients because only the biggest companies in America (10 per cent of business enterprises) chose to consult professional accountants or be audited prior to 1933, and only listed companies were compelled to be subsequently (Montgomery 1912: 195). In contrast, in Britain a long tail of smaller companies was audited. Indeed, as Table 2.1 shows, numerically the smaller companies were by far the British auditors' largest market. This factor may have been due to the differences in the legal requirements discussed earlier, but perhaps more likely is the differing demands of the respective capital markets, since many of these small British (what became defined in 1908 as private) companies had already opted for the services of auditors, probably more as accountants than auditors, prior to being compelled to be by the 1900 Companies Act (Matthews *et al.* 1998: 245).

Not only were American audit clients bigger, they were, as Keeble (1992) and others have documented, also more professionally managed than the British. As Chandler has pointed out, while in the first half of the twentieth century the large British companies were often still essentially federations of old family firms, the American giants had a unified and centralised structure where management was departmentalised and professional. The American railways, for example, were almost certainly ahead of the British in terms of the generation and use of financial and cost accounting data as early as the 1850s. According to Chandler (1977: 110): 'By 1860 the railroads probably employed more accountants and auditors than the federal or state government.' This was at a time when the British railways accounts, as we discussed in Chapter 2, were often a shambles. Even in 1899, a British visitor across the Atlantic found that the 'failure [of British railways] to adopt tried and proved methods of handling traffic, the outdated mode of management organisation and the lack of adequate accounting and statistical procedures were roundly condemned' by American managers (Irving 1976: 218).

Regarding industrial companies, again the scale of American concerns meant that of necessity they needed good accounting systems in order to run the business. Chandler has shown that even by the 1870s the Americans had sophisticated accounts departments and, as we detailed in Chapter 5, were well ahead of the British in the use of internal audits. Chandler (1990: 455) uses the model accounts produced by US Steel in 1902 to illustrate the backwardness of British accounting, since de Paula's equivalent innovations at Dunlop did not come until the 1930s (when it still only employed 28,000 workers, a sixth of the size of US Steel 30 years earlier; Johnman 1986: 239). Chandler (1962: 60–1, 1977: 222–3, 268, 386, 404, 408, 431) described the systems found in many leading companies and concluded that in the 1920s:

> in a great many other American industrial enterprises, tactical and strategic decisions and operational and entrepreneurial activities came to be based on data dealing with anticipated market and economic conditions as well as those concerned with past and current performance.
>
> (1962: 293)

The size and (perhaps consequently) the professionalism in the management of American companies had a major impact on the nature of the external audit in three main ways. First, American companies were far more likely to present the auditor with a good system of bookkeeping, indeed he could insist that a trial balance be presented to him, and: 'If the trial balance is not correct, it is no part of an auditor's duties to locate the error or errors in it' (Montgomery 1934: 73; Chandler 1962: 212, 230; Myers 1985: 63). This was not a stipulation British auditors could make. In other words, from an early date the Americans were conducting 'pure' audits. It is possible that this, and not the regulatory system, was the main reason that the American auditor had the greater need to justify his existence to his client with helpful advice. It certainly meant that the Americans, unlike the British, did not have to attend to the arithmetical accuracy of the bookkeeping but were free to test their client's work and focus on the balance sheet.

Second, the size of client meant that the ability of the auditor to check everything disappeared quicker historically in America. Or: 'The necessity of reducing the audit time spent on checking book-keeping details became more apparent as American business increased in size' (Moyer, quoted in Chandler *et al.* 1993: 456). So the larger scale of their clients goes a long way to explaining why sampling took root earlier in the US than in Britain.

Third, the professionalism of American management meant that the auditors could place greater reliance more often and at an earlier date on their client's internal controls than was the case in Britain. Again this left the American auditor more time to concentrate on the balance sheet.

To recapitulate, perhaps the regulatory system, certainly the nature of bank financing, but most importantly the sheer scale of audit clients gave the American audit its early form. From at least the First World War, American auditors were offering their services to large companies with well organised accounting functions who did not require their accounting to be done, but did require independent verification that their balance sheet was in order when they went to the banks for funds. Hence the emphasis of the American audit from the early days was on the balance sheet. The large size and better organisation of clients in America also meant that the audit firms had to rely at an earlier date and more frequently both on sampling and on their clients' own internal control mechanisms. But of course they were able to do this, in contrast to the British auditors, because their superior clients had better controls, often including internal auditing departments. As a result the Americans adopted the balance sheet audit, in the American sense of the term, perhaps 40 or 50 years before the British.

This analysis makes clearer why throughout our narrative the British appeared to take auditing innovations from across the Atlantic. The question then arises as to whether the American audit was responsible for or influenced the adoption and timing of these innovations by the British.

The diffusion of American audit ideas in Britain could have come about in a number of ways. First, the American firm, Arthur Andersen, which set up in England in 1957, brought their American ideas with them (Matthews *et al.* 1998: 44). As one Andersen man remarked:

> In the 1960s, Arthur Andersen was a firm very unlike the other major firms, because...it had all the techniques based on what had emerged in the United States. The processes the firm went through, and its structure, were very different from those of old fashioned English firms. And then in the late sixties, the English firms changed and transformed themselves.
>
> (Interview with Plaistowe)

Second, a number of the major British accounting firms, Cooper Brothers, Price Waterhouse and Touche Ross, for example, had American branches or went into partnership with American firms and these could have been a conduit for new ideas (Matthews *et al.* 1998: 53–5). A third possible factor was explained by another respondent in interview: 'through the sixties, there was a tremendous amount of American investment in this country...They were buying up companies, investing in companies and having an influence on business here, and of course their auditors followed the new rules' (Interview with Hardcastle). We have noted that American subsidiaries insisted that their British auditors adopt US practices, such as attending stock-taking; and, for example, the Coopers Manual had separate sections on dealing with American owned companies.

However, all these factors would seem to be of marginal impact at most. Unlike Cooper Brothers, Arthur Andersen do not seem to have had any discernible influence on British accounting practice, while American subsidiaries were a small fraction of the clients of British audit firms, most of which in turn did not have American off-shoots or partner firms. Moreover, it was not the case that knowledge of the techniques, or rather ignorance of them, was a factor in British backwardness. Most of the methods were well known and, as we have emphasised above, after a fashion and on occasions they were used in Britain decades before they became generally adopted. Indeed, we argue below that the British took on the new ways at their own pace and for their own reasons, and our brief look at the history of the American audit now allows us to better identify these reasons.

Bigger clients and the rise of the pure audit

As we detailed in Chapter 2, from the start of the professional audit there were large reasonably well-run British companies, principally the utilities, where the auditors would conduct an audit somewhat along American lines. But as we have also noted earlier, for the most part British companies lagged behind the American in both size and organisation, and this was probably the main factor in determining the nature of the British audit. Because British auditors were frequently required to make up the books for their clients this set the pattern for the audit since they had no option but to focus on the transactions in the profit and loss account, where possible to check everything, and to insist on the arithmetical accuracy of the figures. Similarly, because their clients were smaller the British would be less likely to need to resort to sampling than the Americans, while on the other hand they were less able to rely on the client's internal controls. The British auditor, therefore, usually did not have the opportunity given to American auditors to concentrate on the balance sheet.

But if the reasons for the differences between American and British audits in the first half of the twentieth century were the scale and professionalism of their clients, this reveals one of the main driving forces behind audit innovation in Britain since British companies were growing in size and professionalism throughout this period. The British audit clients came progressively to resemble the typical American client, which would explain why the British audit grew increasingly to resemble its transatlantic equivalent.

Again, business historians, particularly Wardley (1991: 282), have recently attempted to down-play the growth in scale of British companies through the twentieth century. Any attempt to estimate company size, of course, runs up against the almost insuperable problem of what measurement to use. Measures such as total assets, usually used in present day studies, suffer from historical problems of valuation and price changes. Wardley's preferred measure – market value – is also flawed by its reliance on the vagaries of prices on the stock exchange. Wardley nonetheless argues that at constant retail prices the biggest company (British Telecom) in 1985 was only three times larger than the biggest in 1904/5 (Midland Railway), a slower growth rate than the economy generally (ibid.: 282). However, this result is based to some extent on the fact that the top ten largest companies (and 22 out of the top 50) in 1904/5 were railways, whereas in 1985 the nationalised railway was excluded. In fact, comparing like with like, the largest company by market value in 1985 (British Telecom) was ten times larger than the biggest non-rail company in 1904/5 (J & P Coats). Moreover, the importance of movements in share prices is indicated by the fact that even if we include the railways the most valuable company in 2000 (BP Amoco) had leapt to about 14 times larger (allowing for inflation) than the largest 1904/5 company – the Midland – a result almost entirely due to the boom on the stock exchange (*Financial Times* 2000: 7–11).

Therefore, although still not a definitive measure, the workforce is probably the best gauge of company size for our purposes; it avoids price changes, and in terms of scale and complexity of client it probably best quantifies the task facing the auditor. Table 9.3 therefore sets out the growth of the largest British companies from 1907 to 2000 for a range of sizes, from the largest company to the 50th largest, measured by their workforce. Again the picture is distorted by the amalgamation and nationalisation of the railways between 1907 and 1955: and also what Table 9.3 does not show is that the largest non-rail employer doubled from 30,000 employees (Fine Cotton Spinners and Doublers) in 1907 to 60,000 (Unilever) in 1935, and all but doubled again to 115,306 (ICI) in 1955 (Jeremy, 1991: 93–114). Table 9.3 does reveal that the 10th, 25th and 50th largest employers approximately trebled in size between 1935 and 1970 and, assuming these companies shared roughly in the 74 per cent increase in output per person employed in the whole economy in this period, meant these companies grew five-fold in output terms – double the approximate 2.4 fold increase in GDP at constant prices in the same period (productivity and GDP data from Liesner 1989: 13 and 38). Table 9.3 also indicates that growth was generally more rapid in the 1955–70 period compared to 1935–55.

This growth pattern is borne out by Hannah's figures on industrial concentration. The share of the largest 100 manufacturing companies in total net output, which had stagnated since 1930, increased from 22 per cent in 1948 to peak at 41 per cent in 1978 (Hannah 1983: 180). The trend was downward slightly since then, to 37.5 per cent by 1990 (*Business Monitor: Report on the Census of Production*). Increased concentration was entirely due, according to Hannah (1983: 144), to merger activity. From a low point in 1950, mergers gathered momentum to reach a peak in the most sustained period of activity in the 1960s. In the ten years, 1957–67, 38 per cent of quoted companies were acquired by other quoted companies (ibid.: 150). Mergers remained high until collapsing in the depression of the mid-1970s, picking up again dramatically if briefly in the late 1980s (Matthews *et al.* 1998: 92).

Table 9.3 Largest companies in Britain by size of workforce 1907–2000

	Employees	Companies	Annual increase (%)
1907			
Largest	77,662	London & North Western Railway	
10th largest	25,000	Armstrong (Sir W. G.), Whitworth	
25th largest	12,000	Joicey (Sir James)	
50th largest	6,147	Associated Portland Cement Manufacturers	
1935			*1907–35*
Largest	222,220	London Midland & Scottish Railway	6.6
10th largest	30,000	Guest, Keen & Nettlefolds	0.7
25th largest	18,697	Boot's Pure Drug	2.0
50th largest	10,000	Combined Egyptian Mills	2.2
1955			*1935–55*
Largest	115,306	Imperial Chemical Industries	−2.4
10th largest	60,000	Woolworth (F. W.)	5.0
25th largest	26,000	Rank Organisation/ Odeon Theatres	2.0
50th largest	18,104	Smith (W. H.)	4.1
1970			*1955–70*
Largest	228,000	General Electric	6.5
10th largest	93,329	F. W. Woolworth	3.7
25th largest	52,400	Metal Box	6.8
50th largest	33,400	Bowater Paper	5.6
1980			*1970–80*
Largest	188,000	GEC	−1.8
10th largest	101,387	Consolidated Goldfields	0.9
25th largest	57,000	Sears Holdings	0.9
50th largest	36,000	Hanson Trust	0.8
1990			*1980–90*
Largest	247,912	British Telecommunications	3.2
10th largest	109,501	BTR	0.8
25th largest	64,900	Rolls Royce	1.4
50th largest	39,189	Rank Hovis McDougall	0.9
2000			*1990–2000*
Largest	191,407	Compass Group	−2.3
10th largest	85,113	Lloyds TSB Group	−2.2
25th largest	54,350	Glaxo Wellcome	−1.6
50th largest	35,517	GKN	−0.9

Sources: Jeremy, 1991: 93–114; *Times 1000*; *Financial Times* 500.

Note
Excludes state and foreign owned enterprises.

This corporate growth, of course, implied a significant decline in the family control of the larger British companies, which tended to be the ones with less professional management. According to Channon (1973: 75), families remained in control of 54 per cent of the 100 biggest manufacturers in 1950, but only 30 per cent by 1970. British companies were becoming larger and they were also becoming more complex. According to Channon, 29 per cent of British manufacturing companies were multinational enterprises (with at least six overseas subsidiaries) in 1950; by 1970, the figure was 58 per cent. Also, 25 per cent of Channon's sample had diversified their businesses away from their core activity in 1950, but this had risen to 60 per cent by 1970; those companies adopting the multidivisional structure had increased from 13 per cent to 72 per cent in the same period (ibid.: 24, 60, 67, 78). Growth in the scale and complexity of British companies then took place throughout the first three-quarters of the twentieth century, but was particularly significant in the 1950s and 1960s, and this fits in with the timing of the diffusion of the new auditing techniques in Britain, as shown by Figure 9.1.

With the increased scale and complexity of British companies and the decline of family control went the introduction of more professional management. Employment in administrative jobs in manufacturing grew from 492,000, or 8 per cent of total employment in 1907, to 1,201,000 or 20 per cent of employment in 1948; by 1990 this had further increased to 1.6 million, or exactly a third of the manufacturing work-force (Hannah 1976: 72; *Business Monitor: Report on the Census of Production*). This growth in corporate bureaucracy applied particularly to the financial function. As Table 2.1 shows, and we discussed in Chapter 2, from 1951 to 1991 the number of qualified accountants working in industry increased over five-fold, and understandably the majority of them performed the accounting work of the companies often previously conducted by the auditors; in fact they were usually recruited from the companies' auditors. These recruits became accountants and chief accountants in the growing number of accounting departments, but also financial controllers (another post copied from America), and, of course, finance directors with a place on the board, an executive position which came to prominence in Britain only in the 1950s and 1960s (Matthews *et al.* 1998: 215).

The reasons for the increased employment of accountants by companies are not hard to find. Given the growing accounting needs of the larger more complex companies, it was cheaper for them to employ their own accountants than to use the auditors. This is borne out by our questionnaire and interview evidence. One respondent to the postal questionnaire, an auditor with Kemp Chatteris, wrote in his explanation of the decline in auditors doing their clients' accounts: 'companies became concerned at the costs of outside help and saw the benefit of improving their own accounting capacity'. Another put the move: 'mostly as a cost reducing policy by clients'. The increased employment of accountants was also linked to the growth in management accounting, since as an accountant with Theodore B. Jones put it: 'management realised that effective management required the prompt production of regular periodic management accounts. These were prepared by the company's own staff who, over the 1939–65 period, became increasingly professional and more highly qualified'; again, 'management required to know the trading position at frequent intervals throughout the year'. Accountants doing the management accounts could also of course produce the year-end financial figures. As another interviewee explained: 'the need for up-to-date and reliable management accounts followed through to the annual accounts' (Interview with Hewitt).

As clients' professionalism increased, the accounting function of the audit fell away. As noted previously, Table 2.2 indicates and Figure 9.1 charts that, whereas in the decades up to and including the 1950s almost two-thirds of auditors frequently also drew up the accounts of their clients, this figure fell consistently to a little under a quarter by the 1990s. Even in the 1960s auditors of mainly quoted companies frequently also drew up their accounts, whereas by the 1990s this figure had fallen away to virtually nil. The breakdown in Table 2.2 responses relative to the size of companies audited confirms the reasons for the decline in accountancy. Among the whole sample across the entire period, only a quarter of those who audited mainly quoted companies frequently did the accounts, whereas over a half to two-thirds of those auditing smaller companies did so. As we pointed out above, the persistence in the number of smaller clients accounts for the fact that over half of the trainees still made up their clients' books at least occasionally even in the 1990s. The implication is, therefore, that the growth in the size of clients and the concomitant growth in their employment of accounting staff capable of doing their own books, led finally to the dominance in Britain of the pure audit by the 1970s.

The importance of the growth in the size of clients to the advent of the pure audit was articulated by many of our interviewees. An auditor with Mellors, Basden & Mellors said client growth:

> was quite a significant change because it meant that the accountancy aspect of the practice diminished. . . . Ford Motor Company had quite a number of accountants, chartered, certified, incorporated but I don't think Raleigh [the bicycle makers] had more than one [qualified accountant] until about 1950.
>
> (Interview with Hewitt)

Respondents to the postal questionnaire were also asked to explain briefly the change in the practice of auditors making up the accounts. Well over 80 per cent of those offering an opinion put the decline in the practice as due – 'Largely because clients seemed more often to have staff qualified to prepare accounts.' 'The client on average became larger and employed better internal staff' was how one explained it; while another was more specific: 'in general clients were smaller at the start of my career. Take-overs had not got underway'.

The balance sheet audit

The rise of the pure audit provided both a challenge and an opportunity for the British auditors. It was a problem in that when the audit involved also making up the accounts clients could clearly see they were getting something for their money. Now, as this unofficial accounting role of the auditor disappeared, our interviews suggested that clients were increasingly likely to view the audit as a 'damn nuisance' (Interview with Aspell). As the chairman and senior partner of KPMG International recalled in the late 1990s:

> I always remember a client saying to me: 'I ought to get more out of my annual audit than a ruddy great bill for telling me I got my sums right'. The provision of management information and the advice that comes from it is a lot more useful than even six or seven years ago.
>
> (Interview with Sharman)

The loss of the accounting function was, therefore, probably, in turn, behind much of the drive from the 1960s onwards for increasing the usefulness of the audit to the client, embodied in features such as the management letter. In other words one unofficial audit function was substituted for another.

On the other hand the reduction of accountancy work gave British auditors the opportunity to shift the focus of the audit more in the direction their American cousins had adopted 50 or more years earlier, namely to the balance sheet. Since British auditors were less concerned with making up the books recording the day to day transactions of the client they were more able to concentrate on the major audit issues of verification of balance sheet items. The increased attendance at stock-taking and the circularisation of debtors from the 1960s, indicated in Tables 6.1 and 6.2, represented this growing focus on the balance sheet. This trend, it should be noted, was decades after stock-taking and debtor confirmations became the rule in America. The British audit changed in its own time and for its own reasons. And Tables 6.1 and 6.2 also confirm what these reasons were, since the practices were primarily a feature of the larger quoted company audits. As clients got bigger and more professional British auditors were increasingly presented with pure audits which allowed them to concentrate on the balance sheet.

But, of course, the rise of the pure audit was only a permissive factor; there were other more active forces at work, also provoked by the increased size of clients, pushing British auditors in the direction of the balance sheet. First, since the clients were getting bigger and more complex the auditor could do less checking of transactions and had increasingly to rely for audit assurance on verifying balance sheet items. As we quoted earlier, one senior PW man explained: 'if you get two balance sheets right, the difference between the two would show up in the profit and loss account. So rather than audit the profit and loss account to death we concentrated on making sure the balance sheet was right' (Interview with Stacy).

A second factor was also possibly switching the audit emphasis towards the balance sheet. The decline of the family firms and increased scale of British companies had made them more reliant on external sources of capital, particularly the stock market. Between the late 1940s and the early 1970s domestic capital raised on the London Stock Exchange increased almost ten-fold in value at constant prices, and by the late 1960s external sources of finance for industry outstripped internal sources for the first time (Wilson 1995: 189–90). Consequently investors, particularly the institutions (which held 60 per cent of all equities by the 1970s; ibid.: 191), and the growing army of investment analysts were increasingly interested in the accuracy of company accounts, especially the declared profit figures and the question of solvency. This was articulated by Stamp and Marley in 1970:

> no one would deny that the function of the auditor, in lending credibility to financial statements, has been growing in importance, rapidly and steadily, over the last fifty years...Such financial reports are relied on heavily by investors, creditors, security analysts, Government, and others. The role of the auditor, in lending credibility to these financial statements, is vital in establishing and maintaining confidence in the capital markets.
>
> (Quoted in Lee 1977: 87–8)

On this view it would seem reasonable to argue that the emphasis of the audit would shift onto the balance sheet and a concern with, for example, the level and soundness of debtors and the level and value of stock and work in progress, a major factor in the calculation of profit, and also one most easily manipulated (Interview with Tweedie; Woolf 1997: 192).

To sum up then, the growing size of clients and the increasing occurrence of the pure audit both left scope for and brought about the need (either because of a declining ability to check transactions or from the demands of the capital market) to switch the emphasis in the British audit from transactions to balance sheet verification.

Sampling and the systems approach

With the operations of the largest companies growing perhaps five-fold from 1935–70, the increased size of audit clients also made the old style of audit simply untenable, and another of our interviewees timed and explained the change:

> from 1946 to 1966, everything went up in scale, and the number of transactions increased tremendously. As the volume went up and the

systems and the nature of business itself became more complex, obviously the audit procedures had to change. You had, on the one side, businesses merging, integrating, taking over, consolidating, and making technical changes, and on the other side you had the profession... struggling to keep the lid on from the audit point of view... You couldn't carry on casting all the books yourself.

(Interview with Jones)

As another respondent put it, there were two main responses to the problem: 'No longer could we pretend to tick everything. So we had to begin to think a little about systems and look at sampling' (Interview with Livesey).

The increased size and complexity of clients clearly indicated the necessity for a greater reliance on sampling, and was behind the many and various types of statistical sampling which were, as Table 4.1 shows, increasingly employed. The second reaction to the increased size of client, as Table 5.1 reveals, was that the auditor had to rely more and more on the client's own systems. Again both Tables 4.1 and 5.1 indicate that the incidence of statistical sampling and the systems approach was closely associated with the size of clients, and to a much lesser extent the size of the audit firm. Clearly then the growth in the size of clients from the 1960s on was the key factor, since big companies were usually the only ones to have internal control systems and internal audit departments on which the auditors could rely, or would justify the use of sophisticated sampling techniques.

It is interesting to note, therefore, that rather neatly the same underlying trend – the growing scale of clients – that meant that auditors could do proportionately less substantive checking, was the same one which meant that they did not need to do so because they could rely on the larger client's control systems.

Finally, it should be remarked that the impact of the escalating size of clients on the audit did not stop there. The increased use of the management letter (Table 5.2) is partly related to the growth of the systems approach since comments on the internal controls was the initial purpose of the letter. Also, the growing use of the audit programme (Table 3.1) and of the audit manual was related to the increased size of audit jobs. The bigger the job the more planning that was required and, as a number of our respondents indicated, the more was the need for firms to discipline their larger labour force.

Commercial pressures for change

The growing size of clients was not of course the only factor bringing about change in audit techniques. As we noted above, the 100 largest firm concentration ratio peaked in the 1970s and Table 9.3 shows, in terms of the size of workforce there was a distinct slowing down in the growth of companies in the 1970s and 1980s, and in the 1990s an unmistakable decline.

Therefore changes in audit techniques after the 1970s are likely to have been driven mainly by considerations other than client size.

What then were the other considerations? The factors affecting the rate of diffusion of technological change in manufacturing which are given greatest prominence in the literature are, of course, movements in the relative cost of the factors of production and other market pressures, and there would appear to be two price factors that had an impact on the innovation of audit techniques – the cost of labour and competitive pressure on fees.

From the 1950s on, labour was becoming more expensive for accountancy firms. Traditionally, articled clerks paid a premium, typically £500 (or £10,650 at 2004 prices) in 1950, for the privilege of being trained (Matthews and Pirie 2001: 401–2). Although the premium was usually repaid to the clerk spread out over their five year period of training, audit firms were in effect using free labour. This fact had obvious implications for the way the audit was conducted. For one thing low labour costs meant there were few time pressures on the bookkeeping audit. Talking of the 1950s, one of our interviewees said: 'We were paid badly, and time wasn't of the essence. If you spent another week or so on an audit, it wasn't a question of needing to be cost effective' (Interview with Engel). Another recalled: 'there was no constraint of having to finish within two months or whatever it was, and there was no sort of timetable. It was a very leisurely occupation really' (Interview with Venning). Again: 'it was a slave trade really, but on the other hand, although we used to work long hours, we weren't pressurised into working very fast because the costs were low. I mean, a shilling an hour! It was a different era' (Interview with Evans). The bookkeeping audit then could afford to be detailed, and another auditor of that era explained:

> The way we used to audit, using cheap labour, meant you covered a pretty high percentage of transactions. In a solicitor's office you'd do every transaction. You'd check everything through ... An audit could be much more labour intensive than it is today, and I think we would take on a lot more detailed work than would be affordable today.
>
> (Interview with Kenwright)

By the 1950s the increased demand for accounting recruits, deriving from the rapid expansion in the demand for audit and other work, was outstripping the supply of suitable candidates. This supply was itself reduced as chartered accountancy became progressively an all-graduate profession; whereas only 8.6 per cent of respondents to our questionnaires who qualified in the 1950s had gone to university, by the 1980s the figure was 87.5 per cent. Therefore, as audit labour changed from a buyers into a sellers market our questionnaire evidence indicates that whereas 88 per cent of respondents qualifying in the interwar period paid a premium, by the 1950s only 30 per cent did so, and the last premium reported was paid in 1958.

Increasingly firms had to pay attractive salaries to their trainees. By 1967, Cooper Brothers were offering £850 (£9,600 at 2004 prices) and Peat Marwick Mitchell, £800 (or £9,020; I am grateful to Prof. J. R. Edwards for these data) as starting salaries for an articled clerk; and the figure is around £20,000 today (Hays Accountancy Personnel).

By the 1990s trainees were being so well paid that the heads of audit firms interviewed considered it a problem. The senior technical partner at Robson Rhodes said:

> The biggest change is in the finances, because when I qualified I was paid very little, and articled clerks were a source of cheap labour. Nowadays, here in London, we pay the equivalent of articled clerks £18,000 per year when they start. Therefore, they are a very expensive form of labour when you take into account our having to pay the colleges £4,000 tuition fees per year, and they are only with us 26 weeks of the year when you take off all the time they are on study leave... economically, it's crazy.
>
> (Interview with Carty)

This trend in the cost of labour had obvious repercussions for the audit process. It meant, indeed, that regardless of the other factors at work, the bookkeeping 'check everything' audit was doomed by the increasing cost of labour alone. Many interviewees made this point: 'labour has got too expensive to be able to give the blanket coverage on transactions' was how one auditor expressed it (Interview with Kenwright). So it is an interesting question, but one almost impossible to answer, as to the relative importance of the cost of labour compared to the other factors involved, particularly the growing size of clients, in the demise of the bookkeeping audit. Probably it was just a coincidence that a number of factors were operating in the same direction at the same time.

Figure 9.1 indicates a significant slowing down in the innovation of our selected techniques from the 1980s to the 1990s. Although not easy to prove, as we discussed earlier, this might be because the opportunities for the innovations had become saturated, perhaps because the majority of audit clients were now of sufficient size to warrant, for example, the systems approach. More likely the cause of the slowdown in process change was due to underlying factors which altered around 1980, changing the appropriateness of the innovations of the 1960s and 1970s, or at least of their further expansion in use. Indeed, in view of our discussion of the trends in client size earlier, it seems likely that whereas up to the 1970s the main driving force for audit change was the increased scale of companies, after then commercial pressures became more important.

From the late 1970s the economics of the audit was being squeezed from the supply side in terms of costs, and on the demand side from the clients. On the supply side there was the continuing increased cost of junior labour, in what was still a highly labour intensive industry. As a partner with Robson Rhodes put it:

> it was becoming clear that as labour got more expensive...something had to be done. It was economic pressure: 1) people wanted things finished by a certain time, and 2) we were getting more expensive. One had to start thinking: 'Well we did three months last year; can't we get away with a month?'
>
> (Interview with Venning)

Also, of course, it was not just the salaries of junior staff that were going up (Higson 1987: 324). As another interviewee noted:

> the big difference is that the audit firms themselves, because of the size of salaries paid to senior members of staff, are much more conscious of the time spent. We keep rigorous time records...even more so today with the increase in competition, which there wasn't so much of in my day among the audit firms. And you get what we never had in those days – estimates before jobs were started. They [audit firms] are much more cost conscious.
>
> (Interview with Engel)

To this supply side pressure were added demand side developments. Audit clients had, from the late 1970s, begun increasingly to question their fees. As one interviewee described it:

> I remember at an annual general meeting in 1981 a shareholder banging on about audit fees. That was my first recollection of anything other than a rubber stamp at an AGM, and that marked the time when audit fees started to come under increasing pressure. We now get involved in competitive tenders for other people's audits and frequently defend our own.
>
> (Interview with Heywood)

Possibly the first example of tendering in the private sector was when Peat Marwick Mitchell won the British Aerospace audit in competition with four other leading firms in 1977 (*Accountancy* February 1978: 10; Interview with Grenside).

Under this increased competitive pressure came the growth in the practice of auditor switching by companies. In 1986, for example, British Rail changed auditors from Peat Marwick Mitchell to Price Waterhouse, and when Guinness took over Distillers, the audit moved from Arthur Young again to Price Waterhouse (*Financial Times* 15 December 1986). A retired senior partner with Peats wistfully remembered: 'At one time companies thought it was bad publicity to change the auditor. Then it became common practice for major companies to put their audit out to tender' (Interview with Grenside). Another senior partner explained:

> the economics of an accounting practice have changed very substantially. And clients...are asking people to bid for work and fee charges are one of the things they take into account. So it's more competitive and the cost base has substantially changed.
>
> (Interview with Carty)

In the recession of the early 1990s, competition manifested itself in general reductions in the audit fees charged by the large firms, and allegations of what became known by another American term 'low-balling' – cutting fees perhaps below cost price to attract new work – were made. Price Waterhouse in a well known instance offered the Prudential insurance company a 40 per cent discount when the £2.4m audit job went out to tender in 1990 (*Accountancy Age* 14 April 1994: 2). In a very public wrangle in 1995, Stoy Hayward, who had been the Royal Automobile Club auditors for 16 years, sent a letter to the client's members complaining that the club planned to switch its audit to Price Waterhouse, whom they accused of pricing the job as a loss-leader in order to gain consultancy work (*Daily Telegraph* 22 April 1995; *The Mail On Sunday* 23 April 1995).

If we delve a little deeper, what was fundamentally driving this increased demand side pressure on auditors was increased competition among their clients themselves. This in turn was a result of the much discussed globalisation of business, and the opening up of British companies to greater foreign competition. As a result of the General Agreement on Tariffs and Trade rounds, world and Britain's tariffs had been falling since the 1950s. In 1947, the average tariff in the industrialised world was around 40 per cent, but by the early 1990s this figure had dropped to less than 5 per cent (Griffiths and Wall 1997: 659). In addition, technical change in the shipping and aircraft industries, as well as the other reductions in transport costs and the remarkable developments in international telecommunications allowing the movement of funds around the world at the click of a computer mouse, have all contributed to the creation of a highly competitive global market (Mackintosh *et al.* 1996: 396). Between the early 1950s and the late 1980s, world trade grew at double the rate of industrial production. Britain was not only at the heart of this change but was further exposed to competition after its entry into the European Common Market in 1973. Already heavily dependent on trade, foreign trade as a share of national income in Britain grew from 20 per cent in the 1960s to 26 per cent in 1980. Imports as a percentage of total sales in manufacturing in Britain increased from 17 per cent in 1968 to 36 per cent in 1989 (Matthews *et al.* 1998: 187–8). Therefore, when world depressions occurred in the early 1980s and early 1990s, most British companies were fully exposed to the blast of world competition and needed to cut their overhead costs.

These deep structural economic changes had their reflection in the audit process, and the changes in audit practice (apart from the impact of IT) that have come about since 1980 have been primarily due to the commercial pressure on costs. As clients sought lower costs, audit fees were an obvious target. In turn, audit firms were forced to compete among themselves for business and to cut their own costs. As a senior PW partner explained: 'the other major change in audits is the pressure on costs. Undoubtedly the cost of an audit, measured anyway you like, has reduced over the last twenty-five years' (Interview with Stacy).

This cost pressure had a major impact on audit processes, and lay behind a trend towards what perhaps euphemistically was called greater 'efficiency'. Gwilliam (1987: 418) explained that: 'An underlying motive for improved efficiency has been increased price or fee competition in the market for auditing services.' As Turley and Cooper (1991: 34) put it, the 'overwhelming' influence affecting audit procedure in the late 1980s was ' "fee pressure" and the need for cost effectiveness and efficiency'. Turley and Cooper argued that this commercial pressure led to a retreat from the systems approach and compliance testing; and Higson (1987: 307) noted a reduction generally in the actual testing of accounting records, the fundamental tool of the audit. To compensate for this, and as a justification for less testing, of necessity greater reliance had to be placed on the use of the auditor's judgement: in the assessment of risk, in the use of analytical review techniques, and with the concept of materiality. A typical interviewee of Turley and Cooper (1991: 35) stated: 'the key emphasis is on collecting the minimum amount of evidence we need to support an audit opinion'.

Interestingly then, while the main interest of the increased commercial pressures on auditors has tended to be focused on its impact on their independence from client management (Beatie *et al.* 2001), our analysis would suggest that the effect might have been equally as great on audit techniques, possibly leading to a decline in the quality of audit assurance.

Summary and endnote

The decline of the bookkeeping audit and the rise of the balance sheet audit and systems approach from the 1960s can largely be explained by the growth in the size of the British auditor's clients due to mergers and takeovers. This increased scale meant that as the clients were more professionally managed they could do their own accounting and present the auditor with a pure audit so that the focus of the work could shift from transactions to the verification of balance sheet items like stock and debt. At the same time the auditor could rely more for audit assurance on testing the client's own internal controls and this was also necessary because the increased scale meant that a smaller proportion of the accounting could be tested. Two further factors operating at this time were the increased cost of audit labour which also meant that less detailed audit work could be afforded, and computerisation, which complicated the audit by taking away the audit trail, but was of benefit because it allowed more clients to do their own accounting and the computers improved audit productivity in, for example, statistical sampling.

Around 1980 the audit changed again under pressure from clients who in an increasingly competitive world environment needed to reduce costs including audit fees. In turn auditors had to cut their own costs by further reducing the testing of the client's records and systems, by only targeting areas considered significant and with the greatest risk of error, and by an overall comparative analysis of the client's business and accounting.

Aside from the exogenous but important advent of computers, then, the causes of the developments in auditing over the last hundred years were at bottom determined by structural economic change occurring among the auditor's clients. The audit profession is of course part of the financial services sector and as might be expected of a service industry the conduct of the audit process responded to the needs of the paymaster. Although this is not the place to develop the point (see Matthews forthcoming) our analysis fits in with a marxian formulation of a superstructure of the audit service responding to changes in the economic base of client companies, with computers adding a further element of overt technological determinism.

Our methodology and findings of course do not accord with those of the 'new accounting history' which tends to look to cultural or social constructions, and where there is perhaps a tendency to devalue archival research, or even to deny the possibility of establishing historical fact. Indeed, establishing causes or explanations is often seen as too deterministic (see e.g. Hoskin and Macve 1986; Napier 1989, 1998; Cooper 1997; Funnell 1997; Gaffikin 1998; Keenan 1998; Merino 1998). This book was written from a different perspective, the stance is positivist and the methodology empirical, and if the book has been successful in its aims, I hope it has been an advertisement for its method.

Appendix

Data sources

Oral history

The interviews used in this book are part of the oral history half of a project funded by the ICAEW. Our non-random (what Hammond and Sikka, 1996: 88, have called a 'purposeful') sample of chartered accountant interviewees included: the oldest accountants we could find, a number of whom trained in the 1920s; small firm practitioners; accountants who had 'left the profession' and worked in industry; medium sized or provincial practitioners; the past and present partners in the largest firms and leaders of the profession; women and accountants personally involved in major controversies and scandals. All interviewees were asked a structured list of questions (although with considerable flexibility in view of the heterogeneity of the respondents) broadly broken down into: the social and educational background of the respondents; the nature of their training; their experience in their careers, their opinions on a range of professional issues and particularly relevant to this book – the changes they saw in the auditing process.

The 77 interviews, the majority of which were conducted by my research assistant Mr Jim Pirie, were undertaken between 1996 and 1998, and lasted from between one and three hours. They were usually conducted in the interviewee's home, or at the ICAEW head office, although some were held over the telephone. The taped interviews were transcribed and then edited to cut down their length (well over a million words in total) and to make them read fluently. Every effort however was made to preserve the respondent's meaning or intention. The interviewees were allowed to comment on and make additions and deletions to the transcript. This self-editing had the advantage of providing a check against any inaccuracies but the disadvantage that on reflection some interviewees refused permission for their interview to be used, while with others interesting and valuable details were excised.

The advantages of oral history are that the historian can create data that is not available from any other sources, and indeed the relatively secretive activity of auditing has left a paucity of documentary sources. Oral history puts the historian in control of the data to be generated. Questions could be directed to auditors who had done or were actually performing the work, and at particular issues; for example, did the interviewee attend stock taking in the 1930s?

The potential problems with oral evidence are that there is possible bias and distortion on the part of both the interviewee and interviewer. With regard to the latter Hammond and Sikka (1996: 79) have argued: 'that avoiding bias is impossible'. However, in this project we strove for objectivity and tried to ensure that our questions did not 'lead the witness'. As for bias by the respondents, the obvious point should be made that no sources the historian uses will be without distortion of one sort or another, certainly not autobiography, minutes of meetings, newspaper reports or even, perhaps especially, company accounts. Another weakness of oral data is that the response of one interviewee is obviously not statistically valid, so the question will always arise – how typical is this respondent? Again memories can be unreliable, especially of course among the elderly. The view of the individual respondent therefore has to be subject to what Lummis (1998: 274) has called 'the normal process of maximum triangulation with other sources'. And in this book oral testimony is wherever possible backed up by documentary and other sources.

For a more extended discussion of the strengths, weaknesses and problems associated with the use of oral history in accounting history, together with brief biographies of the respondents and their edited interviews, see Matthews and Pirie (2001) and also Matthews (2000).

The tapes and transcripts of all the interviews undertaken in the project are available from the author (with the consent of the interviewees) to consult and to use in further work.

The interviews used in this book were with the following:

Peter Ainger, Tape no. 50
Gerald Aspell, no. 16
Robin Atkins, no. 51
Brian Atkinson, no. 18
John Beard, no. 32
Derek Boothman, no. 23
Ian Brindle, no. 69
William Brittain, no. 8
Christine Burdett, no. 59
Marjorie Burgess, no. 61
Patricia Burlingham, no. 60
George Carter, no. 77
James Carty, no. 65
Arthur Chapman, no. 33
John Colvin, no. 25

Brian Currie, no. 76
Evan Davies, no. 34
John Denza, no. 11
Stanley Duncan, no. 27
Harold Edey, no. 43
Ian Engel, no. 12
Julian Evans, no. 3
Alan Fabes, no. 33
John Gilliat, no. 14
Parry Goodwin, no. 29
Sir John Grenside, no. 30
David Haddleton, no. 17
Sir Alan Hardcastle, no. 73
John Hewitt, no. 40
John Heywood, no. 35

David Hobson, no. 68

Stanley Jones, no. 1

Reginald Keel, no. 55

Roy Kemp, no. 71

Joseph Kenwright, no. 7

Chris Lainé, no. 75

Philip Livesey, no. 22

Adrian Martin, no. 66

Stanley Middleton, no. 28

Paul Milne, no. 70

Kenneth Mold, no. 15

John Mordy, no. 19

Ian Muir, no. 63

Robert Niddrie, no. 21

John Norris, no. 24

Peter Palmer, no. 38

Izett Partridge, no. 52

Richard Passmore, no. 42

Matthew Patient, no. 45

Margaret Pearce, no. 53

Ian Plaistowe, no. 74

Tom Sanders, no. 37

Martin Scicluna, no. 36

Colin Sharman, no. 62

David Shaw, no. 26

Neville Sims, no. 20

Lord Patrick Spens, no. 47

Graham Stacy, no. 31

Geoffrey Thornton, no. 48

Sir Ian Tweedie, no. 72

John Venning, no. 44

John Whinney, no. 46

Geoffrey Wilde, no. 41

Richard Wilkes, no. 67

Postal questionnaire

Unlike the oral history, the postal questionnaire half of the ICAEW project is unique as a methodology in accounting (perhaps in any form of) history. It was, like the interviews, designed to generate data not available from documentary sources. The questions, 69 in all, ranged like the interviews over aspects of the accountants' background, experience and opinions. The questions were framed mainly using the standard Lickert scale of questioning (indicated in the Tables 2.2–6.2 in this book), requiring the ticking of boxes, although there were also write-in, often open-ended, questions.

A significant feature of the design of the project was that a random sample of 300 names and addresses was taken from the published ICAEW membership lists for each decade in which the accountant qualified (luckily a date also included in the ICAEW list), starting in the 1920s and 1930s (these decades were amalgamated because the 1920s vintage numbered less than 300) and continuing down to the 1990s. Thus 2100 questionnaires were sent out in total, and after reminders were issued the overall response rate was 45 per cent. The purpose of establishing cohorts based on the decade of qualification was that historical trends could be identified. For example, questions on audit techniques were pointed at the respondent's period of training (since this was the most likely time when they were actually performing audit work and first experiences tend to stay in the memory), and this produced the trends illustrated in the tables here. In addition, two of the questions asked respondents for the name of the firm with which they qualified and the type of the companies they mainly audited, which in turn identified any impact these factors might have had on the techniques used, and these results are set out in the lower sections of the tables.

The advantages of postal questionnaires over oral or documentary evidence are, first, as can be seen from the tables, the numbers involved allow the generation of quantitative data that are statistically significant. Second, questionnaires produce evidence that is not and never will be available from any other source. Moreover, third, in common with oral history the questionnaire gives the historian the ability to create the evidence in the specific areas in which they are interested, and where other sources are lacking.

As with all the historian's sources the questionnaire method is not without its problems. All surveys have the weaknesses that respondents might lie or give the answers which they think are expected of them. With the use of historical surveys there is the added problem, as with the interviews, of faulty memories (particularly relevant for the early cohorts in this survey). The questionnaire seeking historical data can in some instances also pose problems with regard to the interpretation of the results; often the meaning of terms used will change, and a question will mean different things to someone who qualified in the interwar period and someone qualifying recently. For example, in the question which was designed to analyse the use of statistical sampling techniques in Britain, some replies were puzzling since (as can be seen in Table 4.1), almost a third of the 1920/30s cohort indicated they used these sophisticated techniques during their training at least sometimes. This would appear to uncover a surprisingly precocious use of statistics in British audits. The replies to the back-up request to state the sampling techniques used, however, indicated that some of the earlier cohorts had misunderstood the question as referring to simple techniques like block testing.

A more extensive discussion of the questionnaire methodology applied to accounting history has also been given in a recent article (Matthews, 2002).

Company reports

Another source used here is a survey (funded by the Leverhulme Trust) of company reports (housed in the Guildhall Library, London) where, for benchmark years starting in the early 1880s, and every 20 years down to 2000, a sample of 200 reports were analysed. Some data for the early 1880s and 1900/1 are given in Table A.1. As discussed in Chapter 2, audit fees and other data cast light on the amount and nature of audit work undertaken. In addition, the wording of a sample of audit reports in the early 1880s is also given (the audit reports for the 121 companies in 1900/1 were too numerous to reproduce in full) which also gives some indication of the nature of the audit process.

Table A.1 Data from audit reports

Company	Year	Total assets (£)	Year end to date of audit report (weeks)	Audit fee (£)
Artisan Labourers and General Dwellings	1882	1,161,853	5	78
Birmingham Railway Carriage and Wagon	1886	602,038	5	105
Bristol and South Wales Railway-Waggon[a]	1886	354,427	6	30
Cardiff & Swansea Smokeless Steam Coal	1881	469,651	12	11
City of London Brewery	1881	1,016,925	4	200
Crystal Palace	1879	1,526,915	6	131
Cunard Steam-ship	1881	2,061,245	16	210
Eastern Extension, Australasia & China Telegraph[a]	1881	3,568,146	26	100
Eastern Telegraph[a]	1881	6,032,720	29	100
Gloucester Wagon	1881	583,780	6	100
Great Western Rail	1880	83,802,944	6	1,000
John Moir & Sons	1883	215,232	6	150
Liverpool Adelphi Hotel	1881	122,885	3	52
Liverpool Exchange	1880	602,638	11	52
London & Glasgow Engineering & Iron Shipbuilding	1881	333,737	9	191
London & Provincial Marine Insurance	1881	289,597	2	150
Marbella Iron Ore	1881	267,782	5	31
Metropolitan Railway Carriage and Wagon	1881	425,011	5	105
National Safe Deposit	1881	276,499	1	31
Orient Steam Navigation	1881	642,317	16	105
Redheugh Bridge[a]	1881	54,239	6	10
West India & Pacific Steamship	1881	520,485	3	150
1880s				
Max		83,802,944	29	1,000
Min		54,239	1	10
Mean		4,580,699	8	139
Stand. Dev		17,322,192	7	197
Median		520,485	6	105
Mode		N/A	5	105
1900/1				
Max		178,611,132	27	1,500
Min		5,000	1	1
Mean		7,259,264	8	172
Stand. Dev		21,503,033	6	258
Median		239,945	6	75
Mode		N/A	5	105

Note
a Converted half-year accounts.

Audit reports for early 1880s

ARTISAN LABOURERS AND GENERAL DWELLINGS

Price Waterhouse & Co., Johnson Brooks, Auditors
  We have examined the above Accounts with the Books and Vouchers of the Company and find them correct.

BIRMINGHAM RAILWAY CARRIAGE AND WAGON

George Beech, Chartered Accountant, Thomas Simpson, Chartered Accountant, Auditors
  We have carefully and continuously examined the Books, Vouchers and Accounts of your Company during the past Year, and in our opinion, this Balance Sheet is a correct Statement of the Company's affairs as shown therein on 31st December 1886.

BRISTOL AND SOUTH WALES RAILWAY-WAGON

W. F. Brookman, S. Tryon Auditors
  Audited and found correct.

CARDIFF & SWANSEA SMOKELESS STEAM COAL

Coopers Brothers & Co., Chartered Accountants
  We have examined the above Statement with the Books and Accounts including the Accounts from the agents, and certify the same to be correct.

CITY OF LONDON BREWERY

Rawlins & Funnell
  Examined and found correct.

CRYSTAL PALACE

Quilter, Ball, Crosbie, Glegg & Welton
  Examined and approved.

CUNARD STEAM-SHIP

Cooper Bros and Co.
  We have compared the above statements with the Books and Accounts of the Company in Liverpool and with the returns from the Agencies, and certify the same to be correct.

EASTERN EXTENSION, AUSTRALASIA & CHINA TELEGRAPH

Henry Dever; Quilter, Ball, Crosbie, Glegg & Welton, Auditors
  Audited and found correct.

EASTERN TELEGRAPH

Henry Dever; Quilter, Ball, Crosbie, Glegg & Welton, Auditors
Audited and found correct.

GLOUCESTER WAGON

Hudson Smith, Williams & Co., Chartered Accountants
Having examined the books, vouchers and other documents relating to the accounts of the Gloucester Wagon Company Limited for the year ending 30th June 1881, we hereby certify them to be correct.

GREAT WESTERN RAILWAY

Deloitte, Dever, Griffiths & Co., Chartered Accountants. Edward Harper, J. Bowen, Auditors
Examined 20th August 1880 Deloitte, Dever, Griffiths & Co., Chartered Accountants. We hereby certify that the foregoing accounts and balance sheet contain a full and true statement of the financial condition of this Company. And that, the Dividends proposed to be declared on the several stocks and shares are bona fide due thereon, after charging the Revenue of the half year with expenses which ought, in our judgement to be paid thereon.

JOHN MOIR & SONS

R. Mackay & Co., Auditors
We beg to report that we have examined the above Balance sheet with the Books, Accounts, and Vouchers of the Company, and in our opinion it is a full and fair Balance sheet. It is properly drawn up so as to show a true and correct view of the state of the Company's affairs.

LIVERPOOL ADELPHI HOTEL

Banner & Lawson
We have audited the accounts of the Liverpool Adelphi Hotel Company Limited to the 31st December 1880 and assuming the valuation of the stocks to be correct. We certify that in our opinion the balance sheet is a full and fair balance sheet and that it is properly drawn up so as to exhibit a true and correct view of the state of the company's affairs.

LIVERPOOL EXCHANGE

Henry C. Beloe and A. J. Gnosspolius
Audited and found correct.

LONDON & GLASGOW ENGINEERING & IRON SHIPBUILDING

James Wink, John Graham, Auditors
Examined and found correct.

LONDON & PROVINCIAL MARINE INSURANCE

Algernon Bathurst, A. C. Meredith Bolton, Lewis Marcus, Auditors
We have duly examined the Books from which the above Accounts are abstracted, together with all the securities held by the Company and compared the Vouchers with the Cash Books, and we hereby certify that they are correct.

MARBELLA IRON ORE

Turquand, Youngs & Co.
We have examined the Books of the Marbella Iron Ore Company Limited to the 31st December 1881 with the Vouchers in London and the Returns from Spain and hereby certify that the above Balance sheet is a full and correct statement of the position of the Company in accordance therewith. With reference to our remark in former years as to 'Depreciation', we are glad to find the Directors are about to recommend the Shareholders to place aside a portion of the above Profits as a 'Reserve Account for Depreciation', in the value of the Company's property.

METROPOLITAN RAILWAY CARRIAGE AND WAGON

Laundy & Co., Chartered Accountants
We beg to report that we have audited the Books of your company for the year ending 30th June 1881, and that in our opinion, the above statements correctly set forth the position of its affairs and comply with the requirements of the Articles of Association.

NATIONAL SAFE DEPOSIT

Robert A. Maclean & Co., Auditors
Audited and found correct, subject to the approval of the shareholders to treat as 'Preliminary Expenses' the balance of the profit and loss account, at 30th September 1881.

ORIENT STEAM NAVIGATION

John Young, Auditor
I have examined the foregoing statements of account with the Books and Vouchers of the Company and find them in accordance therewith. In my

opinion the Balance Sheet is a full and fair Balance Sheet, and properly drawn up, so as to exhibit a true and correct view of the state of the company's affairs. All explanations and information that I have called for from the Managers have been given, and have been satisfactory.

REDHEUGH BRIDGE

D. D. Main, R. Y. Green, Auditors
  Audited and certified.

WEST INDIA & PACIFIC STEAMSHIP

Harmood Banner & Son
  We have audited the accounts of the West India and Pacific Steam-Ship Company, Limited to the 31st December 1881, and have seen the securities for the investments, assessing the valuation of Coal and Stores on hand, and the sufficiency of depreciation written off. We certify that, in our opinion, the Balance-sheet is a full and fair Balance-sheet, and that it is properly drawn up so as to exhibit a true and correct view of the state of the Company's affairs at that date.

Bibliography

Anderson, M. (2000) 'Accounting History Publications 1999', *Accounting, Business & Financial History*, 10 (3): 385–93.

Anderson, R. C. (1981) *A History of Crosville Motor Services*, North Pomfret: David and Charles.

Arnold, A. J. and Matthews, D. (2002) 'Corporate Financial Disclosure in the UK 1920–50: The Effects of Legislative Change and Managerial Discretion', *Accounting and Business Research*, 32 (1): 3–16.

Attwood, F. A. and Stein, N. D. (1986) *De Paula's Auditing*, 17th edn, London: Pitman.

Barker, T. C. (1960) *Pilkington Brothers and the Glass Industry*, London: Allen and Unwin.

Barras, R. and Swann, J. (1984) *The Adoption and Impact of Information Technology in the UK Accountancy Profession*, London: The Technical Change Centre.

Bartlett, S. A. and Chandler, R. A. (1997) 'The Corporate Report and the Private Shareholder: Lee & Tweedie Twenty Years on', *British Accounting Review*, September 1997: 245–61.

Baxter, W. T. (1999) 'McKesson & Robbins: a Milestone in Auditing', *Accounting, Business & Financial History*, 9 (2): 157–74.

Beattie, V., Fearnley, S. and Brandt, R. (2001) *Behind Closed Doors: What Company Audit is Really About*, London: Palgrave.

Benson, H. (1989) *Accounting for life*, London: Kogan Page.

Bigg, W. W. (1951) *Spicer and Pegler's Practical Auditing*, 10th edn, London: H. F. L.

——(1969) *Spicer and Pegler's Practical Auditing*, London: H. F. L. Publishers.

Bigg, W. W. and Perrins, R. E. G. (1971) *Spicer and Pegler's Book-keeping and Accounts*, 17th edn, London: H. F. L.

Bird, P. (ed.) (1971) *A Casebook on Auditing Procedures*, London: ICAEW.

Boockholdt, J. L. (1988) 'A Historical Perspective on the Auditor's Role: The Early Experience of the American Railroads', in Lee, T. A. (ed.), *The Evolution of Audit Thought and Practice*, New York: Garland: 105–22.

Boyns, T. and Edwards, J. R. (1997) 'The Construction of Cost Accounting Systems in Britain to 1900. The Case of the Coal, Iron and Steel Industries', *Business History*, 39 (3): 1–29.

Boys, P. (1994) 'The Origins and Evolution of the Accountancy Profession', in W. Habgood (ed.), *Chartered Accountants in England and Wales: A Guide to Historical Records*, Manchester: Manchester University Press.

Broadbridge, S. (1970) *Studies in Railway Expansion and the Capital Market in England 1825–1873*, London: Frank Cass.

Brown, R. (ed.) (1968) *A History of Accounting and Accountants*, originally published in 1905, London: Cass.

Business Monitor: Report on the Census of Production (2000) London: Central Statistical Office.

Bywater, M. (1985) 'William Quilter (1808–88). Accountant', in Jeremy, D. J. (ed.), *Dictionary of Business Biography*, vol. 4, London: Butterworth.

Campbell-Kelly, M. (1989) *ICL: A Business and Technical History*, Oxford: Clarendon.

Carr, J. G. (1985) *Information Technology and the Accountant: Summary and Conclusions*, Aldershot: Gower.

Carreras Limited, *Directors Report and Accounts*, 31 October 1950: 11.

Chambers, A. D. (1981) *Computer Auditing*, London: Pitman.

Chan, P., Ezzamel, M. and Gwilliam, D. (1993) 'Determinants of Audit Fees for Quoted UK Companies', *Journal of Business Finance & Accounting*, 20 (6): 765–86.

Chandler, A. D. (1962) *Strategy and Structure: Chapters in the History of the Industrial Enterprise*, Cambridge, MA: MIT Press.

——(1977) *The Visible Hand: The Managerial Revolution in American Business*, Cambridge, MA: Belknap.

——(1990) *Scale and Scope: The Dynamics of Industrial Capitalism*, Cambridge, MA: Belknap.

Chandler, R. (1996) 'Lessons of Auditors Responsibility', *The Accounting Historians Notebook*, 19 (2): 1, 22–3.

——(1997) 'Judicial Views on Auditing from the Nineteenth Century', *Accounting History*, 2 (1): 61–79.

Chandler, R. and Edwards, J. R. (eds) (1994) *Recurring Issues in Auditing: Professional Debate 1875–1900*, New York: Garland Publishing.

Chandler, R. A., Edwards, J. R. and Anderson, M. (1993) 'Changing Perceptions of the Role of the Company Auditor, 1840–1940', *Accounting and Business Research*, 23 (92): 443–59.

Channon, D. F. (1973) *The Strategy and Structure of British Enterprise*, London: Macmillan.

Chapman, S. (1974) *Jesse Boot of Boots the Chemists*, London: Hodder & Stoughton.

Chatfield, M. (1977) *A History of Accounting Thought*, New York: Robert E. Krieger Publishing.

Cochrane, G. (1979) 'The Auditors Report: Its Evolution in the U.S.A', in Lee, T. A. and Parker, R. H. (eds), *The Evolution of Corporate Financial Reporting*, Sudbury-on-Thames: Nelson, 164–89.

Collins, M. and Bloom, R. (1991) 'The Role of Oral History in Accounting', *Accounting, Auditing and Accountability Journal*, 4 (4): 23–31.

Cooper, C. (1997) 'Against Postmodernism: Class Orientated Questions for Critical Accounting', *Critical Perspectives on Accounting*, 8: 15–41.

Cooper, V. R. V. (1966) *Manual of Auditing*, London: Gee & Co.

——(1969) *Manual of Auditing*, 2nd edn, London: Gee & Co.

Coopers & Lybrand (1981) *Manual of Auditing*, 3rd edn, London: Gee & Co.

Cottrell, P. L. (1980) *Industrial Finance, 1830–1914*, London: Methuen.

Davis, R. (1996) 'Serving the Public Interest', *True and Fair*, December 1995/January 1996.

de Paula, F. R. M. (1914) *The Principles of Auditing: A Practical Manual for Students and Practitioners*, 1st edn, London: Pitman.

—— (1917) *The Principles of Auditing: A Practical Manual for Students and Practitioners*, 2nd edn, London: Pitman.

—— (1948) *The Principles of Auditing: A Practical Manual for Students and Practitioners*, 10th edn, London: Pitman.

—— (1951) *The Principles of Auditing: A Practical Manual for Students and Practitioners*, 11th edn, London: Pitman.

—— (1957) *The Principles of Auditing: A Practical Manual for Students and Practitioners*, 12th edn, London: Pitman.

—— (revised by de Paula, F. C.) (1966) *The Principles of Auditing: A Practical Manual for Students and Practitioners*, 13th edn, London: Pitman.

—— (revised by de Paula, F. C.) (1968) *The Principles of Auditing: A Practical Manual for Students and Practitioners*, 14th edn, London: Pitman.

de Paula, F. C. and Attwood, F. A. (1976) *Auditing: Principles and Practice*, 15th edn, London: Pitman.

—— (1982) *Auditing: Principles and Practice*, 16th edn, London: Pitman.

Defliese, P. L., Johnson, K. P. and Macleod, R. K. (1975) *Montgomery's Auditing*, 9th edn, New York: Ronald Press.

Defliese, P. L., Jaenicke, H. R., O'Relly, V. M. and Hirsch, M. B. (1990) *Montgomery's Auditing*, 11th edn, New York: Wiley.

Dicksee, L. R. (1892) *Auditing: A Practical Manual for Auditors*, 1st edn, London: Gee.

—— (1904) *Auditing: A Practical Manual for Auditors*, 6th edn, London: Gee.

Drury, C., Braund, S., Osborne, P. and Tayles, M. (1993) *A Survey of Management Accounting Practices in the UK Manufacturing Companies*, London: ACCA.

Edwards, J. R. (1976) 'The Accounting Profession and Disclosure in Published Reports 1925–35', *Accounting and Business Research*, 6, Autumn: 289–303.

—— (1985) 'The Origins and Evolution of the Double Account System: An Example of Accounting Innovation', *Abacus*, 21, March: 19–43.

—— (1989) *A History of Financial Accounting*, London: Routledge.

Edwards, J. R. and Webb, K. M. (1985) 'Use of Table A by Companies Registering under the Companies Act 1862', *Accounting and Business Research*, Summer: 177–95.

Edwards, J. R., Anderson, M. and Matthews, D. R. (1997) 'Accountability in a Free-Market Economy: The British Company Audit, 1886', *Abacus*, 33 (1): 1–25.

Financial Times (2000) *The World's Top 500 Companies*, London: Financial Times.

Freear, J. (1977) 'Historical Background to Accounting', in Carsberg, B. and Hope, T. (eds), *Current Issues in Accounting*, London: Philip Allan: 1–22.

Freeman, C. and Soete, L. (1997) *The Economics of Industrial Innovation*, London: Pinter.

Funnell, W. (1997) 'The Narrative and its Place in the New Accounting History: The Rise of the Counternarrative', *Accounting, Auditing & Accountability Journal*, 11 (2): 142–62.

Gaffikin, M. (1998) 'History Is Dead, Long Live History', *Critical Perspectives on Accounting*, 9: 631–9.

Garner, S. P. and Hughes, M. (1978) *Readings on Accounting Development*, New York: Arnos.

Gourvish, T. R. (1972) *Mark Huish and the London & North Western Railway: A Study of Management*, Leicester: Leicester University Press.

Gray, I. and Manson, S. (1989) *The Audit Process: Principles, Practice and Cases*, London: Van Nostrand Reinhold (International).

Green, E. and Moss, M. (1982) *A Business of National Importance: The Royal Mail Shipping Group, 1902–37*, London: Methuen.

Griffiths, A. and Wall, S. (eds) (1997) *Applied Economics: An Introductory Course*, Harrow: Longman Group UK.

Griliches, Z. (1957) 'Hybrid Corn: and Exploration in the Economics of Technical Change', *Econometrica*, 25, October: 501–22.

Gwilliam, D. R. (1987) *A Survey of Auditing Research*, London: Prentice Hall/ICAEW.

Hammond, T. and Sikka, P. (1996) 'Radicalising Accounting History: The Potential of Oral History', *Accounting, Auditing and Accountability Journal*, 9 (3): 79–97.

Hannah, L. (1976) 'Strategy and Structure in the Manufacturing Sector', in L. Hannah (ed.), *Management Strategy and Business Development: An Historical and Comparative Study*, London: Macmillan.

——(1983) *The Rise of the Corporate Economy*, 2nd edn, London: Methuen.

Hatherly, D. J. (1978) 'Compliance and Substantive Tests – Can the Auditor Tell the Difference?', *The Accountant's Magazine*, September: 378–80.

——(1980) *The Audit Evidence Process*, London: Anderson Keenan Publishing.

Hays Accountancy Personnel (2003) London: Hays.

Higson, A. W. (1987) 'An Empirical Investigation of the External Audit Process. A Study of the Reaction of Professional Auditors to Recent Changes in the Audit Environment', unpublished thesis, University of Bradford.

——(1997) 'Developments in Audit Approaches: From Audit Efficiency to Audit Effectiveness?', in Sherer, M. and Turley, S. (eds) (1997), *Current Issues in Auditing*, 3rd edn, London: PCP, 198–215.

Hill, N. K. (1979) 'Accountancy Developments in a Public Utility Company in the Nineteenth Century', in Lee, T. A. and Parker, R. H. (eds) *The Evolution of Corporate Financial Reporting*, Sudbury-on-Thames: Nelson, 6–14.

Holmes, A. R. and Green, E. (1986) *Midland: 150 Years of Banking Business*, London: Batsford.

Hoskin, K. W. and Macve, R. (1986) 'Accounting and the Examination: a Genealogy of Disciplinary Power', *Accounting, Organizations and Society*, 11 (2): 105–36.

Howitt, Sir H. (1996) *The History of the Institute of Chartered Accountants in England and Wales 1880–1965, and its Founder Accountancy Bodies 1870–1880*, London: Heinemann.

Humphrey, C. and Moizer P. (1990) 'From Techniques to Ideologies: An Alternative Perspective On the Audit Function', *Critical Perspectives on Accounting*, 1: 217–38.

ICAEW (2000) *Auditing Standards and Guidance for Members*, London: ICAEW.

Innes, J., Lee, T. A. and Mitchell, F. (eds) (1981) *Cases in Auditing Practice*, 3rd edn, London: ICAEW.

Irving, R. J. (1976) *The North Eastern Railway Company 1870–1914: An Economic History*, Leicester: Leicester University Press.

Jeremy, D. J. (1998) *A Business History of Britain*, Oxford: Oxford University Press.

Johnman, L. (1986) 'The Largest Manufacturing Companies of 1935', *Business History*, XXVIII (2): 226–45.

Jones, E. (1981) *Accountancy and the British Economy 1840–1980: The Evolution of Ernst & Whinney*, London: Batsford.

——(1984) 'William Welch Deloitte 1818–1898', in Jeremy, D. J. (ed.) *Dictionary of Business Biography*, vol. 2: London: Butterworth, 57–60.

——(1995) *True and Fair: A History of Price Waterhouse*, London: Hamish Hamilton.

Keeble, S. P. (1992) *The Ability to Manage: A Study of British Management 1890–1990*, Manchester: Manchester University Press.

Keenan, M. G. (1998) 'A Defence of "Traditional" Accounting History Methodology', *Critical Perspectives on Accounting*, 9: 641–66.

Kelly, T. (1987) *The Britsh Computer Indutry: Crisis and Development*, London: Croom Helm.

Kennedy, W. P. (1987) *Industry Structure, Capital Markets and the Origins of British Economic Decline*, Cambridge: Cambridge University Press.

Kitchen, J. (1988) 'Auditing: Past Development and Current Practice', in Lee, T. A. (ed.), *The Evolution of Audit Thought and Practice*, New York: Garland: 24–35.

Lee, T. A. (1972) *Company Auditing: Concepts and Practices*, London: ICAS and Gee & Co.

——(1977) 'The Modern Audit Function: A Study of Radical Change', in Carsberg, B. and Hope, T. (eds) *Current Issues in Accounting*, London: Philip Allan: 87–106.

——(1979) 'Company Audits: 1840–1940', in Lee, T. A. and Parker, R. H. (eds), *The Evolution of Corporate Financial Reporting*, Sudbury-on-Thames: Nelson, 153–63.

——(ed.) (1988) *The Evolution of Audit Thought and Practice*, New York: Garland.

Lee, T. A. and Parker, R. H. (eds) (1979) *The Evolution of Corporate Financial Reporting*, Sudbury-on-Thames: Nelson.

Lee, T. A. and Tweedie, D. P. (1977) *The Private Shareholder and the Corporate Report*, London: ICAEW.

Lee, T. A., Bishop, A. and Parker, R. H. (1996) *Accounting History From the Renaissance to the Present: A Remembrance of Luca Pacioli*, New York: Garland.

Leisner, T. (1989) *One Hundred Years of Economic Statistics*, London: The Economist Publications.

Lenhart, N. J. and Defliese, P. L. (1957) *Montgomery's Auditing*, New York: Ronald Press.

Littleton, A. C. (1981) *Accounting Evolution to 1900*, Alabama: University of Alabama Press.

Loft, A. (1990) *Coming into the Light: A Study of the Development of a Professional Association for Cost Accountants in Britain in the Wake of the First World War*, London: CIMA.

Lummis, T. (1998) 'Structure and Validity in Oral Evidence', in Perks R. and Thomson A. (eds), *The Oral History Reader*, London: Routledge.

Mackintosh, M., Brown, V., Costello, N., Dawson, G., Thompson, G. and Trigg, A. (1996) *Economics and Changing Economies*, London: The Open University.

McRae, T. W. (1964) *The Impact of Computers on Accounting*, London: John Wiley & Sons.

——(1977) *Computers and Accounting*, London: John Wiley & Sons.

——(1982) *A Study of the Application of Statistical Sampling to External Auditing*, London: ICAEW.

Magee, B. (1951) *Dicksee's Auditing*, 17th edn, London: Gee & Co.

Mansfield, E. (1962) *The Economics of Technological Change*, London: Longman.

Manson, S. (1997) 'Audit Risk and Sampling', in Sherer, M. and Turley, S. (eds), *Current Issues in Auditing*, 3rd edn, London: PCP, 234–53.

Manson, S., McCartney, S. and Sherer, M. (1997) 'Audit Automation: Improving Quality or Keeping up Appearances?', in Sherer, M. and Turley, S. (eds), *Current Issues in Auditing*, 3rd edn, London: PCP, 254–72.

Matthew, D. (2000) 'Oral History, Accounting History and an Interview with Sir John Grenside', *Accounting, Business and Financial History*, 10 (1): 57–83.

——(2002) 'The Use of the Postal Questionnaire in Accounting History Research', *Accounting, Business and Financial History*, 12 (1): 1–17.

——(forthcoming) 'The Rise of British Accountancy in the 19th Century: A Technological Determinist Approach'.

Matthews, D. and Pirie, J. (2001) *The Auditors Talk: An Oral History of a Profession from the 1920s to the Present Day*, New York: Garland.

Matthews, D., Anderson, A. and Edwards, J. R. (1997) 'The Rise of the Accountant in British Management Hierarchies, 1880 to the Present Day', *Economic History Review*, 2nd ser., L (3): 407–29.

——(1998) *The Priesthood of Industry: The Rise of the Professional Accountant in British Management*, Oxford: Oxford University Press.

Merino, B. D. (1998) 'Critical Theory and Accounting History: Challenges and Opportunities', *Critical Perspectives on Accounting*, 9: 603–16.

Michie, R. C. (1987) *The London and New York Stock Exchanges, 1850–1914*, London: Allen and Unwin.

Mitchell, A., Sikka, P., Puxty, T. and Wilmott, H. (1993) *A Better Future for Auditing*, London: University of East London.

Montgomery, R. H. (1912) *Auditing*, 1st edn, New York: Ronald Press.

——(1934) *Auditing*, 5th edn, New York: Ronald Press.

Montgomery, R. H., Lenhart, N. J. and Jennings, A. R. (1949) *Montgomery's Auditing*, 7th edn, New York: Ronald Press.

Moyer, C. A. (1988) 'Early Developments in American Auditing', reprinted in Lee, T. A. (ed.), *The Evolution of Audit Thought and Practice*, New York: Garland: 123–8.

Mumford, M. J. (1991) 'Chartered Accountants as Business Managers: An Oral History Perspective', *Accounting, Business and Financial History*, 1 (2): 123–40.

Myers, J. H. (1985) 'Spiralling Upward: Auditing Methods As Described By Montgomery and His Successors', *The Accounting Historians Journal*, 12 (1): 53–72.

Napier, C. (1989) 'Research Directions in Accounting History', *British Accounting Review*, 21: 237–54.

——(1998) 'Giving an Account of Accounting History: A Reply to Keenan', *Critical Perspectives on Accounting*, 9: 685–700.

Nockolds, H. (1986) 'Sir Arthur Bertram Waring (1902–74): Manufacturer of Electrical Engineering Components' in Jeremy, D. J. (ed.), *Dictionary of Business Biography*, vol. 5, London: Butterworth.

Parker, R. H. (1984) *Papers on Accounting History*, New York: Garland.

——(1986) *The Development of the Accountancy Profession in Britain to the Early Twentieth Century*, San Antonio: The Academy of Accounting Historians.

Parker, R. H. and Yamey, B. S. (eds) (1994) *Accounting History: Some British Contributions*, Oxford: Clarendon Press.

Pearson, R. (1997) 'Towards an Historical Model of Services Innovation: The Case of the Insurance Industry', *Economic History Review*, 2nd ser., L (2): 235–56.

Pinkney, A. (1966) *The Audit Approach to Computers*, London: ICAEW.

Pixley, F. W. (1881) *Auditors: Their Duties and Responsibilities*, 1st edn, London: Effingham Wilson.

—— (1910) *Auditors: Their Duties and Responsibilities*, 10th edn, London: Henry Good.

Podolski, T. M. (1986) *Financial Innovation and the Money Supply*, London: Basil Blackwell.

Pollins, H. (1969) 'Aspects of Railway Accounting Before 1868', in M. C. Reed (ed.), *Railways in the Victorian Economy: Studies in Finance and Economic Growth*, Newton Abbot: David & Charles.

Power, M. K. (1992) 'From Common Sense to Expertise: Reflections on the Prehistory of Audit Sampling', *Accounting, Organizations and Society*, 17 (1): 37–62.

Previts, G., Samson, W. D. and Flesher, D. L. (2001) 'The Audit Committee of the Baltimore and Ohio Railroad: 1827–1830', paper presented at 13th Annual Conference of the Accounting and Business History Research Unit, Cardiff Business School.

Reader, W. J. (1976) *Metal Box: A History*, London: Heinemann.

Reed, M. C. (1975) *Investment in Railways in Britain, 1820–1844: A Study in the Development of the Capital Market*, Oxford: Oxford University Press.

—— (1997) 'Accountancy', in J. Simmons and G. Biddle (eds), *The Oxford Companion to British Railway History From 1603 to the 1990s*, Oxford: Oxford University Press.

Robb, G. (1992) *White-collar Crime in Modern England: Financial Fraud and Business Morality, 1845–1929*, Cambridge: Cambridge University Press.

Rosenberg, N. (1982) *Inside the Black Box: Technology and Economics*, Cambridge: Cambridge University Press.

Salter, W. E. G. (1969) *Productivity and Technical Change*, Cambridge: Cambridge University Press.

Schmitz, C. J. (1993) *The Growth of Big Business in the United States and Western Europe, 1850–1939*, Cambridge: Cambridge University Press.

Sherer, M. and Kent, D. (1983) *Auditing and Accountability*, London: Pitman.

Silber, W. L. (1983) 'The Process of Financial Innovation', *American Economic Review*, 73, May: 89–95.

Smith, D. (1982) 'Statistical Sampling and Analytical Review', in Bromwich, M., Hopwood, A. G. and Shaw, J. (eds), *Auditing Research: Issues and Opportunities*, London: Pitman: 141–6.

Spicer, E. E. and Pegler, E. C. (1908) *Audit Programmes*, London: H. Foulkes Lynch.

—— (1911) *Practical Auditing*, 1st edn, London: H. F. L. (Publishers) Ltd.

—— (1914) *Practical Auditing*, 2nd edn, London: H. F. L. (Publishers) Ltd.

—— (1925) *Practical Auditing*, 4th edn, London: H. F. L. (Publishers) Ltd.

Stacey, N. A. H. (1954) *English Accountancy: A Study in Social and Economic History 1800–1954*, London: Gee.

The Stock Exchange Official Intelligence, London: Spottiswood.

The Stock Exchange Official Yearbook, London: Thomas Skinner.

Stoneman, P. (1976) *Technological Diffusion and the Computer Revolution: The UK Experience*, Cambridge: Cambridge University Press.

Sullivan, J. D., Gnospelius, R. A., Defliese, P. L. and Jaenicke, H. R. (1985) *Montgomery's Auditing*, 10th edn, New York: John Wiley and Sons.

Taylor, E. M. and Perry, C. E. (1931) *Principles of Auditing*, London: Textbooks.

Times 1000 (1990), London: Times Books.

Thomson McLintock (1983) *The Thomson McLintock Audit Manual*, London: Macmillan.

Thornton Baker Associates (1981) *Audit Manual*, London: Oyez Longman.

Trebilcock, C. (1969) ' "Spin-off" in British Economic History: Armaments and Industry 1760–1914', *Economic History Review*, 2nd ser., 22, December 1969.

Tricker, R. I. (1982) 'Corporate Accountability and the Role of the Audit Function', in Bromwich, M., Hopwood, A. G. and Shaw, J. (eds), *Auditing Research: Issues and Opportunities*, London: Pitman, 53–68.

Turley, S. and Cooper, M. (1991) *Auditing in the United Kingdom: A Study of Development in the Audit Methodologies of Large Accounting Firms*, London: Prentice Hall/ICAEW.

Waldron, R. S. (1969) *Auditing: A Practical Manual for Auditors by the Late Lawrence R. Dicksee*, 18th edn, London: Gee & Co.

—— (1978) *Spicer and Pegler's Practical Auditing*, 16th edn, London: H.F.L.

Wardley, P. (1991) 'The Anatomy of Big Business: Aspects of Corporate Development in the Twentieth Century', *Business History*, 33 (2): 268–96.

—— (1999) 'The Emergence of Big Business: The Largest Corporate Employers of Labour in the United Kingdom, Germany and the United States', *Business History*, 41 (4): 88–116.

Williams, F. S. (1876) *Midland Railway: Its Rise and Progress*, Newton Abbot: David and Charles.

Wilson, C. (1954) *The History of Unilever: A Study in Economic Growth and Social Change, vol. I*, London: Cassell.

Wilson, J. F. (1988) *Ferranti and the British Electrical Industry, 1864–1930*, Manchester: Manchester University Press.

—— (1991) *Lighting the Town: A Study of Management in the North West Gas Industry 1805–1880*, London: Paul Chapman Publishing.

—— (1995) *British Business History*, Manchester: Manchester University Press.

Wood, B. (1976) *The Process of Local Government Reform, 1966–74*, London: Allen and Unwin.

Woolf, A. H. (1912) *A Short History of Accountants and Accountancy*, London: Gee.

Woolf, E. (1978a) *Current Auditing Developments*, 1st edn, London: Gee.

—— (1978b) *Auditing Today*, 1st edn, London: Prentice-Hall International.

—— (1982) *Current Auditing Developments*, 3rd edn, London: Gee.

—— (1986) *Auditing Today*, 4th edn, London: Prentice-Hall International.

—— (1997) *Auditing Today*, 6th edn, London: Prentice-Hall International.

Yamey, B. S. (ed.) (1978) *The Historical Development of Accounting: A Selection of Papers*, New York: Arnos Press.

Zeff, S. A. (1979) 'Chronology of Significant Developments in the Establishment of Accounting Principles in the United States, 1926–1978', in Lee, T. A. and Parker, R. H. (eds), *The Evolution of Corporate Financial Reporting*, Sudbury-on-Thames: Nelson, 208–21.

Index